Our Last First Poets

University of Illinois Press   *Urbana   Chicago   London*

Cary Nelson

OUR LAST FIRST POETS

Vision and History
in Contemporary
American Poetry

"Often I Am Permitted to Return to a Meadow" reprinted from Robert Duncan, *The Opening of the Field.* Copyright © 1960 by Robert Duncan. Reprinted by permission of New Directions.

"Sonnet 4," "My Mother Would Be A Falconress," and "The Torso" reprinted from Robert Duncan, *Bending the Bow.* Copyright © 1963, 1966, 1968 by Robert Duncan. Reprinted by permission of New Directions.

"Scattering Flowers" reprinted from George Hitchcock, *The Dolphin With The Revolver In Its Teeth,* published by Unicorn Press, Box 3307, Greensboro, North Carolina. Copyright © 1967 by George Hitchcock. Reprinted by permission of the author.

"When The War is Over," "The Room," and "December Among the Vanished," reprinted from *The Lice* by W. S. Merwin (copyright © 1963, 1964, 1965, 1966, 1967 by W. S. Merwin); "Beginning," "The Gardens of Zuñi," reprinted from *The Carrier of Ladders* by W. S. Merwin (copyright © 1967, 1968, 1969, 1970 by W. S. Merwin); "Dead Hand" reprinted from *The Moving Target* by W. S. Merwin (copyright © 1960, 1961, 1962, 1963 by W. S. Merwin); "The Old Boast," "Folk Art," reprinted from *Writings To An Unfinished Accompaniment* by W. S. Merwin (copyright © 1969, 1970, 1971, 1972, 1973 by W. S. Merwin); "The Horse" reprinted from *The Compass Flower* by W. S. Merwin (copyright © 1977 by W. S. Merwin). Reprinted by permission of Atheneum Publishers and David Higham Associates.

"(Newsreel)" from *Shooting Script* is reprinted from *The Will to Change,* Poems 1968-1970, by Adrienne Rich, with the permission of W. W. Norton & Company. Copyright © 1971 by W. W. Norton & Company, Inc.

"(The Floating Poem, Unnumbered)" is reprinted from *The Dream of a Common Language,* Poems 1974-1977, by Adrienne Rich, with the permission of W. W. Norton & Company. Copyright © 1978 by W. W. Norton & Company.

Lines from "The Long Waters," Copyright © 1962 by Beatrice Roethke, Administratrix of the Estate of Theodore Roethke. Reprinted by permission of Doubleday & Company and Faber and Faber.

Lines from "The Rose," Copyright © 1963 by Beatrice Roethke, Administratrix of the Estate of Theodore Roethke. Reprinted by permission of Doubleday & Company and Faber and Faber.

"A Mad Fight Song for William S. Carpenter, 1966," Copyright © 1971 by James Wright. Reprinted from *Collected Poems* by permission of Wesleyan University Press.

Library of Congress Cataloging in Publication Data

Nelson, Cary.
   Our last first poets.

   Includes index.
   1. American poetry—20th century—History and criticism.   2. Free verse.   3. Politics and literature—United States.   I. Title.
PS325.N4   811'.54'09   81-5082
ISBN 0-252-00885-5   AACR2

for my family

Contents

Preface

Our Last First Poets is both a collection of readings of individual poets working in open forms and an analysis of the conflict between vision and history in American poetry of the last twenty years. I have concentrated on a diverse and reasonably representative group of mature poets whose careers were well established by the early 1960s. Indeed, the first poet I consider at length, Theodore Roethke, was by then near the end of his life. These are poets, therefore, whose work merits detailed explication. Moreover, they are poets whose own careers show the effects of the historical pressures of the last two decades. Within these limits, my choices above all reflect my sense of where there was interesting critical writing to be done, either because these poets merit a rereading from this perspective or because few close readings of their work have been published.

To varying degrees and in ways peculiar to their individual situations, each of these poets began the 1960s with a poetic vision largely detached from a sense of immediate political reality. Though often discontented with and critical of American culture, they had until then been able to sustain an aesthetic project seemingly protected from deflation by their sense of the culture's limitations. The public life of the period, however, made aesthetic detachment increasingly untenable, and current events began to threaten their belief in what poetry could accomplish. As a result, the continuing conflict in American poetry between vision and history became especially intense.

This was also the time of a considerable and quite varied resurgence of poetry written in open forms. I use the term "open form" here essentially as a way of making the notion of free verse culturally and temporally specific. Although its early development is associated with Whitman, free verse has since had a diverse and international history. Thus it is helpful to use a term that can reflect the special ambitions contemporary American poets have associated with such practices as mixing passages of varied and unvaried line lengths or continual enjambment. "Open form" is, of course, a term that occurs regularly in manifestoes by contemporary poets, where it often signals a desire for freedom from both poetic tradition and social constraint— ambitions that discussions of free verse have sometimes claimed and sometimes denied. Of equal importance, however, is the recurrent exhortation for American open-form poetry to be open to both the nation's present condition and its past history. Open forms are frequently envisioned as a communal and collective form of writing. Moreover, they draw on the wider tradition in American literature that treats individuals as culturally responsive and representative—a relation that can become redemptive, prophetic, or sacrificial.

Even when contemporary American poetry emphasizes the local, it typically tries, synecdochically, to speak for the nation as a whole. Moreover, it continues to be involved with the project of creating a democratically inclusive aesthetic, an aesthetic that reflects an essentially ahistorical image of American possibility. The ahistorical image, of course, serves in part to compensate for the less appealing realities of public and private life. Yet the faith that made this compensation tolerable—the faith that an exemplary dialogue between poetic vision and historical actuality could persist and perhaps even be beneficial—did not survive the events of the period. As if trying to find forms at once sufficiently expansive and fractured to contain their experience, the poets I discuss have adopted increasingly more open forms as they worked through the last two decades. At the same time, they have become steadily more aware of how political events counter the cultural ideals these forms embody.

American poets working in open forms have, to be sure, regularly been disillusioned by their immediate political environment and by their perception of the general course and meaning of American history. Through the 1960s, however, these two attitudes toward history came together with particular force. Thus Galway Kinnell,

Robert Duncan, Adrienne Rich, and W. S. Merwin, along with many other poets, experienced Vietnam not merely as an unjust war but as a betrayal of a democratic vision of America and as a negative and seemingly irreversible judgment on the whole of American history. Their increasing awareness of ongoing events led to a rereading of America's past, a rereading through metaphorization and totalization that saw the past as culminating in and fulfilled by an intolerable present. This negative and rather spatialized historical awareness— a recurring feature of American literature that was catalyzed again by the war—compelled changes in the poetry of the 1960s and 1970s which spread beyond the immediate preoccupation with America's presence in Southeast Asia. The resulting body of poetry is an instructive and telling introduction to the continuing conflict between vision and history in American poetry.

For the purpose of this book, it does not matter whether the conceptions of American history that inform and constrain this poetry are accurate or deluded. Even the tendency to oppose an individual or collective vision and a sense of historical actuality is problematic, since the opposition between vision and history is itself historically produced. Yet such attitudes toward history have their own life, one that, as others have shown, can sometimes influence actual events. Of course the sense of disaster these poets feel is not unique. American poets have contemplated the loss of an American myth before. No doubt future generations will be reinspired by a myth of America and will in turn be disillusioned. Indeed we may even see a rebirth of a wholly optimistic aesthetic of open forms, though this is unlikely to be either immediate or widespread. The issue here is how these poets situate their immediate experience within their perception of American history, what effect that experience has on their poetry, what resources it leaves them. The conception of history these poets share informs and often undermines the open forms with which they work; it leads them, eventually, to adopt open forms that very nearly destroy themselves. Yet these are forms, as I attempt to show throughout this book, that sometimes succeed precisely because of the risks they take.

In trying to identify those poems that survive the effects of the historical perspective they reflect, I am often led to make strong statements about which poems do and do not succeed and even to offer observations about the kinds of poems that best dramatize and contend with a dark image of American culture. Somewhat surprisingly, much criticism of contemporary poetry remains divided between those who approve and those who disapprove of poets working in more open forms. The poets I discuss are often reviewed and analyzed by critics who essentially either entirely support or entirely deny their accomplishments. Neither audience will be altogether pleased by my more divided loyalties, which evidence a more mixed reading experience. In choosing to record these varying judgments I was guided not so much by a conviction that evaluation is a necessary part of critical writing, though evaluation is probably inescapable when reading one's contemporaries, but by a conclusion that success and failure are often interdependent within a single poet's work. Much of what follows is devoted to close readings of individual poems. My positive readings are often aimed, in effect, at helping to create good poems where many readers will not have known they existed, but these affirmations are connected with other readings that are negative.

It may be best to give advance notice of my positions. Against Roethke's detractors, who remain vocal, my analysis of "North American Sequence" shows it to be a major accomplishment, however flawed. I also argue, and here even Roethke's admirers may disagree, that in "North American Sequence" Roethke's self-prized naiveté becomes a highly self-conscious verbal artifice. In the case of Kinnell, I find much of his early and often-praised poetry weak and sentimental. Many of these poems, however, can now be seen as exercises in preparation for "The Porcupine," "The Bear," and *The Book of Nightmares,* the last of which is repetitive and almost destroyed by internal contradictions, but nonetheless a powerful and important work. Duncan is particularly problematic, since most readers familiar with his work are even more strictly divided, seeing him either as intolerably self-indulgent and pretentious or as one of our major poets. At the cost of offending both groups, I will argue instead that, while much of his work is slack and possibly self-destructive, some of his poems succeed remarkably at registering—and perhaps mastering—a radical play of form and dissolution. For Rich and Merwin, success and failure are even more closely linked. Rich has poems that are didactic and banal; Merwin has poems and many short prose pieces that are facile, self-congratulatory, and so vague as to be empty. Yet both Rich and Merwin have poems sharing diction and subject matter with their failures that are among the most forceful and, perhaps, prophetic in contemporary literature.

Although my evaluative comments are grounded in analyses of the poems' historical situation, I do not want to claim that these judgments have a privileged objectivity. As is always the case with criticism, this book embodies its author's sensibility and enacts its author's relationship with the period it examines. The result is a mixture of explication and advocacy that is also built into the book's structure. Since the poets I discuss are roughly contemporary with one another, I might have tried to present their work as a series of alternative and equally valid reactions to similar historical pressures. Instead, the book is structured as a sequence of chapters moving toward more radically open forms; moreover, my sense of what is appropriately radical, in the context of recent American history, is biased toward an openness grounded either in conflict or in an irreducible plurality. The book's structure mirrors my own position on the political connotations of the American tradition of open-form poetry, since I have doubts about its sometimes more optimistic version in Kinnell and Duncan but instinctively approve of its inverted, ironic version in Rich and Merwin. A critic with different sensibilities could, however, easily alter this arrangement and substitute a different bias, concluding that Rich and Merwin are hopelessly traumatized and placing Duncan and Kinnell in the final chapters that look toward the poetry of the future.

This book also represents a specific theoretical project. Because its historical arguments are frequently worked out through phenomenological readings of individual poems, it challenges two common assumptions about phenomenological criticism: first, that phenomenological criticism is ill-suited to readings of individual texts; second, that a historically based phenomenology is impossible. The practical criticism of the last twenty-five years gives much evidence that the first assumption is incorrect. But the second assumption is more serious. Though phenomenological criticism tends to spatialize its objects of study and thus to slight temporal process and change—even when it describes periodization—it does not follow that historical and phenomenological criticism require mutually exclusive kinds of discourse. This book attempts to demonstrate that they can work together productively, though not that the tensions between them can be abolished, for those tensions are a version of the inescapable interplay of diachrony and synchrony in critical writing.

Neither the phenomenological nor the historical component of this study is offered in a disengaged style. This self-reflexive element in writing phenomenological or historical criticism has received a fair amount of discussion of late, but the further self-reflexive element in reading criticism has not. The subjective and historically constituted character of the reading experience deserves special mention here, for the period I am concerned with is very recent indeed, and many readers will share their culture's characteristic repression of the immediate past. In analyzing contemporary poetry in terms of the political atmosphere of the last two decades, this book challenges its readers to reconsider not only these poets' relationship to that period but also their own. *Our Last First Poets* is not designed as an altogether comfortable reading experience. Its judgments ask to be considered and confronted, though not necessarily to be accepted. I am less interested in convincing the reader that my argument is universally applicable or that it offers the only way to read this poetry than I am in presenting it to the reader and demonstrating that it represents a plausible problematic. Like other modes of analysis that tend to undermine the still common New Critical assumptions about the reader's objectivity and the independence of poetic creation, such as Marxist or deconstructive criticism, the kind of historical phenomenology offered here may seem unsettling and unresolvable.

The polemical element of my argument is most insistent in the first chapter, which uses the limited subject of Vietnam war poetry to introduce the broader issue with which the rest of the book is regularly concerned—the conflict between vision and history in contemporary American poetry. In subsequent chapters, I am less concerned with correlating poetic development with particular historical incidents than with analyzing the pervasive tension between poetic aspiration and a constrained sense of historical possibility. Yet the relationship between the first chapter and the rest of the book is also an aggressive one: the first chapter intensifies and destabilizes the dialectic of vision and history in what follows. In some ways, the burden of the first chapter—the demands it makes of poetry—will make the rest of the book more difficult to read. More prosaically, however, the first chapter also provides introductory comments on several of the poets subsequently treated in greater detail, as well as brief discussions of a number of other poets. The structure of the first chapter in some respects parallels that of the book as a whole; like the book, for example, it ends with a discussion of Merwin and Rich. Chapters two and three are parallel: I discuss two long poem sequences, Roethke's "North American Sequence" and Kinnell's *The Book of Nightmares*, published roughly at the beginning and at the end of the 1960s. Roethke's sequence, which precedes this period of crisis, displays the continuing conflict between poetry and history in a much less traumatic form than Kinnell's. The chapter on Roethke thus provides a reference point both for the analysis of Kinnell and for the rest of the book. The following chapter, on Duncan, is an overview of the work of a poet who has made perhaps the most elaborate recent effort to articulate an optimistic aesthetic of open forms. As these poets move steadily toward more radically open, even dismantled, forms, their work fulfills the need repeatedly articulated in American poetry and prose for a democratically responsive and inclusive aesthetic, while largely undermining its potential for affirmation. This movement culminates in the chapters on Rich and Merwin.

Finally, as I have written elsewhere, criticism is a particularly hybrid kind of discourse—part argumentative demonstration and part a form of literature in its own right. I have worked in this book to balance those sometimes competing functions against one another, recognizing that this really means working out the terms in which writing and analysis are mutually constituted and compromised. This process of negotiation, however, can produce criticism that offers its own kind of literary experience. To that end, I have structured the individual chapters and arranged them within the book so as to condition the way they will be read. Thus the fragility and the appeal of Roethke's synthesis should be intensified by reading that chapter after reading in "Whitman in Vietnam" about a later period when "North American Sequence" probably could not have been written. Similarly, the chapter on Merwin is placed at the end to provide one convincing poetic resolution to the conflict between vision and history that the book has regularly addressed, a resolution that should be at once argumentative and formal.

Acknowledgments

Our Last First Poets has benefited greatly from careful and often genuinely challenging readings by a number of people. Nina Baym, Carol Neely, Paula Treichler, and Richard Wheeler read the entire manuscript. Lawrence Grossberg, Lawrence Jacobs, Carol Kyle, and John Stokes each read several chapters. Paula Treichler read the manuscript twice—in both an early and a late draft—and made many elegant suggestions for improvement.

Both the research for and the writing of the book have been generously supported by the University of Illinois: first by a sabbatical and later by an appointment as an Associate at the University of Illinois Center for Advanced Study.

Several libraries have been industrious in helping me to obtain small press editions: the acquisitions and reference departments at the University of Illinois, the poetry collection at the State University of New York at Buffalo, and The British Museum. Robert Bertholf kindly sent me a poem that no library was able to find.

Earlier versions of chapters one and six were published, respectively, in the *Massachusetts Review* (1975) and *Boundary 2* (1977). A brief section from the first chapter was published as "Levertov's Political Poetry" in *Denise Levertov: In Her Own Province,* ed. Linda Welshimer Wagner (New York: New Directions, 1979).

Finally, I want to thank Satya Mohanty for his scrupulous help in proofreading the manuscript.

CHAPTER ONE

Introduction

Whitman in Vietnam: Poetry and History in Contemporary America

"Where are you, Walt?
The Open Road goes to the used-car lot.

Where is the nation you promised?"

—Louis Simpson[1]

AS THE WHOLE PROBLEM of the interplay between poetry and history in America culminated in Whitman's Civil War writings, so it culminates again in the poetry of the Vietnam war—particularly in the work of those established poets whose careers were significantly affected by the progress of the war during the 1960s. Many poets who began the decade with substantial reputations and reasonably well-articulated personal visions found both their subject matter and their style challenged and invaded by political events they could not ignore. In much the same way that the war appeared to make teaching relevant, it made poetry relevant: both became politicized forms of public address. Yet poets were thereby confronted again with their essential powerlessness in American life; often their work came to embody a kind of urgent impotence. The decade began with a resurgence of open forms aimed at rewriting the myth of American communality, reinvigorating or even reinvent-

---

1. Simpson, *At The End of The Open Road* (Middletown: Wesleyan University Press, 1963), p. 64.

ing the nation's origin. In only a few years, however, an almost unmanageable vision of American history forcefully intruded, a vision
based on a record of self-deception at home sanctioning mutilation
abroad. That sense of history—with its symbolic, bipolar geography—largely ended the innocent optimism of a poetry inclusive of
all American locations. With a terrible irony, the disjunction between myth and reality had been eliminated: many poets believed
themselves to be living in a monstrous satire of the American dream.
Having broken away from colonialism almost two hundred years
earlier, Americans now found themselves among its more grotesque
agents. Against the background of a national policy of government
by the bad poetry of euphemism and rationalization, it was difficult
for good poetry to be other than absurd or desperate. That conflict
has always been present in American poetry, but never more vividly.
Though this is not a book about Vietnam, an analysis of poetry
about the Vietnam war can thus provide us with an extreme but
telling introduction to the more general relationship in America
between poetic form and public life, between personal vision and
our national history. Viewed synchronically, these poets of the 1960s
were the last of our first poets; they wrote as though they were the
avatars of an open exaltation whose death was inscribed in their
work.

Yet the great majority of published Vietnam poems are flat, predictable, and not likely to survive.[2] A few, conversely, succeed as
poems at the expense of making their choice of subject seem almost
coincidental. Such poems often do express a deep and unresolved
horror at murder carried out in the poet's own name and without
his knowing assent. Yet many of them too convincingly master the
anguish and anger at their source. They wish to contain and verbally

---

2. Three anthologies of Vietnam war poems are *A Poetry Reading Against
The Vietnam War,* ed. Robert Bly and David Ray (Madison: Sixties Press,
1966), *War Poems,* ed. Diane di Prima (New York: Poets' Press, Inc.,
1968), and *Where Is Vietnam?,* ed. Walter Lowenfels (New York: Doubleday, 1967). Since their work is outside my subject, I have not commented on
the poetry by Vietnam veterans; their poetry is available in *Winning Hearts
and Minds: War Poems by Vietnam Veterans,* ed. Larry Rottmann, Jan
Barry, and Basil T. Paquet (New York: McGraw-Hill, 1972) and Michael

transform their emotion without themselves becoming part of the inconclusive history of their times. These poems do not so much address a contemporary audience as insulate themselves rigorously from that responsibility. Admittedly, such seclusion, verbally obtained, is itself at the service of an historical imperative; a poem's willed isolation confirms what can and cannot be said to its immediate audience. These poems may reflect the poet's defeated confession that a receptive audience simply does not exist, or his hesitance to speak to his countrymen even if they were willing to listen. A war that daily certified most citizens' individual political impotence did not encourage many to embrace their neighbor's guilt. Many of the poems written in this climate are anonymously private, forwarding their own pain easily, without introversion, and without cost to the reader. This anonymity will increase in time; eventually they can be anthologized, like other war poems with "universal" appeal, without reference to the particular circumstances of their origin. No longer reflecting the historical specificity of Vietnam, they will have succumbed to what Michel Foucault, in another context, has called the "universalizing dissolution into the general form" of war.[3]

These are the most difficult of the Vietnam poems for a contemporary reader to judge, for they give us exactly what we most want— consummation, control, and eventual forgetfulness. Thus these poems wish to draw on their historical sources with false openness, to reestablish an impossible origin before body counts were daily news, when the war was a sheer flat eventfulness not part of the national psyche. But the war reached back and permeated the past, insinuating

---

Casey, *Obscenities* (New Haven: Yale University Press, 1972). For a more sanguine view of Vietnam poetry, see James F. Mersmann's well-informed *Out of the Vietnam Vortex: Poets and Poetry Against the War* (Lawrence: University Press of Kansas, 1974). An excellent overview of the problems inherent in political poetry is Thomas R. Edwards's *Imagination and Power: A Study of Poetry on Public Themes* (New York: Oxford University Press, 1971).

3. Michel Foucault, "Powers and Strategies," interview, in *Michel Foucault: Power, Truth, Strategy,* ed. Meaghan Morris and Paul Patton (Sidney, Australia: Feral Publications, 1979), p. 51. Foucault is speaking here of the Gulag and of "dissolution into the general form of confinement."

doubt into those of the nation's moral victories that once seemed secure, confirming again the recurring suspicion that our very origin entails our death as a people. Charles Olson names us correctly: "We are the last 'first' people." There was malice, he writes, at the root.[4] Even our vision of Edenic repose was fatally apocalyptic.

So these short, inflamed Vietnam poems (there are hundreds of them), confidently denouncing the aggressors among us, are essentially self-deceiving. Nor are the many poems of generous sympathy for the Vietnamese more convincing; they fail to engage what may be the only reality which is truly both personal and historical—the virtual impossibility of genuine (and specific) empathy for a culture so wholly other.[5]

Yet what above all undoes most Vietnam poems, even the poems which are frankly beautiful and original, is an apparent ignorance of how history has usurped both their language and their form. These poems would, in effect, separate public feeling from public speech, as though ambivalent emotions acknowledged in the marketplace can be effectively resolved through poetic language. It is part of the American poetic myth to believe that personal articulation cleanses language. The poet's individual, sacrificial speaking revitalizes all our language at the small price that he suffer his own speech—a suffering the reader democratically experiences as equal to his own. But it is difficult to credit this poetic version of the American dream. The wilderness meadows do not sprout around the poet speaking on the battlefield, nor does a consciousness at ease so readily supplant an embattled mind. Certain poems which render a national agony into language of exalted metaphor must, then, be understood as meticulous acts of historical repression:

---

4. Olson, *Call Me Ishmael* (1947; rpt. San Francisco: City Lights, 1967), pp. 14-15.

5. The opposite approach, a painstaking attention to her own cultural limitations, can be seen in Susan Sontag's well-known essay "Trip to Hanoi." That essay will survive and remain historically relevant. For analyses of "Trip to Hanoi" see Leo Marx, "Susan Sontag's 'New Left' Pastoral: Notes on Revolutionary Pastoralism in America," *Triquarterly*, Nos. 23/24 (1972), pp. 552-75, and my "Soliciting Self-Knowledge: The Rhetoric of Susan Sontag's Criticism," *Critical Inquiry*, 6, No. 4 (1980), 707-726.

Quick on my feet in those Novembers of my loneliness,
I tossed a short pass,
Almost the instant I got the ball, right over the head
Of Barrel Terry before he knocked me cold.

When I woke, I found myself crying out
Latin conjugations, and the new snow falling
At the edge of a green field.

Lemoyne Crone had caught the pass, while I lay
Unconscious and raging
Alone with the fire ghost of Catullus, the contemptuous graces
    tossing
Garlands and hendecasyllabics over the head
Of Cornelius Nepos the mastodon,
The huge volume.

At the edges of southeast Asia this afternoon
The quarterbacks and the lines are beginning to fall,
A spring snow,

And terrified young men
Quick on their feet
Lob one another's skulls across
Wings of strange birds that are burning
Themselves alive.

The poem is James Wright's "A Mad Fight Song for William S. Carpenter, 1966." A note from Wright informs us that "Carpenter, a West Pointer, called for his own troops to be napalmed rather than have them surrender."[6] On the surface, Wright's poem would seem

---

6. *Collected Poems* (Middletown: Wesleyan University Press, 1971), p. 177. It is no small matter that some Vietnam poems, particularly those that make use of factual data, have to be published with footnotes to jog the memory; more footnotes will be required with each reprinting. This is particularly true for a poem like Ginsberg's "Wichita Vortex Sutra"; many of the names he mentions, central figures in the political life of the 1960s, are already meaningless to younger readers. As it happens, Ginsberg himself has provided some of those footnotes; they are printed on pp. 101-8 of Paul

to recover and make unforgettable a telling, demented moment of
our history; yet the poem only focuses on that event because its isolation gives it the power to characterize a broad spectrum of more
ordinary madness; the poem selects an historical incident to render
a whole history manageable. In the context of the surrounding
poems in Wright's general mode of pastoral transfiguration, we
cannot feel that he shows us a career diverted and threatened by
Vietnam. Indeed the poem pretends to demonstrate how little
Wright's verbal muscles can be outmatched: even *this* horror, so
close to us, verges on apotheosis.

   I am not (or at least I hope I am not) merely attempting to take
moral issue with the poem, though political and aesthetic taste often
have morality at their core. Yet any sentiment approaching self-
righteousness is by now irrelevant; the poems which took refuge in
outright accusation are already poetically and historically dead. Actually, I still admire this poem, and I feel it tells us something—
with its image of the suddenly stunned, detached football player
whose head fills with Catullus's metrics—about the distracted, fatal
spirit with which America pursued its dated ideals in Vietnam. Yet
the lesson is offered too easily. Wright does not take the chance of
contending directly with history's real power over the poem. The
pastoral allusion is triumphant and entirely remote; although the
reference to Catullus is juxtaposed with the image of men in Vietnam, its pastoralism is in no way undercut by it. The irony operat-
ing here serves to reinforce the poem's total self-regard. As the last
stanza demonstrates, Wright's poetic securely confers a transcendent
beauty on the demonic.

   George Hitchcock's "Scattering Flowers" partakes of the same
tendency toward exaltation through metaphor.[7] The poem is sus-

---

Carroll's *The Poem In Its Skin* (Chicago: Big Table, 1968). Ginsberg's notes
also correct some of the inaccuracies in Carroll's reading of "Wichita Vortex
Sutra." Carroll takes Ginsberg's declaration of the war's end too literally, regularly misreads the poem's tone, and faults, I think unfairly, Ginsberg's descriptions of midwestern landscapes.
   7. Hitchcock, *The Dolphin With The Revolver In Its Teeth* (Santa
Barbara: Unicorn Press, 1967), p. 30. "Scattering Flowers" is also included
in the collections edited by Bly and Lowenfels.

pended between poeticized madness and irony made almost too bitter through the use of a sanctimonious quotation from Lyndon Johnson as an epigraph, an epigraph that raises too many reactions the poem does not confront: "It is our best and prayerful judgment that they (the air attacks on North Vietnam) are a necessary part of the surest road to peace":

> There is a dark tolling in the air,
> an unbearable needle in the vein,
> the horizon flaked with feathers of rust.
> From the caves of drugged flowers
> fireflies rise through the night:
> they bear the sweet gospel of napalm.
>
> Democracies of flame are declared
> in the villages, the rice-fields
> seethe with blistered reeds.
> Children stand somnolent on their crutches.
> Freedom, a dancing girl,
> lifts her petticoats of gasoline,
> and on the hot sands of a deserted beach
> a wild horse struggles, choking
> in the noose of diplomacy.
>
> Now in their cane chairs the old men
> who listen for the bitter wind
> of bullets, spread on their thighs
> maps, portfolios, legends of hair,
> and photographs of dark Asian youths
> who are already dissolving into broken water.

Curiously, the poem's main strength is its consistent self-deflation. The first two lines are neither perfectly threatening nor sardonic; they are both. The reference to "dark tolling" is overly theatrical, especially since the phrase has no clear context. One could argue that the theatricality reflects a broad recognition that our age has incipient holocaust as its own universal form of bad theater, but even so general a reference would require a more specific context. The next line, "an unbearable needle in the vein," is again perhaps too vague to be more than pretentious. The tone shifts with the next image, however, "the horizon flaked with feathers of rust," since it moves us toward both a radiant visual image and a sense of the air unbreathable from the detritus of war machines. The final three lines take a pastoral image and link it with, perhaps, the small lights on a plane at night. Yet the image remains felicitous, even if it suggests that the fireflies in safer fields at home were for us, in what seemed to many to be our national madness, a temptation to apocalyptic flame.

The second stanza further attempts to amplify the verbal irony. Our democracy has often been willing to render its equality violently; its fire is a leveler with the attractions of all harmonious endings. The image of the dancing girl, with skirts of gasoline almost aflame, is unresolvably ambivalent—as a metaphor she is revolutionary, as a vision of real policy she is horrific. Yet the stanza is ruined by two unhappy images—the accurate but nonetheless maudlin description of children on their crutches and the image of a horse "choking in the noose of diplomacy," the latter a typical case of politics making poetic language banal.

The last stanza more effectively takes our simple rage at the old men whose frustrated power has turned to war plans and compromises this rage verbally. The image is first of all rather romanticized and dated for a war often managed by young men and computers. But the notion is still a source of popular resentment, and it prepares us for the seductions (both literal and verbal) of the last two lines. To kill what we both love and fear is an impulse central to our history. Here the sexual tension which is inescapably part of our heritage of oppressions (of the land and of three darker races) is complicated by language implicating the reader. The sonorities of "already dissolving into broken water" compel our satisfaction despite the sense of elemental disruption.

It does not matter whether these readings were intended to be in the poem. The historical situation evoked by the poem demands that its metaphors be undercut, and the poem partially survives the process because its language is adapted to that end. We are asked, in effect, to believe that the poem's weaknesses are due to historical circumstance, not to the poet's limitations. Ignoring the historical pressure for a reconsideration of form, the poem's solutions are exclusively rhetorical. These rhetorical maneuvers reflect a symbolist tradition that does not survive its contact with a dark reading of recent political events, which can make the tradition appear decadent and over-used. When the symbolist tradition is employed as an unexamined resource in topical poetry, its imagery may seem self-indulgent, since it tends to deflect all attention from external event back to the poet's essentially romantic imagination. Yet what the war called into question, for poetry, was precisely this ability of language to transcend anything. We all know that particular words can be tainted by associations they acquire in public usage. Serviceable, bureaucratic words like "pacify," "relocate," "reconnaissance," become attributes of disguised violence. Phrases like "peace with honor" are riddled with pretence. But more importantly, the whole medium of public discourse becomes a mode of deception, and not even poetic utterance is innocent. "Language," writes Denise Levertov, "you are eroded as war erodes us." The war doesn't end, because *we* are the war; it is the message our history repeats to us each time we speak— "nothing we say has not the husky phlegm of it in the saying."[8]

Because it can address its own permanent verbal tradition, its own history of formal choices, poetry is not always tied in obvious and unavoidable ways to social forces. Even though such ties are inevitably present, a poet can disguise them, deflect his readers' attention from them, or even deceive himself about their significance, by seeming to contend with a tradition exclusively literary. This deception is not, however, easy to achieve in America, for the great myths of American poetry are very much tied to our sense of ourselves as a people—to our persistent belief in the existence of an inner, spiritual equivalent of the virginal continent that once surrounded us. Except in poetry, that dream regularly takes inverted or despotic form. Parallel to a national history in which the dream of Adamic innocence is mired in violence and greed, we have, since Whitman, a

---

8. Levertov, *To Stay Alive* (New York: New Directions, 1971), pp. 22 and 14.

compensatory poetic of open forms. Williams, in *In The American Grain,* explicitly searches the failed visionaries of American history for their implicit promptings toward a new poetic. It may be pathetically naive to have believed that poetry could be a refuge for a social project of enlightened communality, yet the great poems of this tradition stand because they have always dealt with their own verbal inadequacy, with the almost material resistance language has to our projects for it.

At least in its poetic version, the dream persists. Yet ten years of a war perceived as especially despicable gave even the poetry of openness an intolerable quantity of irony to confront. Even if most open-form poetry tends to avoid complex irony, its readers will bring to it a strong sense of irony about our national goals. To succeed, then, the poetry of the Vietnam war must consequently risk more, openly contend with its coeval public history, and court its own formal dissolution. As Adrienne Rich writes, our age like ourselves is "entering the paper airplane of the poem, which somewhere before its destination starts curling into ash and comes apart."[9] Perhaps contemporary poems which are convincingly American will often be poems about the failure of poetry. That is why W. S. Merwin's eroded voice is unnervingly American, despite the universally modern landscape he derives from T. S. Eliot. Merwin takes his national guilt with him to France; his Vietnam poems are powerful because the war made it almost impossible for him to write them.

Unlike Wright's, Merwin's poetic does not simply encounter and overwhelm the war—a victory by fiat which falsely ignores poetry's own inescapable place in the war of public languages. Indeed, though Merwin has several poems explicitly about Vietnam, the war is not most important for his work as a specific subject; the war is rather an incurable spiritual virus, whose disguises for invasion are protean and omnipresent. Unable to isolate the war's effects, Merwin makes an important choice—not to champion and aggrandize the war's dissolution into the general but rather to foreground the process of dissolution and make it difficult to endure. Merwin's *The Moving Tar-*

---

9. Rich, *The Will to Change* (New York: W. W. Norton, 1971), p. 61.

get, published in 1963, with its first fruition of his special voice of
evacuated despair, suggests his view of the people we would become.
His subsequent books move into and grow out of (the alternatives
are appropriately indistinguishable) the history of his times. "The
thermometers," he writes, are coming "out of the mouths of the
corpses."[10] The war was like that too—a form of helpless self-
knowledge, the ironic belated measure of a disease that ran its course
long before we woke to the moment of the poem.

Merwin's "The Asians Dying" is his most famous poem overtly
infiltrated by the war; it merits an analysis by infiltration, a criticism
surrounded and deadened by the poem's political echoes.[11] I quote
the poem's lines, in the order in which they appear, interspersed with
my commentary. "When the forests have been destroyed," he writes,
"their darkness remains," their heaviness and their thick foliage
weigh on us like our guilt. No defoliation, no consuming fire, is decisive. The landscape, leveled in the outside world, rises again in us.
The shadows amongst the trees are now a brooding absence and an
inner darkness. In our eyes are traces of each obliteration; our will is
choked by compulsion; our sight is layered with erasures:

> The ash the great walker follows the possessors
> Forever
> Nothing they will come to is real
> Nor for long

As readers, we too are possessors, but the poem's images *decay*
through association. The enlightenment the poem offers is experienced, paradoxically, as suffocation. We are possessed by a past which
invades each anticipation; ruinous memories seep into every future.
"Over the watercourses / Like ducks in the time of the ducks"—the
only remaining migration is our residual unrest—"the ghosts of the
villages trail in the sky / Making a new twilight." The only constant
is our discontent, the only change the rhythm of returning nightmare.
Twilight is the moment when consciousness—itself a confusion of

---

10. Merwin, *The Lice* (New York: Atheneum, 1967), p. 17.
11. Ibid., p. 63.

misdeeds—submits to new violence.

The poem is a tapestry of recognition and forgetfulness; its lines comment on one another endlessly. Each image (verbally unique) is immediately enfolded by a torpor of historical sameness; in an age whose destiny is past, each name names everything. The poem is a claustrophobia verbally enhanced by false relief; each new line rediscovers old ground.

But Merwin's fine musical sense always provides for surprises in tempo. These verbal shocks (like their unpunctuated lines) bleed off into silence, but that only increases their hold on us:

> Rain falls into the open eyes of the dead
> Again again with its pointless sound
> When the moon finds them they are the color of everything

These lines are set by themselves on the page. If we could, we might join them to another stanza to deaden their horror. The lines relate a simple fact, one we secretly knew and merely had not thought of, but the image lends the war an unbearable solitude. It is as though a single and essential benediction were lacking at the core of everything we are. It is too late, death cannot be contained. We cannot bury the dead of Vietnam; raindrops hammer at their delicate eyes, we cannot reach out to close them. Already they are the color of everything, for everything has taken on their color: their violated sight is taken up into the limpidity of the air.

Thus, "the nights disappear like bruises but nothing is healed / The dead go away like bruises." Dawn is merely burning darkness. There are no more beginnings. We are not truly healed (nor can the poem heal us); we are uniformly, though not terminally, wounded. The body politic absorbs its crimes; they are its substance: "The blood vanishes into the poisoned farmlands." The war is the absolute limit of knowledge: "Pain the horizon / Remains." Above us, trembling but unfulfilled, "the seasons rock," now unnatural signs that no longer signify, "they are paper bells / Calling to nothing living." For a world that will not be reborn, seasonal change is mockery. And the poem, too, is a paper bell; it tolls no prophecy, for its message was apparent long ago—embedded equally in every historical act and in every line.

"The possessors move everywhere under Death their star," Merwin concludes, but he is naming all of us, not accusing anyone, for the poem too possesses a history it loathes. "Like columns of smoke they advance into the shadows / Like thin flames with no light." What we are has corrupted the elements we are made of; all that we cannot see is unspeakably known to us. "They with no past," he writes, "And fire their only future"; the pronoun reveals not the clarity of distance but a special kind of self-knowledge—forgetfulness and revulsion in contest. The possessors have no past because what they do cannot be distinguished from what they have been. The final line is merely a rebuke, a false seal on the poem's form; fire is the future already with us.

Merwin's poetry shows us that it is not sufficient to speak directly of a traumatic history, that history should permeate the aesthetics of the poem. When historical events overtly enter a poem, it rarely works to use them merely for triumphant rage. Anger can be a more effective wellspring for poetry if it is allowed to compromise the poem in much the same way that it compromises the poet himself. Poetry is certainly one of the few places where language can appear to transcend its historical entanglements—after it first submits to them. Some of the most interesting poems about the Vietnam war are almost destroyed by their subject and their own political futility— Robert Bly's "The Teeth Mother Naked At Last," Robert Duncan's "Up Rising," Allen Ginsberg's "Wichita Vortex Sutra," Michael Harper's "Debridement," Galway Kinnell's "The Dead Shall Be Raised Incorruptible," and Levertov's "Staying Alive." All these poems are visibly subverted by the language of the war they grapple with, indeed they very nearly fail.

More than most Vietnam poems, Ginsberg's long "Wichita Vortex Sutra" is permeated with the managerial rhetoric and political slogans of the war.[12] The poem is an immensely self-conscious but

---

12. Ginsberg, *Planet News* (San Francisco: City Lights, 1968), pp. 110-32.

rather notational diary of a car ride toward the city of the title. Ginsberg records some of what he sees, in descriptive passages often sparse and underplayed though careful and appreciative, and includes fragments of radio and newspaper reports. As he has so many times before, he invokes Whitman and assumes his role: "Come lovers of Lincoln and Omaha, / hear my soft voice at last...O Man of America, be born" (pp. 111-12). Ginsberg is fully committed to the role, but more consistently mild and self-deprecating about its efficacy than his critics usually recognize. That reticence may help substantially to assist the poem in surviving. Ginsberg manages, in effect, to call on Whitman's prophetic posture, to invoke the role and its still powerful symbolism, while exhibiting no conviction that anyone will heed his voice. The language of the war is deplored, but with regret and fatalistic humor rather than with self-righteousness. Much more than most poets, he recognizes that the war for the majority of Americans was only language and photography. "Rusk says Toughness / Essential for Peace," Ginsberg notes, and describes "Vietcong losses leveling up three five zero zero" as "headline language poetry, nine decades after Democratic Vistas" (p. 119). "On the other side of the planet," Ginsberg reminds us, "flesh soft as a Kansas girl's / ripped open by metal explosion." There is "shrapnelled / throbbing meat / While this American nation argues war" with "conflicting language, language / proliferating in airwaves" (p. 121).

Interspersed with this reportage are the vignettes of silent Kansas landscapes and Ginsberg's own comments. He mocks the rhetoric of politicians, pleads with, teases, and challenges his American audience—"Has anyone looked in the eyes of the dead?"—and calls on a pantheon of gods to come to his aid: "Come to my lone presence / into this Vortex named Kansas." Yet Ginsberg's voice never dominates. We no longer have the insistent personal lamentation that carries the listings of his earlier poems. His presence here is intermittent, as if he realizes that while "almost all our language" is being "taxed by war" (p. 126) a poet cannot shape it to his will. The poem, then, seems only partly to belong to Ginsberg. History writes much of the text, and Ginsberg can try to identify what history has written, but he cannot pretend to dominate it. The rhythm of alternating vantage points carries us through to the end; the poem is remarkably effective and even hopeful about the possibility for intimacy and joy despite the war's toll on all of us. Yet the poem is finally only elegiac about the vocation of poetry. There is little left for poets to do, and no convincing reason for them to do even that. Nonetheless, Ginsberg manages a gesture whose political significance is precisely its powerlessness. If the war for us is language, he will let it end on his tongue. It is, he writes, an "Act done by my own voice" and "published to my own senses": "I lift my voice aloud" and "pronounce the words beginning my own millenium, I here declare the end of the War" (pp. 128, 127). It is a poignant, extraordinary moment, utterly gratuitous though an exemplary lesson and grandly Whitmanesque in its way. Yet it gives back to the rude history written by politicians all but the speech of vision and witness.[13]

Hearing Ginsberg read "Wichita Vortex Sutra" during the war was exhilarating. In a large audience the declaration of the war's end was collectively purgative. The text of the poem retains that fragile, deluded but dramatic effectiveness because it registers its unresolvable

---

13. The bitter-sweet catharsis of declaring the end of the war has been received very differently by Ginsberg's critics. In a review of *Planet News* that lacks the sympathetic and quite informative ambivalence of her subsequent essay on *The Fall of America*, Helen Vendler describes "Wichita Vortex Sutra" as depressingly inferior to "Kaddish" and cites Ginsberg's declaration of the end of the war as a particularly futile exercise of "pure will power," *Part of Nature, Part of Us* (Cambridge: Harvard University Press, 1980), pp. 195-203. Charles Molesworth more convincingly captures the impact of this climactic moment in the poem: "It stands as a moment of poetic daring, an attempt to use the words of the language for their proper ends of communication and community, rather than for deceit and destruction.... But the putative start of a new millenium is cast in personal terms; as long as Ginsberg is forced, either by poetic 'logic' or by a greater awareness to say 'my' millennium, the poem must remain lyric rather than prophetical," *The Fierce Embrace: A Study of Contemporary Poetry* (Columbia: University of Missouri Press, 1979), p. 53. My only difference with Molesworth's analysis is that I believe the poem is irreducibly *both* personal and prophetic. The unstable mix of the two impulses gives the poem its force and testifies effectively to its historical situation.

ambiguities with such clarity. On the other hand, a text like "Pentagon Exorcism" (pp. 143-44), essentially an unmodulated chant that
is hardly a poem at all, retains none of the drama of its most appropriate public occasion—the 1967 March on the Pentagon. The presence of the two texts—one successful the other mediocre—in the
same volume highlights the problems Ginsberg's critics have with
his work. To write about Ginsberg is to write about trying to find a
rhetoric that records your ambivalences without being overwhelmed
by them. The appeal many of his critics make to the eventual judgment of time is not very useful either, since no judgment of Ginsberg's mixed career will be complete that does not consider his place
in the poetry and public life of his time—a place that includes
not only what he has written but also his exemplary personal
confrontations.

   Equally problematic, perhaps even more so, is Levertov's "Staying
Alive."[14] The long poem sequence is decisively thwarted by the same
historical imperative that brings it into existence. Levertov's whole
career speaks to a mysticism whose verbal interest is continually
risked by comparison to a real world more resistant to ecstatic ascent.
All that justifies her personal expansiveness is the traditional American poetic myth—that what is experienced as our national madness
is in essence the misdirected primal energy of the continent itself, and
that the poet can symbolically redirect that force toward affirmation
and growth. Until Vietnam, Levertov managed to handle her inheri-
tance at a distance, overcoming discrete incidents of violence through
integration into larger verbal rhythms, subjecting personal grief to
purgation. She avoided encountering the larger myths of our history and kept her poetic territory elsewhere and self-enclosed. Her
earlier poetry nurtures a vision exceedingly fragile, almost evanes-
cent. The poems declare their own articulation to be a substantive
human action, though the assertion is continually vulnerable. Yet
with *To Stay Alive* a moral commitment to practical action outside
poetry enters the poetry itself. Moreover, she demands that her vision
prove equal to direct confrontation.

---

14. Levertov, *To Stay Alive*, pp. 21-84.

In several introductory poems reproduced from earlier volumes, she establishes, rather poignantly, the crisis that led her to a new and more provisional poetic form in "Staying Alive." The "Olga Poems" give witness to her entire career to that point; they are evidence that intimate, personal death can be made fruitful through verbal transformation. "A Note to Olga (1966)" hesitantly extends this claim to a social setting; at a political demonstration, her sister's death surprisingly proves a resource. The next four poems pit this vision of poetry "whose language imagines *mercy, loving kindness*" against her experience of the war:

> the mucous membrane of our dreams
> coated with it, the imagination
> filmed over with the gray filth of it [p. 13]

In our own bodies, this knowledge "numb within us / caught in the chest" contends with a Whitmanesque faith that our "understanding manifests designs / fairer than the spider's most intricate web" (p. 13).

Levertov's sense of the war's human cost for us is precise and telling, though her litany of its distant violence lies heavily on her tongue: "the scheduled breaking open of breasts whose milk / runs out over the entrails of still-alive babies" (p. 14). Brutal and accurate as these lines may be, they are essentially clichés of violent war. We can hear in them a history of violence verbalized at a distance, perhaps even specific rhetoric like that of the English reaction when Germany invaded Belgium in the First World War. Moreover, our own physical security makes the language flat and unconvincing. We have no historical ground for sympathetic identification; such words will not come to us. Williams argues that our poetry must seek the Indian in our hearts, but he never truly finds that voice. To give voice to the land, to give voice to Vietnamese pain—these passionate quests are generated by internal needs, they are motivated by self-interest; at worst, they are ironically a kind of poetic colonialism, pathetic evidence that our history shapes and uses our poetry whatever our intentions. Levertov tries to remember "when peaceful clouds were reflected in the paddies" and of the Vietnamese says "it was reported their singing resembled / the flight of moths in moonlight" (p. 15). The first image is weak because of its postcard conventionality; the second is almost patronizing; it suffers from the same untraversable difference she tries to indict with "it was reported."

These poems are made of personal defeat. Levertov admits she cannot "see except dulled and unfocused / the delicate, firm, whole flesh of the still unburned" (p. 16). She fears an insect has come to see through her eyes. The wellspring of her own humanism fails her; the lines opposing poetry and love to the war ring flat. We believe her despair and her revulsion, but her mystical language is hollowed out by the events which drive her to use her vision as an opposing force. "Nothing we do," she confesses, "has the quickness, the sureness, / the deep intelligence living at peace would have" (p. 14). The admission dismantles the poetry, for she does not pursue her own depression far enough. If she were truly to drop "off the limb of / desperation"—not, as she writes, "plumb into peace for a day" (p. 56), but into a poetry of numb self-extinction—she might then find a voice which could survive its times intact. Such a voice for Levertov might have an indestructible lightness that even Merwin (who rarely deceives himself about historical realities) cannot find.

The alternative she chooses in "Staying Alive" does not entirely succeed. The poem's title is deliberately a more process-oriented version of the book's title, as if to warn us that no conclusive poetic victory can follow. Yet such a victory is precisely the poem's goal; she would create a poetic world in which love is the greater power, but she cannot. The poem's openness to historical circumstances, its broad Whitmanesque inclusiveness, is essentially a challenge to do battle. She borrows the patchwork form suggested to her by Williams's *Paterson,* including journals, letters, conversations, newspaper reports. Williams, however, managed with a delicate humor to lead us into believing that even the most thwarted political rhetoric could be maneuvered toward a communal poetic speech. Yet when Williams in 1924 wrote that we build "battleships *for peace*"[15] he had a

15. Williams, *In The American Grain* (1929; rpt. New York: New Directions, 1956), p. 177.

somewhat different historical situation to contend with; it had its own very bitter ironies, to be sure, once the idealism of the First World War was undone by the realities of trench warfare, but irony itself is no longer available as an uncompromised response. There is little workable irony, little nostalgia to be recovered, from the legacy of children disemboweled and villages napalmed for peace. In the very complacency of its venality, the rhetoric of this war (whose language for many poets seemed the core of our self-knowledge) is an impossible adversary.

If conventional irony will not function effectively, neither will anger. The poetry always falls short of the rage we bring to it. Levertov herself knows that well enough. Indeed all her comments about the war's effect on language testify to her sense of the futility of the poetic enterprise. "I'm / alive to / tell the tale," she wrote in her second book, "but, not honestly: / the words / change it."[16] That recognition has to be confronted in these poems where the words are so much more necessary and yet so inadequate. As she suggests in *The Poet in The World,* poetry will not serve well simply to verbalize a prior conviction.[17] Thus her anguish at Vietnamese suffering finds only conventions of violence as its outlet. The hidden subject of "Staying Alive" is this blocked and subverted expressiveness, the poet's despair that appropriate images of pain—so specific and telling as to be unforgettable—are unachievable. Anger in contemporary poetry is thus perhaps best rendered as an emotion no longer possible. The Vietnam poems most likely to survive may be those that emphasize not moral outrage at the private suffering so easily visible in televised images but the very translucence and inaccessibility of those images.

Levertov herself moves toward that kind of treatment in *The Freeing of the Dust,* which includes her first fully successful Vietnam

---

16. Levertov, *Here and Now* (San Francisco: City Lights, 1957), p. 26. For further comments on the tensions in Levertov's poetry see Charles Altieri's excellent chapter on her in his *Enlarging the Temple: New Directions in American Poetry during the 1960's* (Lewisburg: Bucknell University Press, 1979).

17. Levertov, *The Poet in the World* (New York: New Directions, 1973), pp. 16-19.

poems. "The Pilots," based on direct experiences in North Vietnam of the sort very few established American poets have had, records her touching reticence in questioning captured American pilots.[18] Since her hostility cannot survive their actual presence, she is reticent about asking them if they knew "precisely / what they were doing, and did it anyway, and would do it again," if "they understood what these bombs / are designed to do / to human flesh." In no way does this reticence lessen the horror at what the bombs do, yet it does complicate the poet's ability to act and speak; it complicates them with a poignancy exactly right for Levertov's poetry. If "these men understood these acts," she writes, "then I must learn to distrust / my own preference for trusting people." In "Modes of Being," another poem in the same volume (pp. 98-99), Levertov uses a form that emphasizes the disjunction between her own consciousness and the history taking place in Vietnam. Four sections dealing with her own reactions are separated from but interspersed with three italicized passages about the prisons in South Vietnam:

> *Near Saigon,*
> *In a tiger-cage, a woman*
> *tries to straighten her*
> > *cramped spine*
> *and cannot.*

The flat narration establishes Levertov's respect for suffering that is, finally, not her own. Free herself to take pleasure in nature, she can neither forget nor fully maintain the connection with the unspeakable mutilations of the tiger cages:

> > Joy
> is real, torture
> is real, we strain to hold
> a bridge between them open,
> and fail,
> or all but fail.

---

18. Levertov, *The Freeing of The Dust* (New York: New Directions, 1975), pp. 30-31.

Levertov ends the poem with a passage that recalls the imagery of the conclusion to Wright's "A Mad Fight Song for William S. Carpenter, 1966." Here, however, the almost hieratic description of an impossible bird testifies to an apotheosis we desire that cannot be:

> What wings, what mighty arch
> of feathered hollow bones, beyond
> span of albatross or eagle,
> mind and heart must grow
>   to touch, trembling,
> with outermost pinion tips,
> not in alternation but both at once,
> in one
> violent eternal instant
> that which is and
> that which is . . .

The connective tissue to bind together the various forms of eventfulness into one body will not be fleshed out in the body of the poem. Its verbal reach fails, a victim, however indirectly, of the same reality in which a man in a tiger-cage *"tries to stretch out his hand / and cannot."* The poem gestures toward a language of radical fusion it cannot find; it is unable to name the wingspread with which it would take flight. Then the poem testifies to the rude irony language can intrude, for it can at least be said that Levertov's history and that of the Vietnamese prisoners are each "that which is and / that which is . . ."; they are linked by language that certifies only what experience cannot absorb. The poem trails off in ellipses, irresolute in the presence of its own metaphors.

In their own rather different ways, both "Staying Alive" and "Modes of Being" testify to a sense of the end of a poetic of open optimism. "Modes of Being," I think, succeeds because it accepts and indeed uses the forces that undercut its ambitions. Inevitably, though, both poems help to sour us on the verbal possibilities present in Whitman and Williams. Yet the opposite alternative, to parody their poetry, their open acceptance of American things and places, is equally unworkable. It will not suffice to invert Whitman's voice for mockery, as Kinnell does in the second section of "Vapor Trail Reflected in the Frog Pond." "I hear... America singing, / her varied carols," Kinnell writes, "I hear: / crack of deputies' rifles practicing their aim on stray dogs," and he proceeds with a tortured burlesque of Whitmanesque incantation, concluding his list with the sounds "of the soldier as he poisons, burns" and demonically imitates the barbaric yawp "with open mouth, crying strong, hysterical curses."[19] Such irony is grounded in self-pity and will not preserve the poetic tradition it addresses. Apparently we must instead watch the Whitmanesque poetic openly fail, something which Kinnell, however, was not yet able to do. He shifts the tone of the last section of his poem, trying to channel the violence above "rice paddies in Asia" into a vision of human communality: "they gaze up at the drifting sun that gives us our lives / seed dazzled over the foot-battered blaze of the earth." Elsewhere in Kinnell's poetry, the metaphoric transformation of violence into ecstasy works some of his most powerful effects. Here it is gratuitous and, in the light of the history he has cited, absurd.

One might argue that once poetic forms have been used successfully they cannot be retroactively compromised by later use or subsequent historical events. Established poetic forms pre-exist the moment when the poet begins to write. It may even be possible to conceive of new forms, at least speculatively, outside historical demands. Yet in the moment when the poet writes, history enters into and qualifies every verbal choice. Earlier in this discussion, I criticized Wright's use of metaphoric transfiguration, especially at the ends of Vietnam poems. His advocates could well point out that such a fascination with endings is not only an ancient given of our poetic tradition, but also possibly part of the biological heritage of a conscious species. Even if those arguments are correct, the most durable poetic form will still be altered by the pressures applied to it in each recurrence. Our pleasure in endings is, if not undermined, at least rendered historically particular, specific, by a war which did not end for us even when peace was declared. Forms wait, outside history, to be used, but to use them is a political act. We may fairly

19. Kinnell, *Body Rags* (Boston: Houghton Mifflin, 1968), p. 7.

limit criticism to a description of a form's hermetic texture, for even a single metaphor can verbally contain its own resonance. Forms are obtained and bounded by internal structures, and that self-sufficiency is part of their attraction for us. Yet a formal choice is also a response to historically imposed necessities, as any Vietnam poem will prove; a formal boundary is maintained both by internal and external forces.

Poetry and history are especially dependent on one another in America, both because our history has its own formative poetic myths and because our poetry continually addresses the world at large. For our poetry, this address has two dimensions. First, its poetic is a dream of the people we might become; it therefore rarely pretends finality, it prophesies possibilities. Second, American poetry is singularly addressed to the poetry of the future; its projects are given to us to complete. Much of our formal experimentation is a way of extending a challenge to the next generation, of preserving, to quote Charles Olson, "the will to change." Only in poetry do we find reflected Williams's image of Burr's dream—a democracy in permanent and celebratory revolution.

American poetry, as Williams, Roethke, and others conceive it, continually flowers out of its failure. As a formal model the flower is fulfilled by divesting itself of its petals. This opening-outward of form is an historical benediction, a democratization and purgation of guilt. As Kinnell writes, "the petals begin to fall, in self-forgiveness."[20] Yet the experience of recent history now denies many poets the rhythm they previously required to generate their poetry— the alternation between the anticipation and the unravelling of form. As Adrienne Rich writes, in one of her many poems where history surfaces as the aftertaste of every emotion, "I twist last year into a knot of old headlines / —this rose won't bloom."[21]

It is impossible to separate our national purpose from our poetic vision. The poetry of open forms has always depended on an imagined

20. Kinnell, *Flower Herding on Mount Monadnock* (Boston: Houghton Mifflin, 1964), p. 58.
21. Rich, *Diving Into The Wreck* (New York: W. W. Norton, 1973), p. 27.

geography simultaneously in us and at a distance; the war, perversely, parodied that doubleness. The distant jungles of Vietnam are like an overheated, fantasized version of our own continent on its first discovery. At that impossible remove, we acted out again and again the perpetually thwarted dream of a humanized wilderness. The land and its people resist our benevolence, and once more they are devastated. The intimate elsewhere of Olson's composition by field degenerates into a history of self-deceptions here and mutilations there. The experimental renaissance in American poetry of the 1960s suddenly appears decidedly frenetic. Set beside our history, our poetry becomes merely compensatory.

Not only Levertov but many other established poets discovered their aesthetic mysticism untenable in an age of bloodshed whose idealism was unashamedly hypocritical. A few—Bly and Duncan are the chief examples—found refuge in specifically mythic transmutation. Duncan calls up an immense evil figure of Lyndon Johnson: "the very glint of Satan's eyes ... now shines from the eyes of the President / in the swollen head of the nation."[22] Bly makes him the vehicle of an ancient death wish reborn: "As soon as the President finishes his press conference, black wings carry off the words, / bits of flesh still clinging to them."[23] Unfortunately, all myth has its unavoidable attractions; a mythic poem of political accusation will secretly channel the poet's own apocalyptic yearnings. "This joy I love," Bly writes, "is like wounds at sea. . . . The panther rejoices in the gathering dark."[24] Duncan's furiously antiwar "Up Rising" is ironically the obverse of his remarkable love poem "The Torso"; both figure a vast being and both employ images of sexual ascension from darkness.

Bly and Duncan have survived and in some ways grown as poets, but they are not unchanged by their war poetry, and they may lose many of their readers. Duncan's self-contained visionary poems

22. Duncan, *Bending The Bow* (New York: New Directions, 1968), pp. 82-83.

23. Bly, *Sleepers Joining Hands* (New York: Harper and Row, 1973), p. 21.

24. Ibid., p. 21.

("Often I Am Permitted to Return to A Meadow" is a good example) have given way to his Poundian "Passages" sequence, in which every formal resolution is almost masochistically subverted. Bly's carefully bounded associational poems have grown into either longer, interrelated occasions for violent reverie, as in the final title section of *Sleepers Joining Hands*, or the uneven prose poems of *The Morning Glory* and *This Body Is Made of Camphor and Gopherwood*. These prose poems, essentially an effort to recover his earlier vision, have stunning moments, but they are often lax and arbitrary. Bly's phenomenological method now has an increasingly surrealistic edge that includes a destructive element he may not fully understand. For a while, Levertov too retreated to her earlier mode, but in *The Freeing of the Dust* and *Life in the Forest* she has begun to use forms that show a new willingness to challenge her own previously secure mysticism. Nevertheless, the rest of her career will be colored by that first failed confrontation with history. Moreover, the readers who resented her political period may never entirely trust her again.

Some of the poets who have dealt effectively with the war, who have found a voice giving witness to history without falsely mastering it, may have given their careers over to it. Kinnell's experience of the war helped him to overcome the naively Whitmanesque catalogues of his earlier poetry and, finally, to lend his vision of death a quality both local and archetypal. His poem "The Dead Shall Be Raised Incorruptible" provides a bitter, unsettling irony (*"Lieutenant! This corpse will not stop burning!"*)[25] which proves a major turning point in his book-length poem sequence *The Book of Nightmares*. The book's earlier poems offer the first genuinely particular incarnation of Kinnell's sense that emptiness is at the core of all phenomena. The Vietnam poem then risks the book's hermeticism by extending this vision to an historical reality. As a result, however, Kinnell achieves a formal solution whose cyclical closure is at once private and public. The book is clearly Kinnell's masterpiece, usurping most of his previous writing, yet it is so final a work that it is

---

25. Kinnell, *The Book of Nightmares* (Boston: Houghton Mifflin, 1971), p. 41.

difficult to imagine Kinnell writing another major poem. Kinnell's *Mortal Acts, Mortal Words* (1980) has a few effective passages but no single poem of the quality of the best work in *Body Rags* or *The Book of Nightmares.*

Alternatively, Ginsberg will no doubt continue writing, but it remains to be seen whether his long project, begun with "Wichita Vortex Sutra" in *Planet News* and continued in *The Fall of America* and *Mind Breaths,* can be anything but the continuing (and virtually unchanging) verbal residue of the rest of his life. The only other alternatives for him are extreme—to carry his Whitmanesque rhythms into pure sound or to escape into religious mysticism. In many ways, Ginsberg's open-ended lifetime poem is rendered harmless by our history. The confidence that a poem can and will continue is enough to make our history, whose tempo is set by a national repetition compulsion, endurable. All poetic relief has become, as Merwin shows us, evidence of historical complicity:

> When the war is over
> We will be proud of course the air will be
> Good for breathing at last
> The water will have been improved the salmon
> And the silence of heaven will migrate more perfectly
> The dead will think the living are worth it we will know
> Who we are
> And we will all enlist again[26]

The rush of deluded expectation that opens Merwin's poem cannot be easily assigned to one political viewpoint. If we read the series of claims as enthusiastic demagoguery, then the lines, with their frenetic unpunctuated pace, belong to a supporter of the war, and Merwin's tone is distinctly sarcastic. Yet the lines can also be read more slowly, so that they convey a hushed and self-consciously ironic desire for relief from a war that seems even to make the air unbreathable. Through lines two to four also runs the widespread American conviction that an appropriate politics can redeem nature itself. The promise that "the silence of heaven will migrate more perfectly" echoes the displaced religious sentiment in our democratic idealism,

---

26. Merwin, *The Lice,* p. 64.

an idealism whose frustration regularly produces violence. So the cultural myths Merwin here exaggerates touch more of us than a casual reading would suggest. Nonetheless, the irony throughout is unavoidable, and it intensifies with "The dead will think the living are worth it," although the sanctimonious encouragement politicians offer toward sacrifice has this grotesque sentiment as its underlying logic. Building toward a still stronger irony, Merwin inserts the pathetic "we will know / Who we are" into this poetic version of oratory, and by then none of us can be certain we will not "enlist again." The last four lines communicate an irony whose object is compulsive and terrifying. Their tone is so mixed that our horror cannot be extricated from the ambiguous and benighted sense of triumph and affirmation.

If this poem is a fair model of a viable relationship between poetry and history in America, it suggests that the challenge to our poetry now is to create poems that turn rhetorical disintegration into a species of poetic assertion:

This would not be the war we fought in. See, the foliage is
heavier, there were no hills of that size there.

But I find it impossible not to look for actual persons known
to me and not seen since; impossible not to look for myself.

The scenery angers me, I know there is something wrong, the sun
is too high, the grass too trampled, the peasants' faces too broad,
and the main square of the capital had no arcades like those.

Yet the dead look right, and the roofs of the huts, and the crashed
fuselage burning among the ferns.

But this is not the war I came to see, buying my ticket, stumbling
through the darkness, finding my place among the sleepers and
masturbators in the dark.

I thought of seeing the General who cursed us, whose name they
gave to an expressway; I wanted to see the faces of the dead when
they were living.

Once I know they filmed us, back at the camp behind the lines,
taking showers under the trees and showing pictures of our girls.

> Somewhere there is a film of the war we fought in, and it must
> contain the flares, the souvenirs, the shadows of the netted brush,
> the standing in line of the innocent, the hills that were not of
> this size.
>
> Somewhere my body goes taut under the deluge, somewhere I am
> naked behind the lines, washing my body in the water of that war.
>
> Someone has that war stored up in metal canisters, a memory he
> cannot use, somewhere my innocence is proven with my guilt, but
> this would not be the war I fought in.[27]

This is Adrienne Rich's "(Newsreel)," the ninth poem in her two-part, fourteen-poem sequence "Shooting Script." Since each of the poems works on its own, the larger structure is not simply used to contain associative formlessness at the level of particular poems. Skeletal structures are frequently more self-conscious and uncomfortable than those articulated through narrative continuity or covert verbal rhythms. Here, the larger structure shows both characteristics—accumulated interpenetrations of private emotion and historical event, as well as an overt structure with, presumably, some claim to more comprehensive vision. As we might expect, the sequence as a whole provides for multiple entrances and interpretations. Yet this very plurality of connections also serves (I think both intentionally and courageously) to undermine the carefully achieved coherence of the individual poems. The two impulses, for coherence and for disjunction, are at war. We cannot rest satisfied in any individual poem because the sequence continually challenges us to a wider and less conclusive perspective. Such risks to our sense of verbal containment and resolution are generally either unpleasant or unwanted. Significantly, political references, too, are generally unwelcome in poetry, so the structural subversions parallel and intensify the subject matter. The form is uniquely suited to its times.

On examination, these verbal and structural qualifications are apparent within the individual poems. "(Newsreel)"—even the title is disquieting. In what political or emotional context is a newsreel par-

---

27. Rich, *The Will to Change*, p. 62.

enthetical? As a communication, how can a newsreel be merely di-
gressive, a clarification threatening comprehension? Given the political irony integral to poetry—an irony compounded of relevance and
impotence, each inescapable—the word "newsreel" is further compromised as the title of a poem. As it happens, several of the poems
are parenthetically dedicated, but only this poem is individually
titled. The title echoes the title of the sequence ("Shooting Script")
and thereby announces both the poem's method (a sequence of
visual images) as well as its subject (our confused internalization of
historical process).

Newsreel—the images are so clear, but they vanish and leave us
puzzled: "This would not be the war we fought in. See, the foliage
is heavier." It is as though we act (and record our actions) through a
gray perceptual film, a hopelessly clouded mental newsreel. It is not
my war, I know my war. Its images are in me, though I cannot recall
whether I fought or not. Yet somehow, in a self I cannot recover, in
features I cannot now recall, are assembled those images of my war.
Now (and thereby even from the first instant) this newsreel renders
those images equitable and properly ordered: "Somewhere there is a
film of the war we fought in, and it must / contain the flares, the
souvenirs. . . . Someone has that war stored up in metal canisters, a
memory he / cannot use, somewhere my innocence is proven with
my guilt." In a few frames, casually recorded, I appear without these
muted surroundings. My presence is definitive, even if the image has
since been discarded. In some peripheral, ordinary human action, I
am set aside and named; inconsequential, like each of my countrymen, I move numb and slow at the center of the vortex of history:
"Somewhere my body goes taut under the deluge, somewhere I am /
naked behind the lines washing my body in the water of that war."

Extraordinarily, in a single voice, plaintive but unforgivable, Rich
summons all the actors in this historical moment: the perplexed foot
soldier, taken up by a process he begins to understand only when
it is too late to resist; the nation unconsciously pursuing new approval for its past ("I thought of seeing the General who cursed us,
whose name they / gave to an expressway") and futilely seeking relief for its collective dread ("I wanted to see the faces of the dead

when / they were living"); and even the poet herself, subtly impli-
cated despite any protest. Each of the sentences can be voiced by any
of the actors; our roles are interchangeable, our guilt and innocence
inextricably mingled.

This collective first-person narrator has its antecedent in a hall of
mirrors. Self and history are paralyzed before absolute, irreconcilable
needs—to be separate and dependent. And the poem, too, in a voice
univocal and omnipresent, collects its lines while giving them over
to the fury and boredom of its age. "(Newsreel)" is a poem of merciless aggression, yet a poem also of ambiguous complicity. The historical relevance is immediate but uncontainable. The form—ten
prosaic black slats on the page—proceeds through a series of equivalent evasions. Each successive statement seals the poem's moment
while at the same time opening the poem to the past and the future.
Ironically, then, the poem is genuinely Whitmanesque, certifying his
vision of bountiful death in an open form appropriate to our times.
One of the very few wholly successful Vietnam poems, it may also
be a prophecy of the poetry of the future—a poetry whose forms
cling tenaciously to their own dissolution. It is with this aesthetic
criterion in mind that I should like, in what follows, to examine some
of the poetry of our recent past.

CHAPTER TWO

The Field Where Water Flowers:
Theodore Roethke's
"North American Sequence"

I think of American sounds in this silence:
On the banks of the Tombstone, the wind-harps having their say,
The thrush singing alone, that easy bird,
The killdeer whistling away from me,
The mimetic chortling of the catbird
Down in the corner of the garden, among the raggedy lilacs,
The bobolink skirring from a broken fencepost,
The bluebird, lover of holes in old wood, lilting its light song,
And that thin cry, like a needle piercing the ear, the insistent cicada,
And the ticking of snow around oil drums in the Dakotas,
The thin whine of telephone wires in the wind of a Michigan winter,
The shriek of nails as old shingles are ripped from the top of a roof,
The bulldozer backing away, the hiss of the sandblaster,
And the deep chorus of horns coming up from the streets in early
   morning.

[CP, 204]¹

MY DECISION TO PLACE a chapter on Roethke after a discussion of the influence of the Vietnam war on American poetry may first appear improbable. A far less public poet than those I have just discussed, Roethke rarely shows interest in events in American history; indeed, until late in his career he gives little overt evidence of an attempt to come to terms with his national origin. Of course the

---

1. *The Collected Poems of Theodore Roethke* (New York: Doubleday, 1966). Cited internally as *CP*.

obliteration of historical references in Roethke's early pastoralism may itself be a response to history, but that is not my immediate concern here. My concern is rather with the way in which Roethke's work, partly because of these differences, offers a strategic perspective on the poetry of the last two decades.

Roethke's career in several respects parallels those of the poets I will discuss in subsequent chapters. Even more than any of them, his vision was quite fully articulated before he began openly to engage his sense of American history. Like Kinnell and Duncan, he does so in open forms very much in the Whitman tradition. I will emphasize the last phase of Roethke's career, particularly his "North American Sequence," where, as the epigraph above suggests, he opens his greenhouse world to a more literal American landscape. Partly because of the power of Roethke's vision, partly because the period in which he worked was a less traumatic one, the conflict between poetic aspiration and a constrained sense of historical possibility is less intense in "North American Sequence." Nonetheless, like the poets I examined in the first chapter, Roethke finds his vision threatened by its exposure to American culture. The result is a poetry, grounded in loss and courting failure, that in many ways anticipates the poetry of the 1960s.

Midway in Roethke's career, a playful ambivalence enters his poetry. This ambivalence, in which previously secure images become either unattainable or ambiguous, foreshadows the more radical uncertainty of his final poems. In his enigmatic little poem "The Beast," for example, the speaker approaches a great, overgrown door and sees beyond it "a meadow, lush and green" where a "sportive, aimless" beast is playing (CP, 145). Watching the beast, he catches its eye; thereupon he hesitates, falters, and falls to the ground. He attempts to rise, but collapses again. When he is able to stand at last, the beast with its great round eyes has gone: "the long lush grass lay still; / And I wept there, alone." The narrator never actually enters the ,meadow; he falls "hard, on the gritty sill," and does not go beyond. The reader never learns where the meadow is, nor the identity of the ambiguous beast. These things are evocative precisely because they are so gnomic. The poem's symbols have the open-ended

quality of dream images. Indeed the meadow may be the multirefer-
ential field over which dreamers fly; for the poet it is simultaneously
the external world and a forgotten terrain within himself. Other
passages in *Words for the Wind* suggest much the same duality:

> On a wide plain, beyond
> The far stretch of a dream,
> A field breaks like the sea; [*CP*, 124]

> A field recedes in sleep.
> Where are the dead? Before me
> Floats a single star.
> A tree glides with the moon.
> The field is mine! Is mine! [*CP*, 122]

Field, meadow, and plain—with their ravishing openness—make
up one end of Roethke's polarized poetics of nature. At the other end
are spaces of enclosed germination—including, of course, the famous
greenhouse poems. Both types of space have their characteristic in-
habitants. To the fields belong the many species of birds who fly
above them; to the greenhouse, the tiny animals who cluster there—
snail, slug, and worm: "When I was a lark, I sang; / When I was a
worm, I devoured" (*CP, 172*). These animals embody the emotive
qualities of their respective spaces, and they suggest thereby what
human use those spaces have. The greenhouse provides both a retreat
and an organic resource; there the self, "marrow-soft, danced in the
sand" (*CP, 63*). It is a kind of evolutionary swamp which nurtures
the self until it can embrace its wider surroundings.[2] Kenneth Burke
has superbly catalogued the "vegetal radicalism" of the dense, vital
"realm of motives local to the body" which animate Roethke's greenhouse world. Among the wrestling thatches of damp stems, Roethke

---

2. Roethke's own analysis of the greenhouse world, from his "Open Letter," is valuable here: "Some of these pieces, then, begin in the mire, as if
man is no more than a shape writhing from the old rock." And again: "Each
poem...in a sense is a stage in a kind of struggle out of the slime; part of a
slow spiritual progress; an effort to be born, and later, to become something
more," *On the Poet and His Craft: Selected Prose of Theodore Roethke*, ed.
Ralph Mills (Seattle: University of Washington Press, 1965), pp. 40, 37.

discovers "severedness, dying that is at the same time a fanatic tenacity; submergence (fish, and the mindless nerves of sensitive plants); envagination as a homecoming."[3]

The fields offer suitably more expansive possibilities for both growth and threat. If the greenhouse presents a smothering, claustrophobic death, the fields proffer the risk of death through over-extension. The fields challenge us to attempt an excess of becoming; if we accept that challenge, the self may be sacrificed to the landscape: "I fear myself in the field, / For I would drown in fire" (CP, 138). Yet death in Roethke's poetry—whether in greenhouse or field—is always a rite of passage toward rebirth. Often it is willing and even deliberate. The old woman who meditates over her death declares, "I'm wet with another life," and her words point to the self-delivery implicit in rebirth. The new life she is wet with is her own:

The sun! The sun! And all we can become!
And the time ripe for running to the moon!
In the long fields, I leave my father's eye;
And shake the secrets from my deepest bones;
My spirit rises with the rising wind;   [CP, 173]

In these open fields, the secret reserves of the self fertilize a new poetry of expansion. The old woman leaves her father's eye, for in nature's setting she is self-born. But Roethke's lines also have an auto-biographical context; the greenhouse and a field beyond it mapped the natural borders of his childhood—the one a protected space over-seen by his father, and the other a joyous but threatening exposure to the world.[4]

---

3. Burke, "The Vegetal Radicalism of Theodore Roethke," *Language as Symbolic Action* (Berkeley: University of California Press, 1966), pp. 276 and 254.

4. "If the greenhouse was an Eden created and maintained by his father, there was for Ted another one untouched or touched very lightly beyond it. ... I asked his cousin, Mrs. Mortensen, if there were any place on the property that everyone called, 'the field.' She said, 'Oh, sure. Out behind the greenhouse. Ted and I used to play there.' ...

'I want to tell you of a little experience, one of the few really mystical experiences I ever had. Ted and I must have been very young. And it must have

If history were to enter Roethke's poetry at all, it would clearly be most likely to appear during encounters with the second kind of landscape. Put simply, it is easier to forget America in a greenhouse than it is on the prairies. Moreover, in order to personalize landscapes of distance, Roethke would have to take into himself more than their idealized correlatives. Indeed, in *Open House,* where his poetry tries to be ahistorical, the personalized versions of open space are rather strained and awkward, while intimate spaces already show some of the convincing intensity they achieve in the first section of *The Lost Son and Other Poems.*

Roethke's whole career moves toward a poetry that can encompass both these locations simultaneously—toward a textuality extending the body's privacy to an immense landscape and, at the same time, harboring the world within the body's space. In their most conclusive form, the introspective values associated with the greenhouse—meditation, repose, retreat to the womb, death and germination in darkness—are condensed in the image of stone. The values associated with the fields—motion, flight, ravishment, ecstatic self-realization through risk—are condensed in the image of light. Between stone and light, between the earth and the air, stands a poet whose vertical flowering would link them both.[5] "I live in air; the

---

been an oat field that year because we raised food for the delivery horses. The oats weren't that wonderful gray-green; they were ripe and tall. And Ted and I went back there to play. We walked through into the oats and we couldn't see over the top so I think Ted must have been about four and I would have been six. I suppose the field held about five acres of oats and all we could see were the oats and the blue, blue sky, a very hot day. Then we said to each other, "We're lost and nobody knows where we are." It was a very wonderful happy feeling.... [Some time later], suddenly, like all kids, the play was over and we said, "Gee, we'd better start home." So we started but we couldn't find a way out. This seems silly but for two little kids who couldn't see over the top, it wasn't, and, all of a sudden, Ted began to cry.... So I said, "Now, Ted, don't cry. We'll get home all right." And of course eventually we did,'" Allan Seager, *The Glass House: The Life of Theodore Roethke* (New York: McGraw-Hill, 1968), pp. 22-23.

5. Cf.: "An angel with hips of stone / Nestled in my nerves" and "As if a stone had flowered to a bird," *Straw for The Fire: From the Notebooks of Theodore Roethke 1943-63*, ed. David Wagoner (New York: Doubleday, 1972), pp. 78 and 140.

long light is my home; / I dare caress the stones, the field my friend; / A light wind rises: I become the wind" (*CP*, 167). By verbally mediating between stone and light, the poet can link the landscapes they represent. The movement toward a poetry where greenhouse and field can coalesce culminates in "Meditations of an Old Woman" and "North American Sequence," Roethke's masterpieces. In the second, especially, Roethke seeks a language which will give voice to "the unsinging fields where no lungs breathe, / Where light is stone" (*CP*, 196).

"Meditations of an Old Woman" is the more accessible of the two poems. It has a clear narrative persona, with which the reader can easily identify, and a meditative context that prevents associative leaps and structural breaks from seeming too disruptive. It even, retroactively, makes the more fractured associativeness of "The Lost Son" less threatening. To the extent that Roethke presents a convincing image of an old woman's consciousness, the poem appears to be a *tour de force* of empathic identification. Yet the woman's hesitation between passivity and action, with naturalistic correlatives of pool and river, is really an elaboration of Roethke's own polarity of enclosure and openness. Moreover, giving the two alternatives sexual force and making the choice between nesting and flying a woman's problem is an entirely traditional decision. Roethke's human vision is less new than his excited sense of discovery would lead us to believe. The femaleness of protected resources and the maleness of energy in motion are a poetic given.

These perceptual categories inhere in the language; to fuse them is not so much a narrative or psychological problem as a verbal one. Yet Roethke, as Allan Seager's biography of him demonstrates, saw his poetic enterprise more competitively than his green mysticism suggests. More, perhaps, than he may have known, he was an ideal poet to confront the ground reality of language directly.

It is not until "North American Sequence" that Roethke fully realizes his own combative need for sheer verbal performance. In that poem, he also accepts the cultural pressure behind his art. "North American Sequence" is a more faulty achievement than "Meditations of an Old Woman" because it risks much more, but it is also, finally, a greater poem. It is the only major poem in which Roethke accepts his specifically American roots. Because of that, the poem cannot wholly succeed, but that is its strength. The willingness to fail becomes for Roethke the aesthetic equivalent of his temptation to die. For the first time in his career, it is not merely the mystical speaker who would die, but the poem in which he speaks.

In "The Longing," the first poem in "North American Sequence," the search for light incarnate begins in a demonic version of the greenhouse world.[6] Vitality has degenerated into corruption: "A kingdom of stinks and sighs, / Fetor of cockroaches, dead fish, petroleum" (CP, 187). This resembles the landscape Roethke mentions in his "First Meditation," where the self and the world converge in

---

6. The poems in "North American Sequence," with the years of their first publication in journals in parentheses, are "The Longing" (1959), "Meditation at Oyster River" (1960), "Journey to the Interior" (1961), "The Long Waters" (1962), "The Far Field" (1962), and "The Rose" (1963). As was his regular practice, Roethke frequently made use of passages written in earlier notebooks when he composed the poems.

Despite numerous differences in interpretation, including readings of particular passages that contradict each other, the published studies of "North American Sequence" are generally complementary. Readings of the sequence may be found in Hugh Staples, "The Rose in the Sea-Wind: A Reading of Theodore Roethke's 'North American Sequence,'" *American Literature*, 36 (May 1964), 189-203; Ralph Mills, "In The Way of Becoming: Roethke's Last Poems," *Theodore Roethke: Essays on the Poetry*, ed. Arnold Stein (Seattle: University of Washington Press, 1965); Karl Malkoff, *Theodore Roethke: An Introduction to the Poetry* (New York: Columbia University Press, 1966); James McMichael, "The Poetry of Theodore Roethke," *The Southern Review*, 5 (Winter 1969), 4-25; Richard Allen Blessing, *Theodore Roethke's Dynamic Vision* (Bloomington: Indiana University Press, 1974); Rosemary Sullivan, *Theodore Roethke: The Garden Master* (Seattle: University of Washington Press, 1979); Jenijoy La Bell, *The Echoing Wood of Theodore Roethke* (Princeton: Princeton University Press, 1976). Staples's reading drew effective attention to the patterns of imagery in the sequence, though, as Blessing suggests in what I find the single best book on Roethke, Staples's construction of its spiritual project is somewhat too programmatic. Malkoff's and La Belle's readings are both valuable for their analysis of Roethke's allusions to Whitman, Eliot, and other poets. Although their treatment of particular passages is often sensitive, I would take issue with the sense of selfless spirituality that Mills, McMichael, and Sullivan find in the sequence. I read Roethke's achievement here as much more willed and artificial and give more emphasis to the cultural context of the sequence.

despair: "I have gone into the waste lonely places / Behind the eye; the lost acres at the edge of smoky cities" (*CP*, 159). Here again "the slag-heaps fume at the edge of raw cities" and "the gulls wheel over their singular garbage" (*CP*, 187). This is a specifically American vista and its concomitant sense of a jaded, guilty sexuality is equally American. The speaker calls himself "a loose worm / Ready for any crevice," and the sexual image is not accidental. In "The Longing" this sense of physical revulsion is particularly intense. It is as though the greenhouse life has been distributed all over the landscape, exposed to cultural forces, and left to decay. More significantly, perhaps, the inside of the poet's own body is now vulnerable to the body politic. The once potent vegetable shoots, and those sheath-wet sproutings in the poet himself, have succumbed to an unfulfilled lust that "fatigues the soul"; the figure of the worm now offers a cowardly reversion to shapelessness.

"How," Roethke asks, "to transcend this sensual emptiness?" His answer is his own version of America's ever more belated cultural optimism. Despair, we convince ourselves, is the foreknowledge of our oncoming joy. The very proximity of death will return us to our revitalized origins. For Roethke, then, the very decomposition of the spirit presages its salutary immersion again in the world of the flesh. "What dream's enough to breathe in?" he asks, "A dark dream"— a dream illuminated by the dark light of eyes turned toward the body's depths, a dream of "a body with the motion of a soul." Thus the worm and slug, verging on formlessness and insensate matter, suggest a new beginning for a self ravaged and vulnerable. Shapelessness becomes universality and self-transcendence: "I'd be beyond; I'd be beyond the moon, / Bare as a bud, and naked as a worm" (*CP*, 188). Purgative journeys are apparently pre-eminently *cleansing*; spiritually on the other side of the moon, he recovers a virginal sexuality. Reduced to the empty vertical shape of a man—"to this extent I'm a stalk"—the poet is open to an influx of life outside himself. And the life outside will have to revive him, for even an industrial swamp is democratically procreative. Like Whitman, he pleads simply to participate in unselfconscious becoming: "I would with the fish, the blackening salmon, and the mad lemmings, / The children dancing, the flowers widening" (*CP*, 188).

The wish for otherness is just that—a wish, but it appears to be sufficient. The shift from slag heaps to salmon streams is entirely willful and arbitrary. It is sanctioned by a cultural fantasy that now has post-Freudian justification—the wilderness is still psychologically accessible in all of us. Not in *each* of us, but in *all* of us; collectively we still harbor the continent in its original fertility: thus the plea for otherness and the inclusive listing. One can believe the same thing elsewhere, of course, though Conrad thought the journey to origins needed the analogy of a trip to the Congo, and Lawrence thought it might help to come to the New World. In America, however, one simply embraces all things and places. Nowhere else could a poet be thought other than foolish for flinging together fish, children, flowers, "great striated rocks" and even "buffalo chips drying."

"North American Sequence" alternates rhythmically between periods of emotionally-charged self-exploration and precise though kaleidoscopic descriptions of nature. These different types of discourse are so readily identifiable that a reader could collect and rearrange them to make several more consistently coherent poems. Yet the result would not be so powerful. It is precisely the willed rhythm of movement between inside and outside, between the self and the world, and the complementary alternation between depression and joy, which propel poet and reader into the final vision. The introspective personal sections become increasingly ecstatic and mystical as the poet tries to move more deeply into the organic world he contemplates within himself, but this movement is checked by continuing reversals. The self is repeatedly nullified or emptied; nature again presents its dying face. As a poetic device, this kind of rhythm is unavoidably imprinted with echoes of Whitman's *Song of Myself*; Roethke, then, is compelled to find some way to repossess this rhythm and make it his own. He cannot entirely succeed, however, and his accomplishment here, contrary to Harold Bloom's analysis in *The Anxiety of Influence,* is founded on this very limitation.

Roethke brings this tension to the surface, exploiting it to dramatize the poem's verbal battle. In "Meditations of an Old Woman," he has his title character say that "the body, delighting in thresholds, /

Rocks in and out of itself" (*CP*, 163). In "North American Sequence," the Whitmanesque assurance that this rhythm is preeminently biological is abandoned. The juxtaposition of self and other parallels natural rhythms because the language has usurped nature; nature is a felicitous manifestation of will. The poem itself becomes the "Beginner, perpetual beginner" that the old woman proclaims herself to be.

The poem's continuous rhythm of expansion and withdrawal is reinforced when Roethke watches the tide at the beginning of "Meditation at Oyster River." Since the dying salmon, the mad lemmings, and the opening flowers of the first poem would fulfill themselves as inevitably as the tide, it is appropriate for young crabs and tiny fish to ride the tide shoreward in the second poem of the sequence. Nature begins to respond to the poet's call; the water surrounds him momentarily, and we anticipate his joining the tide, but instead he retreats to a safer perch. The decision is a partial rejection. He resists the natural world even while reaffirming his need for it. Then suddenly he unveils a full experience of the tide that could only be achieved from within the water. Not, however, the literal water at the shoreline, for the tides have been reconstituted in the water of words. The pull and tug is now inherent in the temptation to speak. Perched on his rock, he verbalizes the inward stresses of the oncoming waves—the forward thrust of the tide, the water sculpted by sandbars and fringed by beds of kelp, "topped by cross-winds, tugged at by sinuous undercurrents" (*CP*, 191). He receives the benediction of the tide when the water laps his toes, but only that. Then he appropriates the energy, internalizes it, and dreams of a final cleansing. It would be like ice melting in the spring—weakening, shattering, and flowing, suddenly unburdened of both its human and its natural debris:

> And I long for the blast of dynamite,
> The sudden sucking roar as the culvert loosens its debris of
> branches and sticks,
> Welter of tin cans, pails, old bird nests, a child's shoe riding a log,

As the piled ice breaks away from the battered spiles,
And the whole river begins to move forward, its bridges shaking.

[*CP*, 191]

In a few lines, we move from the "tongues of water, creeping in quietly," to this image of violent evacuation. The shock is considerable, not only because the passage is intrinsically destructive but also because it is a deliberate aggression against the Whitmanesque listing in "The Longing." The import is difficult to escape: there will be no loyalty to nature here except as it can be used to suit the poet's spiritual imperatives. This is an aesthetic alternative to the more literal historical usurpation of the American wilderness—rather less damaging, of course, but in service of needs no less dark. "I have left the body of the whale," Roethke writes, "but the mouth of the night is still wide."[7] Free from the self's restrictive darkness, there is yet the wider darkness of the communal self. Emptied of himself, the poet comes into "the first heaven of knowing," a knowledge revealed when the poem celebrates its power. The power is a freedom to remake nature, almost to obliterate it. Like Whitman, Roethke reconstitutes nature in his speaking voice, though Roethke makes the violence of the process more visible. The poem summons its landscapes only to discard everything but their essential energy. It is not only a mystical, trance-like tone we hear in the poem's final meditation; it is an assertion of priority: "I rock with the motion of morning; / In the cradle of all that is." To this impersonal voice, the tide is now an intimate otherness that originates within: "Water's my will, and my way, / And the spirit runs, intermittently, / In and out of the small waves" (*CP*, 191-92). For an instant his body seems part of the mutual vibrancy of landscape and self, though it is really the text that is holding them together in its net. There his consciousness is dispersed over its own perceptual field: "All's a scattering, / A shining" (*CP*, 192).

The third poem begins by reversing this euphoric mood. The self

---

7. Cf. Roethke in *Straw For The Fire*, p. 69:

> Within me swims another thing: a whale,
> Shapeless yet whole, and worse than Ahab had
> Pursued: not white: a gray amorphous ghost
> Of what we should not be.

retreats to its anguished territory and bodily darkness closes in again, through darkening thickets and contorted ravines. The poem juxtaposes its title, "Journey to the Interior," with its first lines: "In the long journey out of the self, / There are many detours" (*CP,* 193). It is a paradox the poem will nullify by force. The journey out of the self will proceed into a true interior we will share with the heart of a new world.

When we start the third poem, we assume that the poet has symbolically cleansed himself of civilization. The bleak clutter of an industrial wasteland in the first poem was exchanged for a world of sandpipers and herons in the second. Though a collection of trash intrudes again, it is carried away on a flood of water. The problem would seem to be solved, so we expect Roethke's experience to be less compromised. Thus the car that introduces "Journey to the Interior" is divisive and unsettling. Surprisingly, Roethke does not reject this standard symbol of the contemporary wasteland; he embraces it. Roethke provides what for him would seem an unlikely tribute to the teenage myths of the late 1950s. He recalls risking his life to drive eighty miles an hour on a dangerous road, and his celebration of this bravado is no less loving than his catalogues of natural life: "A chance? Perhaps. But the road was part of me, and its ditches, / And the dust lay thick on my eyelids, —Who ever wore goggles?" (*CP,* 193). By now this memory would be hopelessly sentimental, but "Journey to the Interior" was first published in 1961, and Roethke just manages to be innocent of the specific cultural self-consciousness that would have made the passage impossible. Instead, the homage to America's mechanical fantasies is more general; on that level, Roethke is quite aware of his inverted pastoralism. The poet has traded in his greenhouse for an automobile. Nonetheless, at the still center of his car ride he finds the greenhouse again.

Through the windows of the car, Roethke discovers that "all flows past"—dead snakes and muskrats, hawks circling above rabbits, "turtles gasping in the rubble," and even "a buckled iron railing, broken by some idiot plunger." All this detritus of nature's cruelty gathers in a catalogue evoking the rhythms of universal change. The passage obviously extends the breaking of the ice-jam passage in "Meditation at Oyster River." There he wished the self, like thawing ice, could be freed as though blasted by dynamite. Here the violence is more literal and commonplace; it is thereby at first more resistant to visionary synthesis. If this landscape "exceeds us all" it does so only by asserting a brute reality beyond our intervention. That, of course, is exactly Roethke's intention—to demonstrate that even the Darwinian side of America's landscapes can provide the raw material for textual transformation. Thus it would be a mistake to conclude that this "detour" into rude violence is peripheral to the poem's chief ambitions. Structurally and rhetorically, "Journey to the Interior" parallels all the poems in the sequence with its movement through descriptive catalogues to a visionary moment. Its dark world of dying things is not a lapse into a negative apocalypse that the sequence later overcomes; it is a necessary stage in the poem's development. It captures the one purgative experience essential to all visions of American communality—trial by visual fact.

What we see tends simply to contradict what we believe. Moreover, in a nation obsessed with the desire to create an ideal community, belief is generally codified before it is tested against reality. That was very much Roethke's artistic situation when he came to write "North American Sequence." His poetic world had been mapped out long before, and there was little if anything he could discover about it in his last years. What he could do, however, was to expose his vision to history, to open his greenhouse to the world at large. That is what he does most daringly in "North American Sequence." The result is a poem whose visionary synthesis must virtually contradict the catalogues of loss on which it is founded. The poem's transcendent moments depend so much on sheer assertion that they are always on the verge of becoming merely manic artifice. Yet Roethke's power of conviction just manages to sustain our trust in his vision. He convinces us that on the edge of our cultural hysteria is a zone of beneficial calm:

> I rise and fall, and time folds
> Into a long moment;
> And I hear the lichen speak,

And the ivy advance with its white lizard feet—
On the shimmering road,
On the dusty detour. [*CP,* 194]

Roethke succeeds for a moment in fusing a traditional opposition in American culture. The machine and the garden are brought together and shown to have a common core. Indeed, the machine is hurled into what is left of the garden and, at least as a metaphor, gets closer to the garden's source than did any of America's historical expeditions. Roethke's vision from the car is almost a mechanistic recapitulation of Wordsworth's boyhood memories in *The Prelude* of running, then stopping short to see the earth still whirling past him. For a moment, Roethke believes that not he but the things around him are moving.

The poem builds to a new pastoral ecstasy, though it is an ecstasy dependent on a poetic will symbolized by an onrushing car. As so often in his work, Roethke describes his meditative immersion in the physical world in terms of elemental transformation—earth to water, air to fire, stone to light. In "The Dream" (*CP,* 120), where sea and shore meet wood and meadow, the image of a woman changes a field to a glittering sea. Here in this willed poetic space where all dying things commingle, he declares, "I rise and fall in the slow sea of a grassy plain." These wide plains of vision gather the separate things of America into a common dance of death. In the territory of her poem, Roethke's old woman recovers all her past in her present, both love's worst day when "the weeds hiss at the edge of the field" (*CP,* 157) and the meadows where she remembers herself as a young girl—"running through high grasses, / My thighs brushing against flower-crowns" (*CP,* 161). In "North American Sequence," the prairie recalls the more public fuming wastes at the opening of the sequence and foreshadows the far field of the eternal near its close. Floating on this field of American locations, the poet tries to find them all a place in his greenhouse Eden. Outside history, the new greenhouse will nurture a set of landscapes themselves imprinted with history's image. Each time is to be a collection of times, each moment a whole cycle of moments. Each voice and every movement

will be democratic. Making himself the stage for this drama of simultaneous events, Roethke gives voice to America's special version of
negative capability. He is bereft of purposeful motion—"beyond my
own echo, / Neither forward nor backward, / Unperplexed, in a place
leading nowhere" (CP, 195)—committed to being only one unique
vehicle for the country's self-expression. Roethke verges on an image
of himself emptied, almost unborn, yet ripe, with the nation's earth
filling his mind. He wants, as Galway Kinnell has described it, to
make himself "vacant as a / sucked egg in the wintry meadow, softly
chuckling, blank / template of myself."[8] For Roethke, to unveil this
empty, original form would be to see his own face reflected in a
generalized image of the genesis of the nation's natural life.

   In the closing stanzas of "Journey to the Interior," Roethke begins
to articulate the shape and texture of an image that has hovered, half-
voiced, throughout his career—the central form of forms. As we
shall see, the notion of a form of forms runs through Robert Duncan's work as well. For Roethke it is not so much a mystical talisman,
though if Roethke's visionary passages are severed from his descriptive reveries, the form of forms would be reduced to that; it is more
his obsessive creation and re-creation of a central project that can
never be wholly achieved because our history continually denies it.
This primary form must combine erosive, temporal flux with sub-
suming, atemporal pattern. His phrase for this aboriginal goal is
"the flower of all water." In the midst of the natural processes
gathered together by the poem's advancing and retreating tide,
Roethke asserts that these opposing rhythms are fulfilled in a single place: "I see the flower of all water, above and below me, the
never receding, / Moving, unmoving in a parched land, white in the
moonlight" (CP, 194). Every fluted wave, all the endless curving
arcs of water, rise up through him to turn inward on a central flowering. The passage suggests that he has discovered the hidden paradigm of sheer fluidity, but the image is really a fiction sustained by
intratextual associations. "I rehearse myself for this," he admits, for
"the stand at the stretch in the face of death." Each poem in the se-

---

8. Kinnell, *Body Rags* (Boston: Houghton-Mifflin, 1968), p. 59.

quence is a new rehearsal, and the sequence as a whole is a series of rehearsals. Roethke's verb implies not so much a preparation for the inevitable as an elaborately staged ritual that will enable him to possess the inevitable within the poem.

Throughout "Journey to the Interior" our anticipation of that end is partly anxious. From the opening car ride, "where the shale slides dangerously / And the back wheels hang almost over the edge," through the descriptions of a conventionally picturesque town rendered foreboding, to the catalogue of vulnerable or dying creatures, a sense of threat continues. His images are adaptations of his more secure pastoralism, but with a new nervousness. Earlier in his career, he could write of a wish to hear "a snail's music" (*CP*, 163), and we could accept this as an extension of his greenhouse attentiveness to minute and soundless motion. Now a surreal uneasiness invades these dreams. When he claims to "hear the lichen speak, / And the ivy advance with its white lizard feet," we may reasonably wonder if these images communicate not only heightened awareness but also a sense of inexorable violation.

A similar ambivalence is at work in Roethke's evocation of the flower of all water; it is set against a sterile background—"a parched land, white in the moonlight." The flower, it seems, both opposes and fulfills its surroundings. Roethke casts his vision as an affirmation; "the spirit of wrath," he writes, "becomes the spirit of blessing." Yet the final line extends Whitman's dream of a democratized, luxuriant death to an image whose joy could easily turn to terror: "And the dead begin from their dark to sing in my sleep." Ten years later W. S. Merwin would be writing lines like these to summon the communality of collective dread.

At its moment in time, the end of the 1950s and the beginning of the 1960s, Roethke's poem can offer these images of collective renewal straightforwardly; they are not yet totally undermined by their historical context. Within a few years, Roethke's optimism would have appeared complicit with more dubious cultural enthusiasms. To maintain some independence for his vision, Roethke might have had to distance himself from arguments for open forms outside the world of poetry, at the risk of damaging his vision by its own defensiveness.

By the mid-1960s "Journey to the Interior" would have been undone by too many bitter ironies. As at other points in American history, the image of a hawk circling above its prey would have had a military correlative. Similarly, the ruined landscape of "The Longing" and the catalogue of dying things in "Journey to the Interior" would have been ineluctably demonic in five years, merely commonplace in ten. By then, Roethke could hardly describe the rippling tide as "burnished, almost oily" without being literal and therefore unintentionally comic. Yet I am not arguing that "North American Sequence" would not have succeeded had it been written later; I am saying it could not have been conceived at all. Like the car Roethke recalls driving, the poem's route skirts disaster; it travels the edge of his historical moment, hanging halfway over the abyss. From our perspective, the poem is filled with poignant vulnerability. Like many credible American affirmations, it is designed to age instantly, to appear from the outset to have been written in the past. We can believe, then, that the dead have sung in Roethke's sleep, even though we know that their voices in our darkness would be more harsh.

"North American Sequence" draws its strength from Roethke's acceptance of the categorical frailty of its vision. Like us, he knows that the poem's Edenic pastoralism is already a nostalgic artifice. It exists in the poem's "long moment" and nowhere else; it is, Roethke writes in the next poem, "a vulnerable place, / Surrounded by sand, broken shells, the wreckage of water" (*CP*, 197). This place is Whitman's shoreline, the narrow vantage point where continent and sea may be exchanged so rapidly that neither seems troubled by its past. Roethke returns to this territory in "The Long Waters" to show us that he, like Whitman, can still perform this aesthetic sleight of hand. Moreover, he tells us, he can play this game with the same ingenuous rapture: "How slowly pleasure dies!" he exclaims, then later: "I embrace the world."

If there is excessive bravado in these claims, it is touched with saving self-mockery. This playfulness is made possible by the poem's confidence in its own textual ground. As we enter the fourth poem, "North American Sequence" now contains its own reserve of organic life. Like the country at large, the poem is itself a wellspring of energy. When Roethke returns to descriptive reverie in "The Long Waters," he is recovering familiar poetic territory. Indeed it is territory now incorporated in the poem's form. When he moves from meditation to description, he is no longer duplicating a transition from the self to the external world; instead he is balancing two kinds of poetic language. The rhythm of excursus and return is a verbal rhythm. As the language moves forward, the natural settings already detailed are carried along as well. Each particular animal and place, exact in its isolation, echoes the other things the poem describes. It is therefore no longer necessary to worry that the land is finally unknowable. Whatever can be seen and named suffices: "Whether the bees have thoughts, we cannot say, / But the hind part of the worm wiggles the most" (*CP*, 196). The part of nature that can be aesthetically co-opted serves, synecdochically, to redeem the rest. It is not only the poem, then, which is renewed by these successive visual catalogues; nature itself is revitalized when the poem gives attention to its changes.

The catalogues in "The Long Waters" are variously humorous and reverent. Thus "the worm's advance and retreat" comically invokes the motion of the tides, and Roethke even proceeds to ask protection from such essential rhythmic force. Yet there are also intense and almost overawed descriptive celebrations: "A single wave comes in like the neck of a great swan / Swimming slowly, its back ruffled by the light crosswinds" (*CP*, 197). Both these images draw attention to the poem's power of vision, to its ability at once to specify and to exaggerate. Whatever the poem sees, it changes and perhaps also fulfills. Throughout "The Long Waters" Roethke is supremely confident of his transformative resources. That security enables him to move between the comic and honorific without disrupting the poem's tone. Overshadowed slightly by the darker vision of "Journey to the Interior," yet also partly freed by that preceding poem's purgative fear, "The Long Waters" establishes a new perspective of bemused respect. In that gaze, both "the butterfly's havoc" and "the heaving sands" are at home.

Roethke has generalized his greenhouse ambience. What was once a quality of perception dependent on a particular place has been

adapted to any location. That alone would not represent a radical development in Roethke's aesthetic. We might expect that he would, in
Bachelardian fashion, internalize the greenhouse world and become
capable of extending its nurturing warmth to the rest of his experience. A series of little greenhouse poems about different miniature
landscapes would naturally follow. But a long poem sequence, moving rapidly through a wide range of settings and emphasizing the act
of poetic transformation, is another matter. It asks whether the American landscape at large can become a greenhouse for the questing self.
That is one of our culture's founding questions. Roethke's private
greenhouse space thereby suddenly becomes both characteristic and
public.

That sense of larger ambitions lends a covert uneasiness to the first
four sections of "The Long Waters." The uneasiness is anticipatory.
We know that the variations in mood are building to a need for
another visionary synthesis. Another verbal resolution will have to
draw these new images together. Salmon leap for insects, ivy puts
down roots, a fisherman dawdles over a bridge. Each of these things
is unique, yet they share a common rhythm; their separate actions
verge on communality. That union will have to be verbal, for it is not
given to us in the natural world. Indeed, our sense of verbal expectation is increased by allusions to the language of resolution used earlier
in the sequence. Roethke names the gestures of plants, animals, and
men, then he summarizes those names in the poem's demonstrated
rhetoric: "These waves, in the sun, remind me of flowers" (CP, 197).
This statement can be rationalized—trout and pine trees may gesture
as instinctively as unfolding flowers; they can register on the eye as
successive waves of phenomena. Yet the memory Roethke invokes is
really of a relation to the poem's language. In these descriptive sections, Roethke relaxes into a daydream of naming in order to gather
energy for a new articulation of the poem's depths. Once again, he
will speak of the flower of all water.

As with each of the first three poems, the penultimate moment is
one of self-abnegation. He claims to be merely the passive recipient of
the vision, to be first the land's breath and only then its voice. "I
have come here," he writes, "without courting silence," and the irony

Our Last First Poets   50

in a poet's making that particular assertion is apparent. Yet he is in a sense merely the vehicle of imagery already present in the landscapes described. Of course, he has selected, arranged and vocalized those settings; he has given them whatever imperative toward communal form they now display. Nonetheless, the poem increasingly communicates a sense of inevitable force that gives Roethke's posture of passivity some justification. Having set all this in motion, he can step back and pretend innocence. "I remember," he writes, "the dead middle way, / Where impulse no longer dictates" (*CP*, 197).

Roethke would have us believe that he is no longer governed by the fatal self-pity of the first poem. His need to be reborn is collective, involuntary, and it can be realized through the instinct of the elements to play at metamorphosis. Nature, or at least nature apprehended, is a series of analogies. Moreover, those analogies converge on one another in the poem's space. There they do not merely clarify one another, they touch. And in touching they waken to a new life, "as a fire, seemingly long dead, flares up from a downdraft of air in a chimney" (*CP*, 198). Roethke wants to speak from the point where these forces meet. He wants to occupy the verbal shoreline, the textuality, between self and other. Ambiguously, then, he can be both witness and agent, actively propounding a vision of selfless empathy. The destination of all he sees and describes, he is also the point of departure for its fresh emergence. He will consummate all nature in a single form, while scattering everywhere seeds of himself. The eyes of his poem see inwardness everywhere:

> I see in the advancing and retreating waters
> The shape that came from my sleep, weeping:
> The eternal one, the child, the swaying vine branch,
> The numinous ring around the opening flower,
> The friend that runs before me on the windy headlands,
> Neither voice nor vision.
>
> I, who came back from the depths laughing too loudly,
> Become another thing;
> My eyes extend beyond the farthest bloom of the waves;
> I lose and find myself in the long water;

> I am gathered together once more;
> I embrace the world. [*CP*, 198]

These are the last two stanzas of "The Long Waters," and they present what is so far Roethke's fullest vision of the form of forms. Rather than a single unifying figure, his vision is a series of parallel and perhaps equivalent images. In that sense, it merely testifies again to the poet's desire to make multiple images seem simultaneous. Yet this "shape" that rises out of the poem's "advancing and retreating waters" does carry the impulse further. Part of that effect is simply cumulative, but the cumulative force still requires suitable language with which to stage its re-emergence. Roethke makes several passes at that language here, and they provide a dramatic glimpse of the synthesis toward which he is working.

The passage is a kind of retrospective and anticipatory summary of Roethke's poetic goals. It reaches back through "North American Sequence" and uses it to gather together the poet's previous work. The sequence of equivalent descriptions serves to conjoin all the paired opposites Roethke has celebrated during his career. At their center is this ambiguous "shape" now openly used to contain a variety of restorative images. Like Yeats's image of the dancer, from which Roethke drew inspiration, the shape he sees is paradoxically both an object and an action. In two of his most well known love poems, Roethke saw this universal form manifested in a woman's body; he called it "a shape of change, encircled by its fire" (*CP*, 119) and marvelled at "the shapes a bright container can contain" (*CP*, 127). Here the shape is encircled as well by the play of light and movement about an opening flower; it is an eternal figure, summoning child and vine branch to its common ground. Like the body of the old woman in Roethke's "Meditations," the form of forms is at once dense and airy.[9] It is a universal shape of change through which all birth and death must pass.

9. "My shape a levity," Roethke's old woman sings, "What's left is light as a seed." She is "a shape without a shade, or almost none," but her body is also a resting place and the accumulated dry bones of all she has been. She may be no more than "a bit of water caught in a wrinkled crevice," but her slight frame is still a curved harbor for the world about her. Rather than choose

The figure Roethke wants to describe is partly a very abstract and generalized extension of a body image primitive enough to represent all embodiment. Like the shape of the human body bent by age or curved in foetal sleep, it would resemble the earliest curled form shared by men, animals, and plants.[10] To the extent that the image is organic and relatively static, Roethke's early greenhouse poems account for its imperatives toward growth and change. Yet Roethke also extended this archetype to inorganic matter. Through much of the middle part of his career, therefore, bodily process is used to draw the elements into association with the body image. When we breathe, for example, the body fills with air, and when we sleep, the body acquires the heaviness of stone. As stone and light, earth and fire, permanence and change coalesce verbally in the body image, it becomes an increasingly representative figure—the enduring and decaying house where each of us lives.

Yet the body that is so verbally allusive is not really the natural body but the body of the poem. The rapturous and playful catalogue in the conclusion to "The Long Waters" dramatizes the collective force of the poem's language. We are to imagine, with Roethke, that the descriptive and exclamatory appositives in the first of these two stanzas impinge on a single figure. They do so here, in the text we read. With the poem's senses dispersed in several landscapes, the poem itself is at once the poet's body and the thinking of the world's body. "Small waves," he wrote earlier, "repeat the mind's slow sensual play" (*CP*, 131). Now he has learned that the poem that counterpoints such likenesses between external physical movement and

between the passive body and the body in motion, the pool or the river, she must overcome the illusory distinction. She must initiate a series of associations which unify all change in a single figure. Then she can speak of airy, impersonal self-dispersal ("I live in light's extreme; I stretch in all directions"), and simultaneously draw herself into a heavy center ripe with her own past ("I'm thick with leaves and tender as a dove...I recover my tenderness by long looking"—[*CP*, 173]).

10. Cf.: "The touch of waters: the dark whorls, the curled eddies," and

A mother's lap
Coiled like a snail,
A dolphin's curl
of downy bones.

Straw For The Fire, pp. 154 and 95.

his own perceptual processes can create and contain their entire interaction: "So the sea wind wakes desire. / My body shimmers with a
light flame" (*CP*, 198). "I roam elsewhere," he writes, "my body
thinking" (*CP*, 195). The poem draws each of these elsewheres together, so that the rhythm of the tides is transferred to the poem's
breathing.

The shape emerging from the poem's waves seems both familiar
and separate, both a friend and the poet himself. It reflects everything of himself he had forgotten, yet makes him "become another
thing." It is both personal and archetypal. Thus it emerges at once
from the poet's sleep and from the ocean's depths. It is greeted with
tears of relief and benediction that flow from himself and from the
ocean's salt water. The poet is himself, he is a stranger, and finally he
is everyone. Only through the poem's disguise can he maintain this
multiple role. It is a role that American poets have often assumed
in more blatantly prophetic form. Nor is this the first time Roethke
himself has sought to become a representative and unifying figure.
Yet "North American Sequence" is perhaps the first time he hints
that the slug and worm of his private greenhouse poems are actually
vestigial culture heroes, explorers working toward the source of a
greenhouse Eden that belongs to all of us.

The "I" in the last two stanzas of the fourth poem in the sequence
stands not only for Roethke and for the poem itself but also for a
broad American audience. We too are gathered into the poem's
voice. As a speaker, the poet fills the traditional American role of
prophetic witness. That role had been functioning covertly in
Roethke's poetry for some time, but "North American Sequence"
makes it considerably more apparent. As a result, the quality of sheer
performance becomes central to the experience of the poem. Roethke
is trying for a definitive reintegration of self and nature, and we watch
him try over and over again. That sense of continual recapitulation,
of assaying yet another time the same textual synthesis, makes his
creative effort here more patently self-conscious and deliberate than
it has ever been before. What some critics experience in Roethke's
poetry as embarrassing self-promotion, too artificially orphic, becomes
the actual subject of "North American Sequence." In the process,

Roethke's vision acquires a new credibility. We no longer have to believe that the vision exists outside the poetry, that it is so pervasively real it is "neither voice nor vision." We only have to recognize that Roethke wants the vision to succeed and that his desire is characteristically American.

The composite landscape of "The Long Waters" is unashamedly synthetic. It is a made place where the poet can summon all of nature's seasons to one mind. By shuffling together a collection of natural sites, the poem would create a varied but harmoniously accessible textual space, a continent on the printed page open to all of us. The project, of course, cannot literally succeed. Yet Roethke accepts the provisional status of his poem's solution, and he even admits that its implicit contradictions are as much comic as mystical. That gives the poem a genuine poignancy; it cannot achieve what it sets out to do. Moreover, each time the poem makes large claims for its vision, the purely verbal quality of those claims will make them seem mere posturing.

The ecstatic synthesis of these two stanzas gives us a glimpse of a personal and cultural unity that will not be. It echoes the partial and anticipatory conclusions of the first two poems in the sequence, recovers the more dramatic synthesis at the end of "Meditation at Oyster River," and leads us to expect yet more radical summations from "The Far Field" and "The Rose." Yet these parallel statements of formal apotheosis are also equivalent and even interchangeable. Delayed, diverted, repeatedly almost achieved, the poem's form is imminent throughout. It is a tentative form in continuous motion, at once scattered and whole. "I lose and find myself," Roethke writes, and the poem too is "gathered together" and dissolved in "the long water."

Roethke would like to exist simultaneously in visionary transcendence and ironic deflation. Thus it is appropriate, though unsettling, that each of his verbal resolutions is discarded when the next poem in the sequence begins. As Richard Blessing has observed, "The narrator has slipped back into spiritual despondency in the space between poems."[11] Each of these regressions brings us up short, yet they are

---

11. Blessing, *Theodore Roethke's Dynamic Vision*, p. 127.

implicit in the precarious rapture of the preceding vision. If we can learn to move back and forth between the dark and light of vision at will, we will have internalized the poem's lesson. It is a lesson addressed both to Roethke's own sometimes violent emotional reversals and to the country at large. For the American dream of a humanized wilderness must have its darker side as well.

Into that darkness once again the sequence descends at the beginning of the fifth poem, "The Far Field": "I dream of journeys repeatedly: / Of flying like a bat deep into a narrowing tunnel" (*CP*, 199). This repeats the movement toward and into closed space that opened "Journey to the Interior." The visionary synthesis at the end of "The Long Waters," then, is not a natural given; it is a feature of the poem's performative force, and Roethke will have to work his way toward it again through fear and loss. We have, however, brought with us a sense of the potential interchangeability of human artifacts and natural life, so the car of "Journey to the Interior," which returns as well, no longer seems to violate the poem's wider focus. Roethke imagines being trapped in a sand-rut "Where the car stalls, / Churning in a snowdrift / Until the headlights darken." The image of the car wheels churning echoes the description in "Meditations of an Old Woman" of a "journey within a journey," lost, "the gate / Inaccessible," possessed of tremendous futile energy, like "two horses plunging in snow, their lines tangled" (*CP*, 158). It is a paralysis of fear endured in slow motion, yet savored, as when Roethke (elsewhere in the same volume) imagines that a meadow mouse which escapes after he captures it must now live under the owl's eye, like a "paralytic stunned in the tub, and the water rising" (*CP*, 227).

The feeling of paralysis amidst danger, one of the most common dream events, puts Roethke in touch with one of his childhood memories—the field "not too far away from the ever-changing flower-dump," whose end drops off into a culvert. There collects, as in the ice-flow passage of "Meditation at Oyster River," a mixture of human and animal debris: tin cans, tires, and "the shrunken face of a dead rat, eaten by rain and ground-beetles." There too he finds a tom-cat, shot by a watchman, "its entrails strewn over the half-grown flowers."

A few years later, Galway Kinnell describes a similar scene more vividly in "The Porcupine"; its effect on both poets is comparable, as Roethke begins to think of himself emptied, simplified by death.

First, however, he needs to elevate these specific images into a general image of death that can be a more manipulable verbal resource. "At the field's end," he writes, "one learned of the eternal"; these deaths are the common voice of all the worldly things the poem has assembled. He suffers for them, but his "grief was not excessive," for there are also "warblers in early May." The natural rhythms of life and death give him, in the poem, a context for contemplating himself with "another mind, less peculiar" (CP, 200). Perhaps, he muses with a playfulness resembling that of the poetry he wrote for children, he'll return in another life as "a raucous bird, / or, with luck, as a lion." The choices are all willed and fanciful, even the more primitive ones. He writes of lying naked in sand, "Fingering a shell, / Thinking: / Once I was something like this, mindless," and he thinks he might "sink down to the hips in a mossy quagmire." The image of envagination and the empty shell invoke both the evacuated, archetypal template of the self and the moist greenhouse where it acquires its face. Yet the birds and far field suggest the vast reaches of air and the self opened to the infinite. "The Long Waters" laid the groundwork for a figure unifying self and world; "The Far Field" extends that synthesis to the two poles of nature introduced early in Roethke's life—the close greenhouse and the wide field.

Roethke is working to create a far field, deep and open but as close as the page he writes his poem on, whose verbal rhythms can unify greenhouse and field and do so not for himself but for all of us:

> I learned not to fear infinity,
> The far field, the windy cliffs of forever,
> The dying of time in the white light of tomorrow,
> The wheel turning away from itself,
> The sprawl of the wave,
> The on-coming water. [CP, 200]

This is the far field where the poem's many waters will gather to flower together. There all outward movement returns to itself, folding disparate things into a single flowering: "The river turns on itself, / The tree retreats into its own shadow" (*CP,* 200). The field will fold together all North American landscapes, as mountain meadow water and a glacial torrent flow together in the alluvial plain. Thus each distant spring, each American tributary feeds our inward reservoir, while the self, brimful of its inwardness, overflows everywhere. From the center of this Whitmanesque self, as from a single stone, spread concentric rings of water, carrying reflected and diffused light ever outward: "The pure serene of memory in one man,— / A ripple widening from a single stone / Winding around the waters of the world." This outpouring water is also a benediction and an embrace, both freeing and bringing home what it touches. The poet's vision, conferring on each thing the dignity of its single name, meanwhile draws each thing within its reach to possess it. In the final lines of "The Far Field," a collective consciousness can appear to be cleansed of longing, for it contains everything. An omnipresent force in nature, the poet's will suffuses inanimate matter and sets it to dream in words: "A man faced with his own immensity / Wakes all the waves, all their loose wandering fire" (*CP,* 201).

"I have come to a still, but not a deep center," he writes, "a point beside the glittering current." There "My mind moves in more than one place, / In a country half-land, half-water" (*CP,* 201). This mediating land, the territory between self and world, between earth and water, is the textuality the poem maps out for itself. Into this land, and into his poem, he must die to be reborn as a collective figure. "I am renewed by death, thought of my death." Yet there is not one death, but many, and each is a renewal. Each time the self is lost, it is regained in the image of the world, in every immediate dying change before his eyes: "The dry scent of a dying garden in September, / The wind fanning the ash of a low fire." "He is the end of things, the final man," the first and last man—Adamic, for the end of things is foretold by a true beginning; each final man begins his life anew. The self—mysterious sea-cave in which the world drowns to breathe again—will be repeatedly buried and uncovered by the tides.

In the body of the poem he can become, as he puts it elsewhere, "A phoenix, sure of my body, / Perpetually rising out of myself" (*CP*, 209).

At the field's end, hovering over the ever-renewing grave of the sea, Roethke recovers the lost innocent self in a new image of his text as a body. Now the sea-shape of this body, foolish and ancient, green and dying ("In robes of green, in garments of adieu"), can forgo all anxious postures. Its form, sea-blessed, is not imprisoning slime or unmoving stone. It is the site of all changes, the nexus where movement must pass whether to be contained or freed. "The body," he writes elsewhere, is "but a motion in a shoe" (*CP*, 237). All movement is thereby imprinted with this image of the empty self—all things fulfill themselves under the sign of the body, whose shape of change is the sign of the form of forms. "Flesh, flash out of me," he writes in a notebook,[12] but the need to be free of a body is supplanted by the discovery of his body anywhere in North America he looks. "The flesh," he once wrote, "can make the spirit visible" (*CP*, 106). Thus "the flesh fathers a dream" (*CP*, 263) as wide as the world. "And I became all that I looked upon" (*CP*, 247). The greenhouse body grows until the far field itself is enfleshed.

The greenhouse world of his childhood, which Roethke explicitly summons to his side in "The Rose"—the final poem of the sequence—now nurtures even the farthest bloom of the waves. "The leafy mind" of his early poems "that long was tightly furled" (*CP*, 11) has thick leaves opening in every elsewhere. Roethke thinks of roses in a tiny childhood world at last granted its true space, in greenhouses six hundred feet wide. He remembers his father lifting him high over the elaborate hybrids: "And how those flowerheads seemed to flow toward me, to beckon me, / Only a child, out of myself" (*CP*, 203). In "The Rose," the distant field flowers through the poet— out of the ground on which he stands. "There are those to whom place is unimportant," he writes in the poem's first line, "but this place, where sea and fresh water meet, / Is important" (*CP*, 202). The rose of baffled wonderment in the first poem ("The rose exceeds, the rose exceeds us all," *CP*, 188) is transformed into a figure

---

12. Quoted by Seager, *The Glass House*, p. 169.

for a self exceeding the limits of time and space, yet supremely flowering in its place:

> But this rose, this rose in the sea-wind,
> Stays,
> Stays in its true place,
> Flowering out of the dark,
> Widening at high noon, face upward, [CP, 203]

This place is the collective sign of all the sites the poem celebrates and engenders. Roethke therefore catalogues anew the beach and the meadow, the sea and the air, filling "The Rose" with diverse American places in the culmination of his sequence. So that any place, any moment, is the scene of the entire continent's survival. He lists the songs of several birds, "the mimetic chortling of the catbird" and "the bobolink skirring from a broken fencepost," then orchestrates a cacophony of sound—cicadas, the shriek of nails ripped from a roof, horns and bulldozers. But he absolves the raucous clatter of its variety in a comprehensive gesture:

> I return to the twittering of swallows above water,
> And that sound, that single sound,
> When the mind remembers all,
> And gently the light enters the sleeping soul,
> A sound so thin it could not woo a bird, [CP, 204]

"Beautiful my desire," he continues, "and the place of my desire" (CP, 204). When desire is deeply rooted in its immediate place, it can surpass self-mortification to voice the collective will of the land, but only the poem has so flexible and representative a location. The sequence of poems began in a paralyzed "agony of crucifixion on barstools" where "not even the soot dances" (CP, 187). It ends when the crown of thorns smiles and takes flight: "I sway outside myself / Into the darkening currents ... Was it here I wore a crown of birds for a moment?" (CP, 202). "I played in flame and water like a boy / And I swayed out beyond the white seafoam" (CP, 120):

> Near this rose, in this grove of sun-parched, wind-warped
>   madronas,

Among the half-dead trees, I came upon the true ease of myself,
As if another man appeared out of the depths of my being,
And I stood outside myself,
Beyond becoming and perishing,
A something wholly other,
As if I swayed out on the wildest wave alive,
And yet was still.
And I rejoiced in being what I was:
In the lilac change, the white reptilian calm,
In the bird beyond the bough, the single one
With all the air to greet him as he flies,
The dolphin rising from the darkening waves;

And in this rose, this rose in the sea-wind,
Rooted in stone, keeping the whole of light,
Gathering to itself sound and silence—
Mine and the sea-wind's. [*CP,* 205]

The rose is a universal figure, but here it is also uniquely American, symbolizing the cohering self-expression of North America's land. The America that flowers here is, of course, largely a visual one. Roethke has not opened his poetry to specific historical events but rather to a variety of sites, including those that have become industrial wastelands. The landscapes, then, represent both possibilities lost and possibilities yet untried. This attributes a static, spatialized character to American history, a tendency Roethke shares with many other American writers.

The resolution Roethke offers us in "The Rose" is exclusively verbal, almost gratuitously so, yet this fragility increases its force. Culturally and personally, the poem offers a momentary way of attaining a harmony the world does not offer. As Adrienne Rich will do ten years later, Roethke works out verbally a synthesis not available elsewhere in human experience. Unlike Rich, however, Roethke does not really expect the poetry to change his life. For a man at times unhinged by guilt and self-doubt, the poignancy and necessity of a vision that is wholly a willed artifice should be apparent.

"North American Sequence" is an artifice that also reaches out to gather all of Roethke's poetry together. We can hear in it echoes of images recurring throughout his career, though that is true of almost any of his poems. More important is the poem's effort to be the apotheosis of that imagery, liberating its heaviness and its edge of despair. If the rose in the final poem is rooted in stone, then stone thereby flows and looses the weight whereby "his thought is tied, the curving prowl of motion moored to rock" (*CP,* 4). There is energy in even that absolute repose: "I touched the stones, and they had my own skin" (*CP,* 133). "My flesh," he wrote earlier, "is breathing slower than a wall" (*CP,* 135), "I know . . . the stone's eternal pulseless longing" (*CP,* 88), "I know the motion of the deepest stone" (*CP,* 132). He has lodged himself verbally at the center of the earth's most eternal substance, and he feels his spirit, too, bound up in the body's unyielding matter. But the immobility of body and stone is only a thickening of the circle of changes; so the spine, emblem of the body's rigidity, is the vortex of a new unfolding. "I turned upon my spine, / I turned and turned again" (*CP,* 147), he writes, so as to become a rose, "a blaze of being on a central stem" (*CP,* 149).

In the deepest stone starts that slow-moving curve traced later by the opening flower and the cresting wave. The original poles of nature are abandoned for a continuum in motion, where the elements are interchanged and self and other become one another unpredictably. Yet in the final moments of the poem, a further resolution appears. Water and flame, stone and light, the fecund "lilac change" and sterile "reptilian calm," seem almost to coalesce. Here, where world and body interpenetrate the poem's flesh, "North American Sequence" holds its forces in momentary stasis. In the image of the rose unfolded in the sea-wind, at once vulnerable and eternal, intimate and indifferent, the poem voices a dream of all motion taken up by form. Deep within the self, and everywhere outside us, is this far field where water flowers in stone.

CHAPTER THREE

Ecclesiastical Whitman: Galway Kinnell's *The Book of Nightmares*

> I give my blood fifty parts polystyrene,
> twenty-five parts benzene, twenty-five parts good old gasoline,
> to the last bomber pilot aloft, that there shall be one acre
> in the dull world where the kissing flower may bloom,
> which kisses you so long your bones explode under its lips. [p. 43][1]

SINCE THE BEGINNING of his career, Galway Kinnell has been trying to create a poetics of death that is at once graphic, mystical, and sensual. In America, such a project is unavoidably overshadowed by Whitman's attempt to make death culturally specific, to redeem death in the guise of an American communality. Kinnell began by competing with Whitman to obtain possession of the earlier poet's overtly prophetic voice. Yet that battle for priority cannot now be won; our history has made prophecy obsolete. Only if a poet can welcome the futility of the role, as Allen Ginsberg has, and turn prophecy into ironic lamentation, can he reoccupy Whitman's position.

---

1. The following books by Galway Kinnell are abbreviated and documented internally: *BR—Body Rags* (Boston: Houghton Mifflin, 1968); *FH—Flower Herding on Mount Monadnock* (Boston: Houghton Mifflin, 1964); *MM—Mortal Acts, Mortal Words* (Boston: Houghton Mifflin, 1980); *WK—What a Kingdom It Was* (Boston: Houghton Mifflin, 1960); *WS—Walking Down the Stairs: Selections from Interviews* (Ann Arbor: University of Michigan Press, 1978). *The Book of Nightmares* (Boston: Houghton Mifflin, 1971) is documented internally by page number only. The

Kinnell's faith and his innocence make that alternative impossible. In much of his work, then, his effectiveness as a visionary speaker is undercut by the brute reality of American history, though it is not until his fourth book, from which my epigraph is taken, that he acknowledges history's power over his poetry. At the same time he realizes that his vision could not be offered to the land by fiat; it would have to be drawn out of the language. The result is his finest work, *The Book of Nightmares,* a ten-poem sequence written roughly ten years after Roethke's "North American Sequence." In many ways, their aims were comparable. Both poets wanted to saturate the language with evidence of elemental transformation; both were working toward a Whitmanesque, sensual vision of death as communal redemption. Yet ten years of difficult and deflating history intervene between Roethke's and Kinnell's poem sequences. Kinnell's project as a result is far more obsessive and fatalistic.

epigraph is from the sixth poem in *The Book of Nightmares;* gasoline and polystyrene (a thickening agent) are the key components of a contemporary formula for napalm.

An illustration introduces each section of *The Book of Nightmares.* Some of these are details from larger prints that acquire a gnomic or mystical quality by being taken out of context. The illustration before the ninth poem shows two figures up to their shoulders in a hole they are digging. One wonders if they are digging a grave. Actually, it is a small detail from a print in George Agricola, *De Re Metallica* (Basel, 1571) that shows a number of men exploring a mining area. The illustration before the third poem shows a man holding a divining rod over a hilly landscape, echoing the reference to divination in the preceding poem. Since the illustration does not suggest what the man with the divining rod is seeking, the effect is ambiguous, at once quaint and portentous. As it happens, this small figure is taken from a much larger print in Sebastian Munster, *Cosmographia universalis* (Basel, 1544), where the context again is mining exploration. The illustration preceding the second poem, "The Hen Flower," shows a woman in Renaissance dress holding a rooster over a flaming pot. Again, we can make connections with a number of motifs in *The Book of Nightmares,* but we cannot tell whether the image itself is symbolic or representational. This illustration reproduces about two-thirds of the title page of Ulrich Molifor, *De laniis et phitonicis mulieribus* (Cologne, 1489), in which two witches are making rain by holding a rooster over a flaming pot. Other illustrations are less obscure. The cover, for example, depicts a stage in the alchemical process, the *nigredo.* This particular version is taken from the *Theatrum chemicum,* vol. 4 (1613), but there are comparable images elsewhere.

My main concern will be to demonstrate how the language of *The Book of Nightmares* is permeated with Kinnell's particular conception of death, but it will be helpful to begin by examining a few of his earlier poems. Kinnell's need for secular images of incarnation will shortly bring him to the New World, but at the outset of his first book his sense of death is largely Christian:

> You struggle from flesh into wings; the change exists.
> But the wings that live gripping the contours of the dirt
> Are all at once nothing, flesh and light lifted away.
>
> You are the flesh; I am the resurrection, because I am the light.
> I cut to your measure the creeping piece of darkness
> That haunts you in the dirt. Step into light—
> I make you over. I breed the shape of your grave in the dirt.
>
> [*WK,* 64]

The tone of authority here is openly arrogant. This tension between darkness and light, Kinnell has Christ tell us in "The Supper After the Last," is the reality that devours us. No hesitation, no doubt, touches this vision. Yet there is a curious quality of dazed intonation. The verbal equivalences are almost chanted, as if the speaker is being used by words whose power is their own. The Savior here is a "wild man" with "the wreck of passion / Emptying his eyes" (*WK,* 63). If we are created in his image, then we are "created / In the image of nothing." Almost all the poems in *What A Kingdom It Was* (1960) depend on this vocabulary for visionary evacuation; the context there is inescapably theological. With his second book, *Flower Herding on Mount Monadnock* (1964), the same vocabulary begins to function as its own justification; it becomes a ritualized, necessary signature for any poetic utterance: "Cells Breathe In the Emptiness" (*FH,* 39). Words like "emptiness," "nothingness," and "darkness" accompany a host of gestures toward loss and self-extinction: "You flinging yourself out into the emptiness"; "the river leaning like a wave towards the emptiness"; "Darkness sticks itself / To empty spines"; "And the dimension of depth seizes everything"; "And the grass, look, / The great field wavers and flakes"; "A last, saprophytic blossoming"; "It burns up. Its drift is to be nothing"; "worn / To the lost grip it always essentially was" (*FH*, 36, 41, 42, 55, 37, 33, 58, 52).[2] Almost simultaneously, W. S. Merwin was using much the same vocabulary to evoke a sense of romantic mystery. Both poets would shortly alter the vocabulary's connotative force—Kinnell by grounding his images of emptiness in a violent and immediate physicality, Merwin by abandoning his romanticism for a poetic of paralysis and loss. For both poets, the change would come partly as a response to their sense of recent American history.

Despite what American New Criticism has taught us about poetic context, in Kinnell's work these invocations of redemptive death are not radically altered by their individual settings. Indeed they are not merely thematically parallel, they serve essentially the same aesthetic and psychological function. Death for Kinnell is a restorative force, as it was for his acknowledged mentors, Whitman, Rilke, and Roethke; it works as a power the poem can call up, a power which is the poem's true source and its only goal. Death is the place where the poem's inwardness and its public rhetoric meet. Death overhears the poem and absorbs all the resonances the poem prompts in its readers.

Kinnell's verbal machinery (I use the word in Kenneth Burke's sense) acts repeatedly to apply that formal, nominative seal to whatever particular events provide the poem's ostensible occasion. Relative quality in Kinnell's poetry is partly a question of how far this continually renewed project succeeds. As we read a succession of his poems, we have to ask how much of our common experience is channeled through each new instance of a familiar ritual.

As Kinnell has acknowledged, he succeeds more fully in long poems. His short visionary poems are unconvincing because his key words are not very powerful without a more elaborate context. His short poems can work, however, when they are chiefly ironic. In a

---

2. Cf. Kinnell's comment in "Galway Kinnell: A Conversation," *Salted Feathers*, 2, No. 3 (1967), n. pag.: "I generally begin [a poem] with some words that come into my mind. These words appear in a kind of mood which I can't describe very well. Starting from these words, I get an idea of the direction that they are leading me and I just follow it...."

short poem, irony can provide a sufficient emotional ground and can
even make a limited subject seem representative. But Kinnell's irony
works only as a form of relief, or a signature for closure. Given
larger ambitions, his irony tends toward sentimentality, so it will not
in itself support a long poem.[3] Kinnell's verbal motives require not
deftly managed synecdoche but a sense of broad inclusiveness established through accumulated detail. So long as the details are American, the method is patently Whitmanesque, and by now culturally
approved and politically safe. Yet our history has soured us for such
projects. If the sequential naming of American things, places, and
people survives at all without ironic compromise, it is only, as Susan
Sontag has shown, in the austerity of the black and white photo-
graph.[4] We can now *see* with Whitman's eyes; the vast poem of
America founders all about us. Visually, we can cross the continent
in a minute. If the trip takes longer, the poem of community succumbs to the obvious visual evidence of violence and greed.

Kinnell's first major long poem, "The Avenue Bearing the Initial
of Christ Into the New World," naively ignores these cultural realities, and, I think, largely fails as a result. As anyone who has read
much poetry by young people in New York will readily confirm, the
subjects Kinnell selects cry out for poetic canonization. The "crone
who sells the *News* and the *Mirror,* / The oldest living thing on
Avenue C," may not have read Dostoevsky, but she seems to know
instinctively that "she is Pulchería mother of murderers and mad-
men" (*WK,* 70-71). In London, fishmongers sometimes exaggerate
their Cockney accents when they hear American voices; more brutally, the residents of Avenue C conveniently suffer in Kinnell's
presence.

------

3. Charles Molesworth argues that Kinnell's main impulse is to move
beyond the irony characteristic of modern poetry toward a poetry of empathy: "Empathy results from a systemic consciousness, an awareness of the
field on which and through which the forces of experience act and make
themselves visible." Molesworth cites sentimentality, a loose oracular structure, and "a didacticism close to the evangelical" as the pitfalls in Kinnell's
chosen mode, *The Fierce Embrace: A Study of Contemporary Poetry* (Columbia: University of Missouri Press, 1979), pp. 98-111.
4. See Sontag, *On Photography* (New York: Farrar, 1977).

There are at least partial solutions to these problems. Ginsberg sometimes succeeds by limiting himself to a particularly flat form of description and by acknowledging that the panoramic listing, in so far as it demonstrates community, is a lie the American poet revives because he needs it. Such poems must either deal overtly with the poet's motives, or they must court disaster (as Robert Duncan does) through deliberate formal subversion. Kinnell in these earlier poems is not yet able to confront his own cynicism and anguish. He is simply used by the tradition. Moreover, in "The Avenue Bearing the Initial of Christ Into the New World" he supplies an unfortunate barrage of mythological, biblical, and literary allusions that turn his pathos into Camp sentiment and his avenue into a Hollywood set. The poem fails (and its ready acceptance by reviewers is a sign of that failure) even though its descriptions, which I confirm as a former resident of the avenue, are entirely accurate.

Kinnell's stance in the poem, to the extent that his impulse to write about the poor of Avenue C is benevolent rather than merely colonialist, is that poetry is a public forum where people can be given a voice they could not acquire themselves, a voice they may not consciously miss, but which the poet decides they need. Williams remained in Rutherford all his life in part for the same reason, and the program can be traced in American poetry back to Whitman. Williams, however, had rather less apocalyptic aims in mind; he does, in one way, transpose the whole of his native landscape to the body of *Paterson,* but he does not share Kinnell's troubled need to believe that poetry confers immediate beatitude on its subjects. "The Avenue Bearing the Initial of Christ Into the New World" declares itself as a transforming fire where the common poor become heroic, eternal versions of themselves. Yet the poet's will to bestow grace is not quite so altruistic. Sanctity distances those who acquire it. The poem's real drama, its covert pain, is Kinnell's own struggle to unburden himself of the photographs his mind has taken of the avenue. He calls it a place "where the drowned suffer a C-change," but the real stage is not the sordid, extraordinary street but the poem itself. The reference to *The Tempest* hints that not only his subjects but

also the artificer himself must be reborn. It is Kinnell who is drown-
ing and would breathe again:

> It is night, and raining. You look down
> Towards Houston in the rain, the living streets,
> Where instants of transcendence
> Drift in oceans of loathing and fear, like lanternfishes,
> Or phosphorus flashings in the sea, or the feverish light
> Skin is said to give off when the swimmer drowns at night.
>
> [*WK*, 82]

Kinnell's poem bears within it the seeds of a purgative journey
through overwhelming sensation. The poet would immerse himself
in the avenue's flood of images so as to acquire a new and broader
selfhood. But the journey here is replaced by the special power of
mythical vision automatically granted poetry itself. As Terry Comito
has pointed out, "All the swarming multiplicity of the scene only
emphasizes the ceaselessness of a dissolution in which human life
seems to share the fate of what it feeds upon," but Kinnell will not
confront the way his descriptions of decay challenge his vision.[5] From
the outset, the poem is a secure site of transfiguration. In Comito's
words again, "America becomes for Kinnell a special myth for the
elusiveness of these 'leaked promises,' for the bitter nostalgia of all
our Nicks and Kanes and Gatsbys for the 'secret country' where we
can rest and be at one with the world."[6]

Instinctively, Kinnell knows that this America exists only in his
poetry, and that the tangible products of history he describes there
threaten even this imaginary redemptive landscape. Hence the under-
tone of brittle desperation in his poetry, for he does not yet know
what to do with this knowledge. For Roethke the problem was not
so acute; his vision, of course, was more fully worked out, yet he still
had to handle his American materials carefully. Roethke could cite,
almost with gingerly reticence, the waste acres at the edge of cities,
a few sounds of bulldozers and hammers, and the traces of human

---

5. Comito, "Slogging Toward the Absolute," *Modern Poetry Studies,* 6,
No. 2 (1975), 191.

6. Ibid., 190.

garbage in a frozen river, without any of this quite forestalling his vision, however much it made his vision a more tentative artifice. Kinnell, writing almost at the same time, describes whole neighborhoods in dissolution, and the vision of communality becomes nearly absurd. By the time he writes *The Book of Nightmares* the process will be complete.

In his third book, *Body Rags* (1968), Kinnell begins to see that Whitman's legacy of a honey-laden American death (as well as the poetic line whose rhythms embody it) can no longer be accepted in unselfconscious innocence. As I pointed out in my opening chapter, Kinnell in the second section of "Vapor Trail Reflected in the Frog Pond" uses Whitman's "I hear America singing" to head a catalogue of less felicitous sounds: "crack of deputies' rifles ... sput of cattle-prod, / TV groaning at the smells of the human body" (*BR*, 7). The device is much too self-conscious; it helps to fragment a poem whose first section shows more promising restraint but whose third section uses Kinnell's usually strong powers of transfiguration in a context that makes them objectionable. The dead of Vietnam, he assures us, will be merely more carrion in nature:

> the flesh a man throws down in the sunshine
> dogs shall eat
> and the flesh that is upthrown in the air
> shall be seized by birds, [*BR*, 8]

These are disturbing, almost cannibalistic images, yet the revulsion they stimulate is contradicted by a sense of consolation. Nature's universals intervene; whether newly born or dying, all "hands [are] rivered / by blue, erratic wanderings of the blood." Roethke could succeed with a related gesture in "Journey to the Interior," risking his own life, noting the violent deaths of men and animals, then overcoming his uneasiness with the observation that "all flows past." Roethke, however, was dealing with a far less intractable sense of historicity; even so, he attempted only a momentary consolation, not the definitive transfiguration Kinnell desires. Kinnell is not yet equal to juxtaposing his vision with historical realities. The juxtaposition is jarring, its verbal ecstasy unearned, though it is interesting to see

Kinnell's images of transfiguration pressured by a sense of history into confronting more challenging and powerful images of violent death.

"The Porcupine" and "The Bear" are the first full fruition of his new sophistication with its harsh realism, though they deal more with American archetypes than with specific historical events. Nonetheless, Kinnell's vision now must be achieved within the poem, and he can no longer write without cost. With these two poems Kinnell abandons the pose of Whitmanesque generosity toward what he describes and openly shapes external events into rites of self-discovery. The poems are sustained by conventions of narrative; they do not attempt new forms because Kinnell is not prepared to risk the privileged status of poetic language. Yet he no longer assumes that his diction of mystical emptiness will touch the reader through a power already invested in the words themselves. He begins to concentrate on the act of writing, rather than resting satisfied with the priestly function of poetic speech.

Though the two poems have many similarities, an important further change in Kinnell's poetic practice takes place between them. Roughly, it is a change from comparison to direct statement. "The Porcupine" is a carefully constructed series of parallels between the animal and the poem's speaker; it is a structurally more sophisticated version of the mythic allusiveness in his earlier poetry. The comparisons between the porcupine and the man depend on the poem's overt mechanics, but they do succeed. In "The Bear," however, Kinnell goes further; he achieves a visionary rhetoric that speaks simultaneously from animal and man. This poem plays a decisive role in his career, more decisive than Williams's early poem "The Wanderer," in which Williams plunges into the Passaic River to be merged with it, much as Kinnell's hunter climbs into the bear's carcass. Both "The Bear" and "The Wanderer" are rites of passage that generate a spiritual metamorphosis. For Kinnell the change is also deeply physical.

To follow this development we must begin with "The Porcupine" (*BR,* 56-59). Its comparisons between man and porcupine are initially lighthearted. Like us, the porcupine "puts his mark on out-

houses" and "chuckles softly to himself when scared." Like us, he
hesitates at thresholds, and "his eyes have their own inner redness."
Conveniently, our paths cross unawares. The porcupine is a lover of
salt, so he gnaws wood-handled tools, all "crafted objects / steeped
in the juice of fingertips." For him, as for us, "the true / portion of
the sweetness of earth" is a human tear. The connection also works
the other way. The scriptures of Zoroastrianism sentence porcupine-
killers to hell, where they will "gnaw out / each other's hearts" in
pursuit of a less substantial sweat—the "salts of desire." The man
of the poem is himself a human porcupine, with a "self-stabbing
coil / of bristles reversing, blossoming outward." His quills, apparent
in feeling and action, grow out of an inward flagellation. He tosses
in bed, under a quilt that mimics the patchwork countryside of farms
over which the porcupine roams, and his restlessness wakes the
woman beside him. The speaker describes himself as a secular Saint
Sebastian, tortured by invisible arrows; his incarnation is for a more
ordinary martyrdom.

The poem's descriptions of suffering are handled with graceful
wistfulness, leaving us just barely wary of what is to come. The
casual, openly artificial, and even gratuitous parallels between man
and porcupine put us at ease for a more radical comparison. Stuffed
with his varied provender, willow flowers and choice young leaves,
the porcupine in the first section drags himself through "roses and
goldenrod, into the stubbly high fields." Then, midway through the
poem, a porcupine sleeping in a tree is shot by a farmer.[7] The porcupine that was "he" becomes "it." The shift from the personal pronoun signals a moment of violent, impersonal apotheosis. As it falls,
it tears open its belly on a sharp branch, hooks its gut, and goes on
falling:

> On the ground
> it sprang to its feet, and
> paying out gut heaved
> and spartled through a hundred feet of goldenrod

---

7. In "Galway Kinnell: A Conversation," Kinnell reports that he had
killed a porcupine a few days before starting the poem.

before
the abrupt emptiness.

The porcupine's death descends like a guillotine; there is its terror, then nothing. But our own emptiness may be anticipated; we can learn to recognize its power to sustain us. We may dream of death as an indecipherable message, but its real impact strikes us in that physical vulnerability we experience in the porcupine's fleshly death. We too have "fallen from high places," but we must fall again, even embrace our own mortality, before we can truly possess our loss. Like Hopkins, another of his spiritual mentors, Kinnell would render his ecclesiastical concerns in images of earthly incarnation.

I too, he writes, have fled "over fields of goldenrod" to discover the self's true home. In the midst of those flowers among whose blossoms the porcupine's guts are scattered

> I have come to myself empty, the rope
> strung out behind me
> in the fall sun
> suddenly glorified with all my blood.

The man's wounds are psychic; the rope of his past is metaphorically intestinal. But all his pain can be transfigured by the image of himself emptied. Beyond fear, in possession of a radiant emptiness, again like the porcupine, he finds himself "softly chuckling." He discovers an image of himself "broken / skulled," shattered and essential, "or vacant as a / sucked egg in the wintry meadow." He is resolved into the "blank / template" of himself, the hollow but potent original mold that shaped him. The template is an image of renewal through regression, reminiscent of Roethke's figures for a primary and almost anonymous selfhood. The goldenrod then is replaced by images of rebirth through disavowed substance, of burdock that "looses the arks of its seed," of thistle that "holds up its lost blooms." The roses of the first stanza become images of desolate yearning: They "scrape their dead limbs / for the forced-fire / of roses." But a wind is moving over the earth, and its force gives witness to a more ethereal or transitory flame.

Both "The Porcupine" and "The Bear" generate increasing emotional intensity as they proceed. Because "The Porcupine" develops in a series of parallel passages, its movement is somewhat uneven, but "The Bear" carries us in an unbroken arc to its destination. Each depends on a highly visual narrative, but "The Bear" in particular is impossible to separate from the images of the hunt it induces in the reader. Unlike many of the more abstract poems preceding *The Book of Nightmares,* these two will survive as integral, self-sufficient works precisely because of their narrative and visual singularity. The special power of "The Bear" is that its very specificity makes it remarkably universal. It is an experience we are unlikely to undergo, but it nevertheless applies to all of us. As Comito observes, "Kinnell's protagonists are sometimes prototypically American in their hunger to find images of themselves in the world."[8]

The solitary hunt undertaken at great risk, a recurrent American motif, traditionally serves as a rite of initiation. The poem does not, however, simply describe a passage into manhood. It is also conventional for the successful hunter to acquire, at least symbolically, some of the powers of his prey. Yet the bear's characteristics are not merely adapted to become human attributes; the figure at the end combines the perspectives of both species with superb economy. The narrative prepares us for that visionary metamorphosis in the second half of the poem. The arctic hunter first discovers the bear when he fills his lungs with its scent.[9] It is a "chilly, enduring odor"; its source can be occupied but not eliminated. The preparations are disciplined and reverential. The hunter coils a sharpened wolf's rib and freezes it in blubber. The bear will not be found unless it willingly takes into

---

8. Comito, "Slogging Toward the Absolute," 190.

9. In "Galway Kinnell's 'The Bear': Dream and Technique," *Modern Poetry Studies,* 5, No. 3 (1974), John Hobbs suggests that Kinnell took the story of the hunt from *Top of the World* (New York: Harper, 1950), a popular novel about Eskimo life by Hans Ruesch. In "To the Roots: An Interview with Galway Kinnell," *Contemporary Poetry in America,* ed. Robert Boyers (New York: Schocken, 1974), Kinnell reports that he heard the story of the hunt indirectly: "Somebody once told me the story of how Eskimos hunted for bears. I guess he had read it in a book, but over the course of a few months I forgot who had told me and I imagined it was told me by someone who had actually hunted with the Eskimos. In any case the story stuck with me a long time . . ." (p. 242).

itself this human instrument; it is a totemic figure for the man and his intent. If the bear swallows the bait, the fat will melt and the bone will pierce his gut. When the bait has vanished, the hunter wanders in circles until he finds the bear's blood staining the snow.

Now the hunter must endure his trial; the dying bear will be his teacher. Where the beast rests, he will rest. Where the beast stretches out to drag itself over unsteady ice with its claws, the man too lies down to pull himself forward with bear knives. He must not only follow the bear's trail, but must also duplicate its movements. In this silent ritual, the animal is the man's dance-master. Then the hunter begins to starve, and he must make a choice—to humiliate himself or to die. If he would live, he must eat the bear's excrement; it is soaked with nourishing blood. Many readers find this scene intolerable. They will not understand the poem unless they realize that the choice *not* to eat the bear's excrement—and some of us may be certain we would not despite starvation—is really the more extraordinary option. He hesitates, as perhaps the bear hesitated at the blubber set out for him, gnashes it down and goes on running.

Now each has swallowed something of the other. The circle will shortly be closed. On the seventh day the hunter will rest, and when he wakens a new world will fill his senses. He sees the bear's body ahead. Possibly, he muses, the bear caught his scent before it died. He eats the flesh raw, cuts the animal open and climbs into its warm carcass to sleep. Into this tomb, which is also the womb of the earth's substance, the hunter descends to dream of death and be reborn.

He dreams "of lumbering flatfooted / over the tundra," of being "stabbed twice from within." Whatever way he lurches, whatever "parabola of bear-transcendence" or "dance of solitude" he attempts, his blood splatters a trail behind him. This is a dream of the bear's ordeal, but with a human edge. It is as though the animal is startled and terrified by a sudden consciousness of its own physicality. Ordinarily the bear is threatened only by external aggressors. Now, like a man self-tortured by every gesture, the bear is wounded internally. Like a man, the animal is driven to outleap its substance. It reaches for a solitude that only men can know—in which the whole material world appears to the mind as otherness at a distance. But the bear falls back to earth; the distance can only be bridged by assimilation.

"The Bear" is a poem about American consciousness in search of its true body. It succeeds in describing a bodily consciousness that is instinctive, communal, at one with the land, but it can only offer this vision at a fatalistic distance. The poet does identify with the hunter, presumably an Eskimo, but to preserve the myth of the hunt he has to choose an arctic setting popularly known as the last wilderness. So the poem is itself a final gesture toward an option most of us have lost. It commemorates a poetic ritual in which the body is finally given to utter its own mortal speech. The poem begins in late winter, in desolation and in need, but it ends when the hunter awakens to hear migratory geese returning in the spring. The dam-bear is waking; the man's sleep has been a gestatory hibernation. When he wakes, he measures time in seasonal and bodily rhythms, not with impossible human yearnings. He now walks, it seems, with the bear's feet—with a "hairy-soled trudge." And he wonders what "was that sticky infusion, that rank flavor of blood, that / poetry, by which I lived?" The mystery of the poem is this—that in America blood is the spirit's true poetry. No longer, therefore, is this Christ's blood; now it is the blood of a land shared by American creatures and the American people. Poetry is now the ritual that traverses the distance between them, the ideal landscape in which they interchange a communality. What Kinnell still must learn, however, is that this violent commingling has a history more immediate and intransigent than any archetype.

The Book of Nightmares fulfills everything Kinnell attempted before it. This volume is so much the fruition of his previous poems— their language, structures, and themes—that many of them now read like its early drafts. To reread the first three books and the other early poems after *The Book of Nightmares* is to find their whole enterprise retroactively pre-empted. Indeed even *Mortal Acts, Mortal Words*, published in 1980, reads like it predates *The Book of Nightmares*.

In this book Kinnell's vision is a wholly verbal achievement, no longer dependent on the reader automatically granting an American

poet the right to Whitmanesque prophecy. Moreover, Kinnell's poetry no longer depends on narrative anticipation for its impact. The
change begun with "The Porcupine" and "The Bear" is complete; we
are now primarily conscious of the poem's language. Kinnell's mystical vocabulary is not simply invoked; it is rendered into complex and
singular images that nonetheless convince the reader a common
source is undergoing metamorphosis. His recurrent terms—death,
emptiness, flowers, darkness, and light—are interwoven with images
of blood, bone, and stone. This verbal tapestry is linked to a number of motifs introduced in the poem's separate narratives, such as
the hen's death, the old man's shoes, and the births of his children.
The result is a matrix of repetition and variation, in which the narratives of the ten individual sections begin to lose their identity through
their relationship to the poem's larger form.

Throughout the book, the pervasive binarism of Kinnell's language
is inescapable. In the first poem he writes that he learned his "only
song" by climbing down to riverbanks to witness the "long rustle /
of being and perishing" (7). Toward the end of the book he walks
out into the fields and out of himself, seeking like the very stones of
the earth "to be one / with the unearthly fires kindling and dying"
(66), but the fields are as much the poem's ten sections as they are any
literal landscape. He describes himself as "dumped alive / and dying" (14) into his bed. Such casually paired terms for life and death
are commonplace enough. Renewal and extinction are linked as always by the temporal process that extends from one to the other. In
moments of change, ends and origins come together. Neither sur-
prised nor enlightened, we are shown a familiar concept and set at
ease. Yet some of the details supporting this theme are unusual: at
birth, his daughter turns blue when her umbilical cord is cut, seeming to die for a moment. Her tie to the resources of the womb's darkness is severed and she begins to forget what she had been, her
"limbs shaking / as the memories rush out of them" (6). That loss
will always be with her, like the imprint of a void and anonymous
self, a self she, like Kinnell and Roethke, would embrace again.
Already her "featherless arms" are "clutching at the emptiness" (7).

From the first pages, it is apparent that Kinnell's binarism is unstable and reversible. Kinnell wants to make the opposite terms of polarities coalesce. His daughter Maud is born "clotted with celestial cheesiness" (6); she glows "with the astral violet / of the under-life." "Cheesiness" suggests both ripeness and cheesy degeneration; "celestial" renders both meanings oxymoronic. Dramatic as Kinnell's narrative is, his main emphasis is verbal. He is less interested in the experience of birth than in the changes he can ring on the words we use to describe it. His daughter's birth occurs at the outset; it establishes the verbal ground on which the rest of the book is written, the vocabulary whose first associations Kinnell will both reinforce and invert.

The verb "to suck," for example, is only used a few times, but it is still given a double meaning. Maud "enters the headhold / which starts sucking her forth" (6); as she "sucks / air" and screams "her first song," she seems both to arrive and depart. The language is forceful but affirmative. Yet we soon read of "the sucked / carcass" of a hen killed by a weasel, and Kinnell later wills his twentieth-century brain to the fly, "that he may suck on it and die" (43). Nothing felicitous remains in those usages, but they are still linked with the earlier connotations. With his lover ("she who lies halved / beside me"), he watches bees "sucking / the blossom-dust / from the pear-tree" (68). In time the bees will be "burned down into flies" and thus be connected with more demonic sucking. Like lovers, the bees will only be whole when paired with their verbal opposites.

The verbal metamorphoses are often more complicated. When Maud awakens, "the green / swaddlings tear open" (5). Her consciousness begins as a ceremonial violence against substance: "a filament or vestment / tears." The sacrament of birth is a rude but celebratory opening. As Maud's "black eye / opens," so too will she someday "open / this book, even if it is the book of nightmares" (8). In the next poem, Kinnell looks into "the opened cadaver / of hen." In a mass of tiny eggs, he reaches toward "the icy pulp / of what is" (13), a cosmic point retaining only the abstract arc of the egg: "I have felt the zero / freeze itself around the finger dipped slowly in." Linked with eggs and origins, the word "open" undergoes a series of changes. He sees the Northern Lights "opening across the sky and vanishing" (13), illuminating themselves so thoroughly that they disappear. The word's ambivalent force increases with "the sweet, excremental / odor of opened cadaver" (37) and the decaying body whose "belly / opens like a poison nightflower" (44). Yet there are also visionary openings. The lovers feel their "bodies opened to the sky . . . the bodies of our hearts / opened" (59). Meanwhile he has described the "opened tail of peacock" and the opened bodies of dead birds. The resonance of the word becomes broad enough for him to write that "a way opens" into "everything I ever craved and lost" (67). Eventually, any use of the word implies all its meanings; none are exclusively positive or negative. In the final pages the openings are kaleidoscopic. A violinist puts his sorrow "into the opened palm / of the wood" (74). Each ordinary opening is imbued with everything opened or closed. The poet feels the bones of his foot "ripple together in the communion / of the step" and "open out / in front into toes." His stride opens outward "to dissolve into the future" (73). An opening is a temporal and hierarchical nexus for a vision embodied in linguistic transformations. Among discarded rubbish on earth and simultaneously in the heavens, "in the hole torn open in the body of the Archer" (74), the dead repossess their beginning in their end. The poem also opens itself in closure; Kinnell compares it to a skydiver "opening his arms" as he falls.

These variations on individual words are also woven together into larger patterns. Each important element of his diction, for example, is cast several times into imagery of death, imagery that occurs in each poem. The individual words are also continually aligned in new combinations. One perceives, overall, a broad vision worked into and out of the language itself. Through these interlocking images, Kinnell would demonstrate that language coheres beneath a surface of differences.

For a poet like Merwin, or for novelists like Beckett and Burroughs, that covert verbal matrix sets conclusive limits to everything we can say. Language for them is a tool whose use and function are predetermined. Moreover, we are shaped and possessed by the words we utter. The mouth, as Merwin writes, is "the door at the base of the skull where now the performers enter each with his eye fixed on the waiting instrument."[10] For those writers, submission to language occasionally prompts the kind of ecstasy Yeats associated with the experience of being taken up and used by historical destiny. More often, however, they see language as either ironic or suffocating. Language is the only form of self-consciousness; it is an index to all human action. Kinnell reacts differently to the same data; for him, as for Whitman, or for Robert Duncan, the celebration of the warp and weft of words is intrinsically liberating. Yet in Kinnell's book the interconnectedness of language sometimes becomes so pervasive that all change disappears before the obsessive reduction of each verbal difference to the same message. At that point, celebration yields to despair, and Kinnell's tone edges toward Merwin's. Yet Kinnell never follows the project to its paralyzed conclusion. His Whitmanesque democratization of language does, however, infuse a strain of melancholy into his poetry. This melancholic joy in the interrelations between words typifies the aesthetic of open forms in American poetry, and it reflects a covert awareness that America's history includes more dubious public achievements. If it willfully and optimistically reverses much that Marxist aesthetics suggests about the social pressures exerted through speech, implicitly arguing that language can overcome history by compensating for it, it also testifies fatalistically to history's inescapable determinism. Yet the dream, however often it is thwarted, persists.

For Kinnell, this dream parts from the modernist revulsion with language as the foremost evidence that human thought degenerates into materiality. Kinnell's poetic travels the same hierarchy in reverse. Like Norman O. Brown, he believes language can redeem the body by elevating it to consciousness. Language and consciousness can come into their own full power only by occupying the territory of the physical world. The mind's descent into the body, like the hunter's dream while he sleeps in the bear's carcass, is a submission to flesh that brings enlightenment:

> And the brain kept blossoming
> all through the body, until the bones themselves could think,

---

10. Merwin, *The Carrier of Ladders* (New York: Atheneum, 1970), p. 94.

and the genitals sent out wave after wave of holy desire
until even the dead brain cells
surged and fell in god-like, androgynous fantasies—
and I understood
the unicorn's phallus could have risen, after all,
directly out of thought itself. [59]

When the brain blossoms through the body, consciousness enables substances to be self-aware. In the verbal connectiveness of *The Book of Nightmares* we are to see the brain blossoming through the body of language, creating a collective life that compensates for a unity the nation has never achieved. The verbal blossoming renders human thought and the materiality of language copresent to one another. Then, as in Roethke's ecstatic visions, the center of the self is everywhere; like an instinct, thought seems to originate in the senses. Inevitably, the imagination is sexualized, and thought becomes an organic origin: "The unicorn's phallus could have risen, after all, / directly out of thought itself." Everything has the potential to flower verbally. Toward the end of the book, he walks out "among the stones of the field, / each sending up its ghost-bloom / into the starlight" (66), his rebirth signaled when "an eerie blue light blooms / on all the ridges of the world" (68).

Kinnell's sense of flowering recalls Williams's dedication to that image throughout his career. For both poets, as for Roethke, flowering is an essential metaphor for unfolding form. As the image of flowering accumulates associations in *The Book of Nightmares,* it unifies what seem contradictory emotions of ecstasy and despair. It is a figure that both dramatizes and transcends its constitutive binarism. Maud awakens as a blue flower opening and grows in concert with all organic life, her hair "sprouting" and her gums "budding." Yet flowering also suggests isolated, self-witnessed form: "the rose would bloom no one would see it" (13). Kinnell writes that Maud will remember, beyond the reach of consciousness, the songs she heard in infancy, not "the songs / of light ... but a blacker / rasping flowering" (7). Later he remembers the hen's "deathsmells, / blooming again in the starlight" (30). Unwilling to accept change, Maud tells flowers not to die (49). But we are already the fruit of dead flowers. In battlefields, "the belly / opens like a poison nightflower" (44); there the only seed is the "wrung-out / blossom of caput mortuum flower" (67). For Kinnell, as for Roethke, the flower suggests a violate, emptied selfhood: "it has a way / of uttering itself in place of itself" (*FH,* 58). The invisible life of a flower "burns up. Its drift is to be nothing" (*FH,* 58). Kinnell dreams of an acre "where the kissing flower may bloom, / which kisses you so long your bones explode under its lips" (43). For Kinnell, as for Baudelaire, flowering mingles death and consummation. When a fly caught in a spider's net gives up its struggle, Kinnell says its wings "flutter out the music blooming with failure / of one who gets ready to die" (35). Then he imagines an old drunk's relief in unconsciousness: "I blacked out into oblivion by that crack in the curb where the forget-me blooms." The mind flowers into emptiness. As the self's flower opens, the germinating seed and the falling petals, origin and end, are combined in the arc of a single gesture. All flowering is secondary, derivative, but in that derivation memory and anticipation are folded together. As Kinnell wrote earlier, "The petals begin to fall, in self-forgiveness" (*FH,* 58).

This rich, obsessive intratextual play of difference and repetition has its apotheosis in a sequence of visionary landscapes. There the figure of flowering is integrated with imagery of light and stone:

> I come to a field
> glittering with the thousand sloughed skins
> of arrowheads, stones
> which shuddered and leapt forth
> to give themselves into the broken hearts
> of the living,
> who gave themselves back, broken, to the stone. [65]

> . . . . .

> I walk out from myself,
> among the stones of the field,
> each sending up its ghost-bloom

into the starlight, to float out
over the trees, seeking to be one
with the unearthly fires kindling and dying. [66]

These landscapes are linguistic fields of force in tension, sites of verbal transformation situated between verbal opposites. They seek to
overcome a melancholic past and a fatalistic future, a history of
remembered and anticipated failure, by combining them in a figural
present. The landscapes call up the elemental underlife of the earth
and draw near to us the movements of constellations. They are composed in a verbal territory neither exclusively internal nor external.
Kinnell has said that "when you do get deep enough within yourself, deeper than the level of 'personality,' you are suddenly outside
yourself, everywhere."[11] His landscapes, at once intimate and open,
recall the landscapes at the end of the last three poems in Roethke's
"North American Sequence." For Kinnell, they grow out of the
secure rhetorical territory, the idealized American space, in which the
transfigurations of "The Avenue Bearing the Initial of Christ Into
the New World" take place. But this terrain has now become an
open, unprotected site for unpredictable verbal changes. What was a
static repository is now a field in linguistic motion.

Established by elaborate verbal echoes and consummated in Kinnell's visionary landscapes, this textual field of change is also reinforced by explicit structural linkage. Kinnell has always been fond
of structures that link beginnings and endings, and *The Book of
Nightmares* uses them extensively. Most of the poems, for example,
either repeat or rewrite their title near their conclusion.[12] Thus we
expect the final poem to echo the first. In both poems a small twig-

---

11. "'Deeper than Personality': A Conversation with Galway Kinnell," ed.
Philip L. Gerber and Robert J. Gemmett, *Iowa Review,* 1, No. 2 (1970),
133.
Cf. Kinnell's "Poetry, Personality, and Death," *Field,* No. 4 (Spring, 1971),
pp. 65-66: "We move toward a poetry in which the poet seeks an inner lib-
eration by going so deeply into himself—into the worst of himself as well as
the best—that he suddenly finds he is everywhere."
12. In several poems a specific image occurs at the beginning and the
end: a reference to "cursed bread" in the first poem, a description of being
"sprawled face down" on a mattress of hen feathers in the second, an image

fire set on old ashes burns in the rain, and a black bear, "his fur glistening / in the rain" and his head "nodding from side / to side," sniffs blossom-smells, eats a few flowers and "trudges away."[13] Kinnell's daughter Maud is born in the first poem, and his son Fergus is born in the last. The balance amplifies the poem's multiple sense of completion and renewal. Thus the first poem is not merely repeated in the last; it is simultaneously completed and begun again. The origin (zero) and the beginning (one) recur in the number of the final poem, ten: "one / and zero / walk off together" (73). The dead, he writes in a gesture against history, "lie / empty, filled, at the beginning" (74).

The old mystical formula, "as above, so below," which Kinnell quotes (68), reaffirms the poem's converging categories of verbal opposition. Temporally—the beginning and the end, past and future, two births separated in time, become copresent; spatially—the various settings, the isolated lovers, the whole physical breadth of the narrative, are clasped together in the poem; and hierarchically—heaven and earth, mind and body, are transformed into self-regarding images of one another. With these opposing terms equated, the poet

---

of an old Crone foretelling the future in the third. In the sixth poem, the first and last sections end with the same exclamation: *"Lieutenant! / This corpse will not stop burning!"* Sometimes the image is altered, but the effect is comparable. The fifth poem has an image of "the gaze / from the spider's clasped forebrains" in the first section and an image of "the light / from the joined hemisphere of the spider's eyes" in the last. There are numerous other repetitions throughout the book. A few examples will suffice. In the second poem Kinnell sees "the cosmos spelling itself" when he reads the shoulder blade of a ram, a common method of discovering hidden knowledge; in the next poem, the Crone reads Kinnell's own shoulder bones. In the eighth poem, a sheriff presses the "whorls / and tented archways" of Kinnell's fingers into a police blotter; in the next poem, he finds himself "alive / in the whorled / archway of the fingerprint of all things." Sometimes the second reference is a comic inversion, a technique that builds to the healing laughter of the final poem. In the second poem, a rooster groans out *"it is the empty morning"* to signal Peter's denial of Christ. Two poems later, a deskman in a cheap hotel forgets to bang *"it is morning"* on the sheet metal door.

13. Both the first and last poems have an image of the Archer: "the Archer lay / sucking the icy biestings of the cosmos, / in his crib of stars" (7); "the hole torn open in the body of the Archer" (74).

can imagine that all speech is simultaneous. The poems, we are to feel, are all equivalent; they traverse the same ground.[14] The form is the emptiness awaiting the words that fill it.[15]

The role that narratives play in this increasingly centripetal textuality is a paradoxical one; they differentiate and fuse the same metaphors. The quantity of textual repetition and variation grounded in the narratives is immense, but one example will demonstrate how the process works. Compare the first passage below, which commemorates Maud's life in her mother's womb, with the second, which describes the death of an old man:[16]

> It is all over,
> little one, the flipping
> and overleaping, the watery
> somersaulting alone in the oneness
> under the hill, under
> the old, lonely bellybutton
> pushing forth again
> in remembrance,
> the drifting there furled in the dark,
> pressing a knee or elbow
> along a slippery wall, sculpting
> the world with each thrash—the stream
> of omphalos blood humming all about you. [5]

---

14. The sense of formal equivalence is reinforced by having each of the poems divided into seven sections, a division that also creates the sort of parallel structures we found in "The Porcupine." Though the breaks here generally come at logical points in the narrative, they are not, however, strictly necessary. They therefore create an almost diffident sense of reoccurrence. In "To the Roots: An Interview with Galway Kinnell," James J. McKenzie asks "Did you have the seven-part divisions of each poem from the beginning also?" Kinnell replies: "No. But the sections seemed to be coming out that way, so I made them all come out that way. It's clear that some of the poems could have been divided into eight or six parts quite as easily" (p. 244).

15. Cf.: "that enormous emptiness / carved out of such tiny beings as we are / asks to be filled" (*MM*, 15).

16. The old man's death is part of an elaborate system of references. In the third poem, "The Shoes of Wandering," Kinnell puts on an old pair of shoes at the Salvation Army, discovering that they fit every knuckle and corn.

Violet bruises come out
all over his flesh, as invisible
fists start beating him a last time; the whine
of omphalos blood starts up again, the puffed
bellybutton explodes, the carnal
nightmare soars back to the beginning. [37]

When Maud is born, Kinnell describes her as "glowing with the astral violet / of the underlife" (6). In the second passage above, the old drunk ends his life in a violet flowering of darkness. His death rewrites the imagery of the womb in a violent degeneration. Maud's nine-month hibernation is later echoed in Fergus's foetal "fishy thrash." Thus if the poem begins with Maud's birth and ends with Fergus's, it also offers the old man's death as an image of its center.

The two births are clasped together about a center which is death furled in darkness, steeped in blood.[17] As we shall see shortly, that center is not only a biological metaphor; it is also an historical weight the poem cannot transcend. Many other images of blood are worked into the text between the children's births, a text drawing up "that underlife / where the canaries of the blood are singing" (59): "the chameleon longing to be changed would remain the color of blood" (13), "memory reaches out / and lays bloody hands on the future" (21). We lurch blindly, Kinnell writes, on a path over a "ground of ground / bones, crossing itself / at the odor of blood, and stumbling on" (22). The obvious reference is to Kinnell's "The

They seem like the "eldershoes" of his own feet, and in the final poems he begins to relive the life of the old man's shoes. In the fifth poem, "In the Hotel of Lost Light," Kinnell lies in the "sag the drunk smelling of autopsies / died in." With his own "body slumped out / into the shape of his," Kinnell begins to relive that life, and, in Whitmanesque long lines reminiscent also of Ginsberg's "Howl," writes an epitaph for the drunk's last days. The narrative recalls the empathy he attempted to achieve with the poor in "The Avenue Bearing the Initial of Christ Into the New World," but here the self-conscious artificiality is openly exploited and his irony, while still sentimental, is more successful.

17. Scattered through the poem are numerous references to the notion, based on the theory of love that Aristophanes proposes in Plato's *Symposium*, that we are each "a torn half / whose other we keep seeking across time"

Bear," but this ground is also soaked with the blood of old battle-fields. He writes later of mortality's "meal of blood and laughter" (29), speculates that we are mindlessly "ready to take on the blood-thirsty creatures from the other planets" (42) and wills his "crooked backbone / to the dice maker, to chop up into dice, / for casting lots as to who shall see his own blood" (43).

Blood and bone finally become almost interchangeable; they are our essential substances, consumed in the fire of breath. Singly alive, the body's song is the song of all creatures alive: "The voice is a particular recognizable voice; at the same time it mysteriously sheds personality and becomes simply the voice of a creature on earth speaking."[18] The poem is full of agonized, almost throttled sounds, "labored breath-takings" and "gasp of lungs." Yet all these rough calls are subsumed in the poem's song, or so Kinnell, with Whitman's sense of voice, would believe. Indeed, if the poem's interconnectedness can become strong enough, these anguished sounds can acquire a new origin as permutations of the poem's repeated references to its own "song." In the final poem, a violinist plays Bach on an instrument whose strings cry and sing "from the sliced intestine / of cat." The bow-hairs are "listening down all their length / to ... the sexual wail / of the back-alleys and blood strings we have lived" (74).

Like the hunter's dream in the bear's body, the poem's song "is a stirring of that ineradicable memory of once belonging wholly to the life of the planet."[19] In the visionary passages in the final poems, Kinnell discovers, to paraphrase Rilke, the earth verbally re-arisen within himself. Yet this vision for American poets has an inescapable cultural analogue, and it answers to cultural pressures for mythic

---

(58). He calls a woman "she who lies halved / beside me" and playfully describes sex as "that purest, / most tragic concumbence, strangers / clasped into one" (58). Earlier he wrote of "two clasping what they dream is one another" (37) and of a wind moving "among the stones, hunting / for two twined skeletons to blow its last cry across" (45). These images of failed love, of bodies clasped together but still unsatisfied, are linked verbally to images of birth. Maud began "clutching at the emptiness" moments after her mother's cervix completed "the slow, / agonized clenches making / the last molds of her life in the dark" (6).

18. Kinnell, "Poetry, Personality, and Death," p. 67.
19. Ibid., p. 69.

resolution. To "belong wholly to the life of the planet" is also to acquire the redemptive collective life of the American land. The textuality of the poem, its body, is everywhere, "skeleton groaning, / blood-strings wailing the wail of all things" (68). Like Roethke, Kinnell opts for verbal changes that empower elemental transformations, but Kinnell's alchemy is more elaborate, surreal, and obsessive. Blood and bone metamorphose into earth, air, water, and fire. "In all the windows / of stone" light and darkness are visible in one another:

> The witness trees heal
> their scars at the flesh fire,
> the flame
> rises off the bones,
> the hunger
> to be new lifts off
> my soul, an eerie blue light blooms
> on all the ridges of the world. Somewhere
> in the legends of blood sacrifice
> the fatted calf
> takes the bonfire into his arms, and *he*
> burns *it*. [68]

In the first poem, Kinnell lit a small fire and saw in its flames "the dead, crossed limbs / longing again for the universe"; in the wet wood he heard "the snap / and re-snap of the same embrace being torn" (3). Into the fire fall raindrops to be "changed." An oath is broken, "the oath sworn between earth and water, flesh and spirit." The oath will be "sworn again, / over and over, in the clouds" and "broken again, / over and over, on earth" (4). The oath is a bond certifying difference, a structuring of discourse. The poem would become a mediating place where the swearing and breaking of the oath are simultaneous. In the final poem, a bear smells the sweat of "a death-creature" who watches from the edge of a wood. Suddenly he knows his own eyes stare back out of the darkness; "he understands / I am no longer here, he himself / from the fringe of the trees watches" (71). Between those two looks, the poems cohere. A "wafer-stone" (the reference to the host is intentional) is skipped across the water "ten times." The ten "zeroes it left" meet and pass "into each other, they themselves / smoothing themselves from the water" (66). The book coheres by a willing reductiveness, a self-sacrificial disintegration of all into one. The book does what we as a nation cannot do: it lets go. It is written in "the still undanced cadence of vanishing" (52). "Still" implies both "as yet" and "motionless"; the full richness of vanishing will be revealed as the unresolvable play between the infolding and unfolding of the poem's form.

In the passage quoted above, the fatted calf burns the flames himself because to be consumed is the self's verbal radiance. The passage fuses the pagan ritual with the image of the burning bush. Sacred and secular coalesce. In an early poem Kinnell has a man in a desert climb Mount Nebo "to look over the far side / Of the hill on which Moses died looking this way, / And to see the bitter land, and to die of desire" (*WK*, 41). Here the Crone's prophecy to Kinnell suggests Moses overlooking the promised land: *"You will feel all your bones / break / over the holy waters you will never drink"* (23). Now the promised land is ours, but the people never enter either. The book's resolution occurs at a similar distance. Our sense of closure is partly empathic or voyeuristic; the poem's closure necessarily excludes us. Inevitably, too, the renewal of the first poem in the last suggests not just structural balance and completion but also a fruitless return to a point of departure. The resolution is temporary: the entire sequence begins again.

As Kinnell lights a fire in the first poem, he speaks "a few words into its warmth— / *stone saint smooth stone,"* ritually invoking the binarism of earthliness and transcendence, death and sensuality. The smooth stone later becomes the "egg / shaped stones" that suggest funereal rebirth and the eucharistic self-absolution of the "wafer-stone." Stones suggest the heaviness of spirit irretrievably immured in substance. The stones of the field "saying / over their one word, *ci-gît"* are an image not only of human death, as on a battlefield of unmarked graves, but also of the earth as the grave of the heavens. The stones that announce "here lies" give witness to the paradoxes of incarnation—enlightened matter contrasting with contained spirit.

The purgative wish runs both ways; ascent and descent yearn for one another and regard one another with melancholic fatalism:

> ... knowing
> the sadness of the wish
> to alight
> back among the glitter of bruised ground,
> the stones holding between pasture and field,
> the great, granite nuclei,
> glimmering, even they, with ancient inklings of madness and war.
>
> [66-67]

The field of stones and the field of stars are reversible; they mirror one another. When Kinnell speaks into the fire, "the singed grease streams / out of the words" (4). The image is ambiguous and unresolvable. Does the binary ritual free the words of their fleshly dross or extract their essence? The problem extends to the metaphors associated with the poem's form. Does the entire fabric of words free language from its material entanglements or establish its conclusive reincarnation? Kinnell takes this paradox of the physicality of language from Whitman, but Kinnell is less at ease in its articulation.

In his essay "Whitman's Indicative Words" Kinnell credits the Whitman line with communicating "that deep rhythm the words themselves will also have when their time comes."[20] Whitman, he claims, draws from words their "prehistoric and infantile resonances" and makes those resonances virginal and new. Whitman's affection for the physicality of speech complements his attempts to verbalize the physical presence of the human body. Kinnell cites the erotic passages from the fifth section of *Song of Myself* and the passages in the final section where Whitman bequeaths his flesh to the world: "I effuse my flesh in eddies, and drift it in lacy jags." Kinnell is particularly attracted to those passages where Whitman describes the body in terms of sheer process and fluid energy.[21] These passages

---

20. Kinnell, "Whitman's Indicative Words," *American Poetry Review*, 2, No. 2 (1973), 9.

21. Cf. Kinnell, *The Poetics of the Physical World* (Fort Collins: Colorado State University, 1969), p. 20: "Poetry is the wasted breath. This is why it

Kinnell correctly connects with Whitman's images of the whole physical world as light and energy in motion: "Something I cannot see puts upward libidinous prongs, / Seas of bright juice suffuse heaven." Such descriptions, Kinnell points out, "may even detach themselves completely from any visible surface."

Kinnell reads Whitman for "incandescent passages" that verge on Norman O. Brown's sense of the "resurrected body." Brown intends the phrase to refer to a rediscovery of the polymorphous perversity of the infantile body, a sensuality that could become conscious in adult life were it not repressed. For Kinnell, however, resurrection is both inescapably religious and a specific cultural necessity. Kinnell quotes the fifth section of *Song of Myself* in his essay, but omits the first two lines, in which Whitman justifies his poem's eroticism as a union between soul and body. The omission is significant precisely because the lines are more relevant to Kinnell than to Whitman.

Kinnell has consistently been a very ecclesiastical Whitman. He celebrates the body in contexts that continually suggest spiritual ascent and affirm the body, in all its instinctual animality, as a genuine vehicle for holiness. Religious rhetoric, however, proves more forceful than any changes one can work on it; though his subjects are now secular, the rhetoric persists. Thus his playful inversion of the fortunate fall proves traditional: "Someday the burlap of your skin / Will pass for linen, by the grace of sin" (*WK,* 49). Like Hopkins, he seeks to show the imprint of the incarnation on all creation.[22] Through his first two books, Kinnell uses Whitman's vision of the body, and even Whitman's catalogues, but his version of Christian

clings to the imperfect music of a human voice, this is why its verbs are so imitative of bodily motions, why its prepositions pile up like crazed longings, why its nouns reverberate from the past as if they spoke for archetypes of earthly life, this is why the poem depends on adjectives, as if they were its sense, which want only to smell, touch, see, hear, taste, to press themselves to the physical world."

22. Cf.:

> Mirrored in duskfloods, the fisherbird
> Seems to stand in a desolate sky
> Feeding at its own heart. In the cry
> *Eloi! Eloi!* flesh was made word:
> We hear it in wind catching in the trees,
> In lost blood breaking a night through the bones. [*WK,* 54]

myth protects him from Whitman's vision of American history. Although the interplay between mysticism and history helps keep Whitman's poetry alive, Kinnell keeps the two separate, lest the whole site of poetic transfiguration be invalidated by historical realities.

Despite his difficulties with the Civil War, Whitman managed to revive his faith in a national openness in which death would be visible but luxuriant, a sensuality democratized to the arms of lovers and the uncut hair of graves. Kinnell's own proclamations—"Now on the trembling pulse let death and birth / Beat in the self as in the April grass" (*WK, 25*)—are less confident. The historical myth has become defunct. We are left, in Susan Sontag's words, with "a kind of garbage plenitude—the reigning inversion of Whitman's dream."[23] In poems like "The Last River," based on Kinnell's participation in the Civil Rights movement, the perversion of Whitman's dream is pointed out with a certain amount of self-congratulation. Later, as in "Vapor Trail Reflected in the Frog Pond," his attitude toward the distorted dream is both angry and ironic. Yet only with *The Book of Nightmares* does historical reality directly impinge on his vision of sensuality.

The sixth poem in the book, "The Dead Shall be Raised Incorruptible," taking its title from St. Paul's First Epistle to the Corinthians, is a sarcastic indictment of Christian man's twenty centuries of determined extermination of his brothers. The particular stimulus, however, is America's Vietnam war, and the generalization to all of Western history does not eradicate the special violence of Kinnell's own generation: *"do not let this last hour pass, / do not remove this last, poison cup from our lips"* (45).[24] Kinnell concludes a description of a rotting corpse with this image, the irony barely controlled: "a mosquito / sips a last meal from this plate of serenity" (44). Then the soul takes wing: "the fly, / the last nightmare, hatches himself."

23. Sontag, "Shooting America," *The New York Review of Books,* 21, No. 6 (April 18, 1974), 21. In *On Photography,* pp. 68-69, the phrase becomes "a garbage-strewn plenitude—the willful travesty of Whitman's magnanimous dream."

24. Cf. Christ's words in Matthew 26:42: "O my father, if this cup may not pass away from me, except I drink it, thy will be done."

The nightmares of the book's title, particularly his children's night-mares and our nightmares of death, are to be eliminated by the book's formal resolution. The book will "invent on the broken lips of darkness / The seal of form" (*FH,* 24). Yet the nightmare of American history cannot be undone. Kinnell anticipates the subject of the sixth poem in the third. There a boy "shipped back burned / from the burning of Asians" sweats "his nightmare out to the end / in some whitewashed warehouse / for dying" (21). In the same poem, Kinnell writes of poetic creation as a "path / inventing itself / through jungles of burnt flesh," a willed illusion echoing the fiction of national destiny. The book's final stanza views that night-mare with cosmic irony, but the irony will not function for Kinnell or for us, only for the poem and perhaps, within the text, for the figures of the poet's children. "Don't cry!" he warns Fergus, and then adds "Or else, cry." The alternatives are arbitrary; each affirms itself as the absence of the other. He tells Fergus to look "on the body, / on the blued flesh, when it is laid out" to find "the one flea which is laughing." From one perspective, this is Kinnell's own body, and he is offering the poem's form to Fergus as a way of dealing with his father's death. It is also one way for Fergus to make use of his own death in the midst of life, by translating his nightmare of death into cosmic laughter.

The laughter here is self-deprecating. The flea recalls those "dreamers not yet / dipped into the acids / of the craving for any-thing, not yet burned down into flies" (58). Yet the flea also signals the upward swing of the pendulum, what Kinnell earlier called our "lech for transcendence" (*WK,* 63). As the poem's final gesture, the flea's laughter echoes the reciprocal humiliation of form in a content both verbal and historical. Form, like ritual, absolves and harmonizes content. But form also takes into itself the irreducible dross of the particular. This "blued flesh," like the rotted flesh the mosquito feeds on in the sixth poem, the poem occasioned partly by the Vietnam war, is also the spirit's ironic tabernacle. It is the flesh, "blue as a coal," to which Maud is born. The book's flesh, its words, would be spiritualized by the endless alchemy of its formal reverbera-tions. But this formal zero is also the hen's quite mortal egg and the bullets expended in war. The cycle repeatedly traverses an historical burden it cannot transcend.

As an accomplished form, as a purely verbal system, the book almost surmounts every obstacle to its fulfillment. Yet Kinnell, following an historical imperative, deliberately subverts the self-referential perfection of the book's formal development. In the sixth poem, near the center of *The Book of Nightmares,* he opens the book to precisely those historical circumstances it cannot undo:

> "That you Captain? Sure,
> sure I remember—I still hear you
> lecturing at me on the intercom, *Keep your guns up, Burnsie!*
> and then screaming, *Stop shooting, for crissake, Burnsie,*
> *those are friendlies!* But crissake, Captain,
> I'd already started, burst
> after burst, little black pajamas jumping
> and falling . . . and remember that pilot
> who'd bailed out over the North,
> how I shredded him down to catgut on his strings?
> one of his slant eyes, a piece
> of his smile, sail past me
> every night right after the sleeping pill . . .
>
> "It was only
> that I loved the *sound*
> of them, I guess I just loved
> the *feel* of them sparkin' off my hands . . ." [41-42][25]

Much of the rhetoric of this monologue is essentially untouched by the verbal matrix of the surrounding poem, and that is exactly the point. It testifies to the anguish that makes the poem's vision at once necessary and insufficient. Like Whitman meditating over the dead of the Civil War, Kinnell confronts those peoples on whom America has conferred eternal life, but unlike Whitman Kinnell realizes

----

25. Cf. Kinnell's comments in an interview (*WS,* 109-10), in which he describes how this passage conflates references to both the Vietnam and Korean wars.

his poetry cannot alleviate that horror. This history, of course, is more than American, "Christian man" having "exterminated ... Jews, Moslems, witches, mystical seekers, / black men, Asians, and ... every one of them for his own good" (42). Yet we have our own particularly American history of genocide—"a whole continent of red men for living in unnatural community / and at the same time having relations with the land." This history did away with the very collective organic life toward which we now aspire with futility. And the compensatory myth of resurrection has its secular American version. "The Dead," we delude ourselves, "Shall be Raised Incorruptible" in America's inclusive form. "Can it ever be true," Kinnell asks, "all bodies, one body, one light / made of everyone's darkness together" (30). The ecclesiastical dream is finally wedded to its democratic realization. Moreover, the verbal interconnectedness of *The Book of Nightmares,* which is its chief accomplishment and its central aesthetic, is itself an expression of a dream of democratic relations.

The verbal interconnectedness Kinnell works into his poem is incredibly elaborate. Through it, the narratives are absolved of their individual anxiety or misery, but they are also thereby dissolved into the play of discourse. The language's interconnectedness absorbs all temporal process, seeking to replace history with its own inclusive space. Yet it cannot transform the national history it acknowledges. In accepting its American heritage, the book obliges itself to fail: our *"corpse will not stop burning"* (41). Form's transforming fire makes flesh, blood, bones, air, earth and water, light and darkness, interchangeable. Yet when this equalizing process is given a national name and an historical past, one variable but democratic substance pervades it all:

> carrion
> caput mortuum,
> orts,
> pelf,
> fenks,
> sordes,

    gurry dumped from hospital trashcans. [41][26]

The book's mythic, archetypal form can never wholly surmount its singular American content. "This earthward gesture / of the sky-diver" is Kinnell's American version of the myth of Christian martyrdom. The formal closure of the poem can never be complete. The first and last section is each "a torn half / whose other" it keeps "seeking across time," and the traversal across time, through history, makes the fusion of the two halves impossible. At once calm and anxious, ethereal and mundane, *The Book of Nightmares* offers us a body suspended between communal fusion and communal disintegration. Vision and history confront one another in Kinnell's major work; they are mutually causative, reactive, and finally irreconcilable. The verbal apotheosis of *The Book of Nightmares* is also its failure.

---

26. Kinnell is sometimes fond of archaic diction, especially when he can show that the history of the language can be drawn out of its contemporary materiality and made co-present in the poem.

CHAPTER FOUR

Between Openness and Loss:
Form and Dissolution in
Robert Duncan's Aesthetic

a poetry
refusing itself like a comet
with a tail of tin cans. [*NP*, 13][1]

Everywhere dissenting, contradictory voices speak
up.... I don't seek a synthesis, but a melee.[2]

The interweaving of all aspects and identities of Man
in one fabric ... the sense of warp and woof of that interweaving
as a design of complicities, drives me to interrupt every simple
satisfaction in me with an errant suggestion, to undo each seemingly
self-contained figure, each sentence, with a phrase contrary to its
syntactical course. [*C*, xxxvii]

ROBERT DUNCAN HAS perhaps the quintessentially American career among poets committed to working in open forms. He
has also probably written more extensively about his aesthetic theory
and about the dynamics of open-form poetry than any other poet of
his generation. Although some of his interests are unique, several
important elements of his aesthetic—the pursuit of a democratic

---

1. The following works by Robert Duncan are abbreviated and documented internally: *AT — As Testimony: The Poem and the Scene* (1964;
rpt. San Francisco: White Rabbit, 1966); *BB — Bending The Bow* (New
York: New Directions, 1968); *BR — A Book of Resemblances* (New Haven:
Henry Wenning, 1966); *C — Caesar's Gate: Poems 1949-50* (Berkeley: Sand

and communally responsive writing, the concept of creation by field, and the image of poetry as an open and unfinished process—are shared by many other contemporary poets. This chapter begins by summarizing Duncan's aesthetic, focusing on the main features of his concept of form; it concludes by reading several of his poems in the context of both his poetic theory and the historical pressures that have either compromised his vision or been subsumed by it.

Like Olson and Pound, Duncan grounds his poetry in a theoretical program both affirmative and querulous, a program that the reader may in turn find both challenging and irritating. Each poet offers captivating moments of lyrical beauty, but each also regularly subverts this lyricism. Then the theory becomes a counter-pressure to the desire to hold an audience. Dominated by theory, poetry can become slack, formless, or enthusiastically sentimental. Yet theory can

Dollar, 1972); *D — Derivations: Selected Poems 1950-1956* (London: Fulcrum, 1968); *F — Fragments of a Disordered Devotion* (San Francisco: Gnomon, 1966), n. pag.; *FD — The First Decade: Selected Poems 1940-1950* (London: Fulcrum, 1968); *I — An Interview* (Toronto: Coach House, 1971), n. pag.; *NP — Names of People* (Los Angeles: Black Sparrow, 1968); *OF — The Opening of the Field* (New York: Grove, 1960); *P — A Prospectus for the Prepublication Issue of Ground Work to Certain Friends of the Poet* (San Francisco: privately printed, 1971); *RB — Roots and Branches* (New York: New Directions, 1964); *SG — The Sweetness and Greatness of Dante's Divine Comedy* (San Francisco: Open Space, 1965), n. pag.; *T — Tribunals* (Los Angeles: Black Sparrow, 1970); *TL — The Truth and Life of Myth: An Essay in Essential Autobiography* (Fremont, Michigan: Sumac, 1968); *W — Writing Writing* (1964; rpt. Portland, Oregon: Trask House, 1971), n. pag.; *Y — The Years as Catches: First Poems 1939-1946* (Berkeley: Oyez, 1966).

For an annotated bibliography of Duncan's separate publications see Gary M. Lepper, *A Bibliographical Introduction to Seventy-Five Modern American Authors* (Berkeley: Serendipity, 1976).

Readers familiar with Duncan's work will be aware that his unconventional spelling—"rime," "delite," "reformd," which I have followed throughout—is intentional, e.g.: "We drop a silent *e* from an unpronounced syllable, daring no more than men in the seventeenth century presumed" (*BB*, ii).

2. Duncan, "Pages from a Notebook," *The New American Poetry,* ed. Donald Allen (New York: Grove, 1960), p. 406.

be constructive, helping to generate "a fountain of living forms" (*TL*, 29) by establishing an arena for action and seeming to protect it from cultural usurpation. The theory of open forms tries to be both a ground for innocent, Whitmanesque openness and a barrier against the realities of political and literary history. Yet the visionary openness and the history are mutually dependent, their balance every-where insecure.

Theory is always partly combative; it is the front line of vision. "Every order of poetry finds itself, defines itself," Duncan writes, "in strife with other orders."[3] Despite his resistance to a more strict and academic formalism, Duncan recognizes that he needs it as an antagonist. Like most poets, he is aware that a plurality of poetries is stimulating; indeed, he admits that absolute allegiance to one doctrine is pointlessly restrictive: "I'm not going to take the closed form versus the open form because I want both, and I'll make open forms that have closed forms in them and closed forms that are open" (*I*). Yet he is also willing to respond aggressively. Writing twenty years after Randall Jarrell's objections to *Paterson,* when Williams had won approval even among academics, Duncan remains unforgiving: "By the time of *Paterson III,* fossil-minded Randall Jarrell correctly saw that Williams had lost his skeleton. The form in process, the form evolving in terms of the survival of themes in a field of creation, took over."[4] The defensiveness of the first sentence qualifies the vision of the second. Duncan's criticism is studded with such battles.[5]

Theoretical positions often have practical consequences that are self-defeating. Because he believes his poems are part of an ongoing process, not independent objects, Duncan refused to be anthologized from 1961 to 1975; the result was a loss of potential readers for his

3. Duncan, "Man's Fulfillment in Order and Strife," *Caterpillar,* 2, Nos. 3/4 (1969), 229. "A new order," he continues, "is a contention in the heart of existing orders."

4. Duncan, "Notes on Grossinger's *Solar Journal: Oecological Sections,*" (Los Angeles: Black Sparrow, n.d.), n. pag.

5. He continues not merely to argue with the New Critics but actually to rail against them, long after their influence, both on taste and on practical matters like publishing opportunities and literary awards, has declined. He

books. After publishing *Bending the Bow* in 1968, Duncan decided
not to publish another volume of collected poems until 1983, feeling
he needed time free from the coercions of publishers' expectations.[6]
Even Duncan's published work can be difficult to find. His prose is
generally published in small-circulation magazines. His early books
are now rare; he has reissued some, adding unpublished or uncol-
lected texts, but eliminating others. Three dimensions of his work—
the books published in his own holograph, his exquisite drawings
and title pages, and his collaborations with Jess—are available only
in limited editions.[7]

Roots and Branches and *Bending the Bow* are weakened by Duncan's commitment to their inclusive, chronological arrangement. His
deliberately fragmented, inconclusive poems demand an integrative,
book-length structure to generate and control interactions between
poems, a structure more elaborate than the listing he borrows from
Pound's *Cantos* for his "Passages" and "The Structure of Rime" sequences. Duncan's books require the sort of organization he observes

defends himself against the most irresponsible criticism and even resents ex-
ceptions to statements of general praise. See, for example, Duncan's opening
comments about M. L. Rosenthal in his preface to the 1972 edition of
Caesar's Gate, as well as his regular comments over the years about Olson's
advice in "Against Wisdom As Such."

6. Cf. *P:* "I want a time and a space to work in that will be, as time and
space were only in the years before others were interested in publishing me,
the time and space of a life of the work itself." Duncan has issued a few
recent poems in limited editions, but they are not easily obtained.

7. For Duncan's lovely covers and title pages, see *The Sweetness and
Greatness of Dante's Divine Comedy* (500 copies), *Faust Foutu* (Stinson
Beach, California: Enkidu Surrogate, 1959—750 copies), *Play Time / Pseudo
Stein* (New York: The Tenth Muse, 1969), *Medea at Kolchis: The Maiden
Head* (Berkeley: Oyez, 1964—528 copies), and *A Seventeenth Century Suite
in Homage to the Metaphysical Genius in English Poetry* (250 copies). Duncan's *The Cat and the Blackbird* (San Francisco: White Rabbit, 1967—500
copies) and *Names of People* (281 copies) are illustrated by Jess, the artist
who has been Duncan's long-time companion.

The longest book in Duncan's beautiful and quite readable holograph is
A Book of Resemblances (203 copies), also illustrated by Jess. A number of
Duncan's limited edition books include his drawings, but the largest collection
is *A Selection of 65 Drawings* (Los Angeles: Black Sparrow, 1970—330
copies).

in Williams: "*Spring & All* in 1933 stands a major realization of
form. Its 28 poems belonging to an open sequence" of "discrete
sharply drawn, contrasting poems that are in turn parts of something else, elements thruout of a melodic structure."[8] Few of Duncan's poems are wholly discrete or sharply drawn, but both those that
are self-contained (such as "Often I Am Permitted to Return to a
Meadow") and those that are not (many of the "Passages") are
complicated by the poems around them. Yet of his three recent collections, only *The Opening of the Field* entirely finds that surrounding form.[9] *Roots and Branches* and *Bending the Bow* could be edited
and restructured.

The procedure might resemble Pound's work on *The Waste Land*,
a surgery Duncan considers damaging: "It had been cut and reor-
ganized to succeed, and had lost in its conscious form whatever unconscious form had made for the confusion of sequence, the 'miscel-
laneous pieces' that did not seem to fit."[10] Since Duncan made this
comment before the draft of Eliot's poem was published, it reflects
his assumption that revision is destructive. Like Ginsberg, Duncan
believes that revision prevents poetry from displaying the uncertainty
and spontaneity of human life. Ginsberg somewhat naively believes
that poetry can fully record nonverbal events. Duncan instead argues
that poetry should record all the dimensions of the writing experience. If the poet in uninhibited in transcribing the verbal complica-
tions he experiences while he writes, his poetry will present a wider
human reality. Yet Duncan's "refusal to censor or correct" (*C,* xxxvi)
is sometimes supported by rhapsodies about an art where "everything was possible, nothing circumscribed the flowering of being

---

8. Duncan, "Nights and Days: Chapter One," *Sumac,* 1, No. 1 (1968),
119.

9. Duncan has said that he "started out from the very first poem in
Opening of the Field to compose a book," "Robert Duncan's Interview,"
Unmuzzled Ox, 4, No. 2 (1976), 83. Now, however, he largely rejects the
idea that a book should serve as a significant structure in itself. Similarly, he
describes "Passages" as "a series having no beginning and no end as its condition of form," "Preface to a Reading of Passages 1-22," *Maps,* No. 6
(1974), p. 53.

10. Duncan, "Nights and Days: Chapter One," 121.

into its particular forms."[11] Like many poets committed to working in open forms, Duncan urges Blakean excess—a poetry "not carefully made but enraptured in making . . . a gesture extravagantly willing itself—a demonstration—a thing done" (*F*). The last phrase refers to Olson's poetics, but the passage generally suggests the Beat poets of the 1950s, particularly Ginsberg and Corso.

Ginsberg and Duncan both believe conventional forms manifest imperialist motives; thus they often regard them with righteous condescension. Closed, conventional forms are "a 'discipline' imposed like a military drill or court manners."[12] More broadly, Duncan finds established forms to be repressive: "Form, to the mind obsessed by convention, is significant in so far as it shows control"—"the tenor throughout is prophylactic"; thought must be contained and directed, or we will be overcome by unmanageable emotions.[13] Such poetry becomes either a protective response to threatening experience or a way of extending psychological dominance over the unknown.[14] Duncan may be right that we employ conventional forms to subdue the chaotic associativeness inherent in language. Yet such forms cannot altogether disguise the forces they encounter. As Duncan himself confirms elsewhere, all forms contend with formlessness. Formal dominance is always partial, flawed, even when it gives the appearance of rigor and stasis. Indeed, Duncan's best poems are those in which carefully wrought forms nearly succumb to a temptation toward dissolution.

Though we cannot absolutely distinguish between open and closed forms, descriptive differences nevertheless suggest tendencies

---

11. Duncan, "From a Notebook," *The Black Mountain Review,* 2, No. 5 (1955), 212.

12. Duncan, "The Lasting Contribution of Ezra Pound," *Agenda,* 4, No. 2 (1965), 25.

13. Duncan, "Ideas of the Meaning of Form," *Kulchur,* No. 4, pp. 61 and 72.

14. Because threat and risk are so ominously present in Robert Lowell's work, Duncan selects him as an example of a poet who uses more conventional forms to repress his experience. Duncan says that Lowell "holds his line and establishes his rime at the edge of disaster" and argues that his poetry is the lesser for not following his terror through to incoherence, "Ideas of the Meaning of Form," p. 66.

in each. As Whitman's catalogues demonstrate, open forms can be more generously and democratically inclusive. They also make it possible, though still difficult, to attend to the immediate event of the writing situation.[15] As Duncan puts it playfully, a closed or pre-conceived "form is the important disregarding of what is going on in order to go on at all" (W). Such disregarding, with its compromises and failures, is evident in the most carefully wrought sonnet, but Duncan is correct in arguing that open forms can foreground the associative risks in language.[16]

Yet the benefits of this free responsiveness do not substantiate a faith in first utterance. If free verse can open the poem to unexpected images or formal imperatives, it can also make them accessible to the poet's intervention. Poetry, Duncan suggests, "is a composition that takes place in the unconscious that the consciousness feels as an imperative towards form."[17] Like Georges Poulet, Duncan believes the actual text of literature is altogether conscious: "the minute it's sounded it belongs to consciousness" (I). If, as Duncan insists, the poet's function is to refine his attentiveness, to become conscious of what is actually happening in the poem, then the poet's heightened awareness must allow for choices and excisions in harmony with the evolving form.

"I evolve the form of a poem," Duncan writes, "by an insistent attention to what happens in inattentions" (TL, 46). Accidents of association, puns, homonyms, etymologies of sense and sound— Duncan considers these essential for poetic forms to be true to the formal potential of the language. Form, he believes, is "not something the poet gives to things but something he receives from things" (TL, 41). The "things" in poetry are words, and Duncan is aware of the coercion exercised by language's connotative history.

---

15. Systematic forms, Duncan argues, tend to mask "the variety of what was actually going on, the lead one sensed in incident, in factors so immediate they seemed chance or accident to all but the formal eye," "The H.D. Book: Part II, *Nights and Days,* Chapter 2," *Caterpillar,* 2, No. 1 (1969), 32.

16. Open forms, Duncan writes, have "the greatest inner tolerance for even conflicting tones, certainties, doubts — the texture of a widely, even wildly, multiphasic personality," "From the H. D. Book: Part II, Chapter 5," *Stony Brook,* Nos. 3/4 (1969), p. 341.

17. Duncan, "From the H. D. Book: Part II, Chapter 5," p. 347.

Words are already symbolic and metaphoric. He has faith, however, that if we pursue the covert associations in words, associations which often have as much to do with sound as with meaning, we can release a democratic force free of all coercion except the imperative toward an infinite variety of forms. Poetry would recover language's instinct for unpredictable metamorphosis. This is at once an optimistic and a fatalistic view of language, one shared by Duncan and Kinnell and one they both trace to Whitman. One encounters such ideas elsewhere, but American poets often believe that the recovery of that democratic verbal resource is a special national responsibility.

To write, then, is to learn a discipline of listening: "We have only to . . . cooperate with the music we hear"—"the reverberations of our first thought in the reservoir of communal meanings."[18] Like Gaston Bachelard, Duncan believes a new image breaks through the surface of single meanings to tap a deep reservoir of connections.[19] "Poetry," Duncan comments, "is language that becomes so excited that it is endlessly creative of message" (I); poets "hear languages like the murmuring of bees. Swarm in the head."[20] The individual image gives us access to the communal memories of the race, communal memories, Duncan feels, that America's collective immigrant consciousness is uniquely able to gather. "There is no isolate experience of anything then, for to come into 'house' or 'dog,' 'bread' or 'wine,' is to come into a company."[21] "Speaking of a thing I call upon its name, and the Name takes over from me the story I

18. Duncan, "Towards an Open Universe," *Contemporary American Poetry,* ed. Howard Nemerov, Voice of America Forum Lectures (United States Information Agency, c. 1965), p. 176.

19. Cf.: "Language becomes throughout a ground of suggestion and association, a magic ground, weaving of phrases echoing in other phrases, a maze of sentences to bind us in its spell," Duncan, "Two Chapters from H.D.," *Triquarterly,* No. 12 (1968), p. 90.

20. Duncan, "Pages from a Notebook," p. 407. Cf.: "In the Hive of Continual Images the Bees, the angelic swarm, build in the visible cells a language in which they dance," Duncan, "Structure of Rime XXVII: Jess's Pasteups," *Quarterly Review of Literature,* 16, Nos. 1-2 (1969), 33.

21. Duncan, "Rites of Participation," rpt., *A Caterpillar Anthology,* ed. Clayton Eshleman (New York: Doubleday, 1971), p. 27.

would tell" (*TL*, 45). Writing is a dialectic of resistance and submission; we are "seized by the language to work purposes we had not contemplated."[22] Yet in the self's dialogue with the wellspring of words, language is reordered. Thus Duncan does not argue for purely automatic writing. Writers answer the language in their own words; they shape a limitless force, giving it visible form and substance.

But form is never monolithic. An apparently consistent surface is actually a fragile trembling among alternatives, inconsistencies, and indecisions. Form not only defines its boundaries in the midst of formlessness, it also reflects and communicates formlessness. "The artist senses in the very transformation of world into art the specter of an ultimate return of created things into their original state."[23] The particular vocalizes, bodies forth the infinite: "Chaos, the Yawning Abyss, is the First Person of Form" (*TL*, 24). All embodiment dismembers and reconstitutes its given substance: "From many roots, words gathered into one stem of meaning, confused into a collective suggestion."[24]

Form is a destiny that dissolves and absolves, combining past and future in the intention of the present. History for Duncan is therefore essentially a formal process. The attraction and terror of form is this capacity to eliminate change and uncertainty, to make chaos fateful. Duncan's analogy for formal realization is Christ's incarnation and passion. In form, eternity becomes mortal. "In every true poet's voice . . . you will hear a counterpart of the Son's sorrow and pain of utter undergoing . . . the poet understands the truth of the anguish of Christ's passion as a truth of poetic form" (*TL*, 75, 76). Amidst the melodies and concatenations of the language, the poet speaks and the potentiality of utterance is momentarily specified. Like the Creator, the poet oversees "the figure of the Son given up into

---

22. Duncan, "Pages from a Notebook," p. 407. In poetry, Duncan writes, it "is the words themselves that speak for us, revealing and betraying us" (*P*, 8). Yet the word's creativity "can only realize Itself in the Flesh, in the incarnation of concrete and mortal Form" (*TL*, 45).

23. Duncan, Introd. to *Translations* by Jess (New York: Odyssia Gallery, 1971), p. x.

24. Duncan, "From the H. D. Book: Part I, Beginnings, Chapter 5: Occult Matters," *Stony Brook*, Nos. 1/2 (1968), p. 4.

the terrible guarantee of the poem" (*C,* xxv). As a poet assumes a single mask, his projected inwardness becomes other, inaccessible: "The Son's cry to the Father might be too the cry of the artist to the form he obeys" (*TL,* 24).[25] Why, the poet wonders, does his form forsake him as it come to fruition?

Poetic form is a fateful intersection, a nexus where incarnation and ascension meet to tell their story.[26] Inspiration "carries the artist through in a state that combines fear for form and faith in form to realize the imperatives of his poem" (*TL,* 23). In the formal consummation, all the disparate elements of the text, its diverging and converging harmonies, are crucified, "as a universe is crucified in me— / Christ-crosst upon the body of my world" (*Y,* 66).[27] "Our sense of completely realizing and being faithful to a form," Duncan comments, is "one of the reasons we withdraw from it. We see the tragedy of fulfilled forms."[28] Perhaps both the tragedy and the temptation of open forms are even greater. The temptation is one of containment—that a radically open form could enclose an infinite variety of content, a temptation that is part of American culture. Yet this containment is also a dismemberment, a passionate unfolding. The process is continuous, moving not in fixed cycles but in diverse and simultaneous renewals and extinctions. "Order is disordering."[29] New forms undo the existing order of forms, and in that disorder new forms begin to work.

Open forms urge us to experience structures that are fluid and

---

25. Cf.: "It is in passion, in suffering, that, even as we cry out, we become workers, organs, instruments of our Art that is fateful or formal. The Christ is the music, the sense of needed form . . . ," Duncan, "From the Day Book — excerpts from an Extended Study of H. D.'s Poetry," *Origin,* second series, No. 10 (1963), p. 43.

26. The writer hesitates, Duncan writes, at "the threshold that is called both *here-and-now* and *eternity*"; when he crosses the threshold, the distinction vanishes, "Towards an Open Universe," p. 177.

27. Cf.: "This god Christ will not rest in an historical identity, but again and again seeks incarnation anew in our lives," "From the Day Book — excerpts from an Extended Study of H. D.'s Poetry," p. 26.

28. Duncan, "Discussion," *A Meeting of Poets and Theologians to Discuss Parable, Myth, and Language,* ed. Tony Stoneburner (Cambridge, Mass.: Church Society for College Work, 1968), p. 32.

29. Duncan, "Man's Fulfillment in Order and Strife," 232.

contingent. Yet open forms can cohere, and even cohesion in motion can suggest finality: "the poem had presented itself as a welling up of words or waters that was yet a well in its fullness, eternal and motionless" (*BR,* vii). Form, Duncan often writes, is a "net" the poet uses to fish for coordinates, coordinates that must be gathered in repeated castings. "Projected in time from a series of works," he writes, "there is an increment of design."[30] Yet form is also eroded as it evolves. This erosive feeling reflects not only the sense of process that is part of any formal consummation but also the simultaneous accumulation of other forms. There is an increment of designs.

Ideally, these multiple and contrasting orders could coexist in the poem as they coexist in the language. Rather than pursue the destiny of a single order, the poet working with open forms could become a protean and democratic creator, entertaining variegated and disordering orders simultaneously. The poem could be a form among forms, dismantling and reassembling its own structures. Duncan proposes a poetry of "heraclitean form" sustained not by anticipating its final accomplishments but by the inexhaustibility of its resources.[31] "Come," he urges, "let us have a lasting sentence" that can survive the grammatical termination of its constituent sentences.[32] Form can evolve through the criss-crossing of many paths to establish a field of intention; "the Composition and we too are never finished, centered, perfected."[33] Like other arguments for an intrinsically unfinished open poetry, Duncan's is partly a way of gaining the freedom to move forward without worrying whether each phrase contributes

---

30. Duncan, "Nights and Days: Chapter One," 106.

31. Such poetry, Duncan writes, reflects "a view of language...as being in process, as immediate happening, evolving and perishing, without any final goal—the goal being in the present moment alone," "Man's Fulfillment in Order and Strife," 231.

32. Duncan, "Beginnings: Chapter 1 of the H. D. Book, Part I," *Coyote's Journal,* Nos. 5/6 (1966), p. 31.

33. Duncan, "Rites of Participation," p. 43. This balance between the unique or particular and the universal or general is paradoxical and even contradictory. If only the immediate event matters, why maintain the existence of a broader eventfulness? If the universal context is the final overriding goal, why should each line not be addressed to it? Duncan wants the best of both positions.

to the emerging whole. Indeed errors and distractions drive the poet to devise increasingly more comprehensive and powerful forms, though ones which in turn can also become more elusive, as they are forced to contain ever more divergence and variation. "Each realized experience of form" becomes "the germ of a new necessity for form or affinity for form."[34] Each form renders itself insufficient. Yet language is "conservative too of all its earlier forms" (*I*), so the imperative to new forms runs counter to the language's instinct for replication.

Form is governed not by the tyranny of predestination, but by the illusive play of history's fatefulness amidst over-riding change. This difficult balance does not survive in Duncan's Vietnam poems, in which history's fatefulness becomes demonic and the celebratory conception of form gathers in an experience of terror. Like Pound's "dynamic form which is like the rose pattern driven into the dead iron filings by the magnet" (a passage Duncan admires), poetic forms will suddenly reorganize accumulated detail.[35] Yet the iron filings are scattered again by each shift in the magnetic forces.[36] A single word may draw a poem into cohering lines of force, or it may undo all that a poem aims to achieve. "Interweaving forms" turn coeval, interactive; image and rhythmic patterns are drawn into formal grids that overlay one another, complementing and contradicting one another. The

> ground is a palimpsest of change:
>   The design
> constantly in reconstruction.
>   Destroyd.
>   Reformd. [*D*, 19]

Duncan writes that *Leaves of Grass* has its form "as the ever flowing ever self-creative ground of a process . . . a pouring forth of

34. Duncan, "The H.D. Book: Part II, Nights and Days, Chapter 4," *Caterpillar*, 2, No. 2 (1969), 40.

35. Ezra Pound, *Guide to Kulchur* (1938, rpt., New York: New Directions, 1968), p. 152.

36. Cf.: "The poem, like music, taking shape upon the air," ("The H.D. Book: Part II, Chapter 4," p. 35), "Formless, and yet taking on all Form"

thought, not a progression but a medium of thought."[37] With these models in mind, the pressure to carry the project further invades all his poetry. For Duncan the whole modern tradition serves as "a directive to work not from preconceived form but towards creative form."[38] His naiveté about which forms are and are not preconceived is partly self-justifying but also a way of intensifying his doubt about the openness of his own poetry.[39] Emphasizing the moment-by-moment shifts in the writing situation not only opens the poem to intrusions but also encourages the poet to question the authenticity of his own consciousness. With "the apprehension of the work's 'life' springing anew in . . . each immediate cell,"[40] the writer must continually renew the decision to write. Like Adrienne Rich, Duncan believes we should consider a work successful if it is true to the process of its creation. "The end of masterpieces," Duncan announces, "the beginning of testimony."[41] The poem's "testimony" will be an act of unfettered witness—or at least an act accepting its own recalcitrance. We can no longer think "of good and bad works but of seminal and germinal works cast abroad in the seas of the world."[42] That, perhaps, is the democratic ideal, to abjure judgment and acknowledge that any text has its place in the play of languages. Yet Duncan himself is not always positive toward other poets' work.[43] His career is marked by acceptances and rejections—both of the poets he adopts as models and of his own work. The ideal of open form, however, is a field democratically accommodating all these interactions.

(C, 19), "changing and rechanging form, deformd" (D, 44).

37. Duncan, "Changing Perspectives in Reading Whitman," *The Artistic Legacy of Walt Whitman,* ed. Edwin Haviland Miller (New York: New York University Press, 1970), pp. 76 and 89.

38. Duncan, "The H. D. Book: Part I, Chapter 2," *Coyote's Journal,* No. 8 (1967), p. 28.

39. Cf.: "Our experience of form throughout," he writes, "is a faith in the principle or voice we follow," Duncan, "Two Chapters from H. D.," p. 98.

40. Duncan, "The H. D. Book: Part II, Chapter 4," 40.

41. Duncan, "Ideas of the Meaning of Form," p. 61.

42. Duncan, "Notes on Grossinger's *Solar Journal.*"

43. See the book reviews Duncan wrote for *Poetry* during the late 1950s and early 1960s.

Duncan's version of Olson's notion of creation by field, a notion Williams also approved and extended, embraces all the connotations of field as open and "multiphasic": "Not one but many energies shape the field. / It is a vortex. It is a compost" (*T*, 12). The field is not a stable area of verbal activity mapped out and definitively bounded by a given text but a spatio-temporal gestalt continuously reprojected and reconstituted. Moreover, the field enlivens all the territory it establishes: " 'Form, Gestalt,' Pound notes: 'Every spiritual form sets in movement the bodies in which (or among which) it finds itself.' "[44] Olson's discovery of "form as a field of things in action" (*I*) has to be complemented by an image of kaleidoscopic forms commingling and counterpointed.[45]

The field is a generalized version of a redeemed American continent, a ground of permission, a naked, exposed territory where all occurrence can enter to encounter its co-existing orders. As with Kinnell, the apotheosis of the particular is the revelation of its full democratic connectiveness. Duncan's dream, a particularly American one despite its diction, is "to compose the true epithalamium where chastity and lewdness, love and lust, the philosopher king and the monstrous clown dance together in all their human reality" (*TL*, 38).[46] Each thing named acquires an endless series of second-

44. Duncan, "The H. D. Book: Part II, Chapter 4," 31.

45. "Poetry," Duncan writes, "has its form in a field generative of forms" (*C*, xxxiv). The total field is "an art where figure and ground may be exchanged freely," "The H. D. Book: Part I, Chapter 2," p. 31. In that field, all randomness, each accident of circumstance, constitutes new forms. There "every thread is central and every figure central to threads and figures"—"the miasma of phrases, drifts of meaning within meaning exhausting any literal reading until the prose swarms with seeds of meaning," "Two Chapters from H. D.," pp. 79 and 91. Creation by field maintains "a melodic coherence in which words—sounds, meanings, images, voices—do not pass away or exist by themselves but are kept by rime to exist everywhere in the consciousness of the poem," "Rites of Participation," p. 38.

46. For such a cosmic celebration, the poet could not pretend to provide more than a humble ground. Indeed, each efflorescence in a field of colors, each harmony and discord in a field of sounds, is part of the wide field where creation is at play. "In composition by field, a color does not glow in itself or grow dim, but has its glow by rhyme—a resonance that arises in the total field," "Introduction" to *Translations*, p. iv. The field is always the scene or

ary names. The self is freed, like the self of Roethke's "North American Sequence," to pursue innumerable rehearsals of selfhood. Each failure, each cruelty, each single death, is absorbed and redeemed in the democratic counsel of its brothers. Selfless, or at least many-selved, free to err because error is absolved in the communal myth, the poet engages in an unplanned, enraptured speaking.[47]

American poets often emphasize their joy in creating open forms.[48] Yet the open "collage of diversities," the idealized American space, has other more worrisome names. If it is "Mnemosyne, the Mother-Memory of Poetry" with its "matrix of meanings" made visible, it is also "the Dragon of the Formless Heavens," the libidinal "Mother of our Formless Nature."[49] The verbal universe that open poetry would articulate in the total field of its activity is also the otherness, the disordering sea that is the source of all phenomena. Duncan often describes that mothering and devouring resource, the resource

---

setting for an unbinding, or unfolding. Each field, paradoxically, may be said to have its origin in its wider outcome: "The world is a field creative of texts," Introd. to *Translations,* p. viii. "Back of the field as it appears in Olson's proposition of composition by field is the concept of the cosmos as a field of fields," "Changing Perspectives," p. 78.

47. As Duncan writes of Pound's *Cantos,* "The rant, the bravado, the sarcasm, the exaltation are purposeful overcharges that touch again and again to keep our sense alive to the disorder, the demand of experience for a higher order of form," "The H. D. Book: Part II, Chapter 5," p. 342. Each apparent digression, each intrusion, brings us to see "the world in the light of a new necessity. An in-forming," "Beginnings: Chapter 1," p. 11.

48. Their manifestoes include numerous injunctions toward the concentration required to cast off repression and there are confessions of frequent despair at the inability to meet the challenge. Yet the theory is also intended, rather less nobly, like the criticism that accepts and admires all open poetry, to affirm the way the broader vision overwhelms each awkwardness and extraneous intrusion. Thus even if the form is irregular, "free verse, later projective verse... deriving from an inner aperiodic formal intuition," the writing experience is supposed to be intrinsically liberating, "The H. D. Book: Part II, Chapter 4," 40. "To compose so in the pure exhilaration of a formal feeling" ("Nights and Days, Chapter 1," 119) is to attend to the immediate verbal event while recognizing that each "minum" of the poem participates variously in "the collage of diversities" (*BR,* x).

49. Duncan, "The H. D. Book: Part I, Chapter 2," p. 28; "From the Day Book—excerpts," p. 25; "Nights and Days: Chapter One," 115.

Robert Bly sees as central to poetic creation, in terms reminiscent of Whitman. Duncan would submit to its power in what he feels is Whitman's mode of bitter-sweet despair, or in the manner of Prospero's melancholic disavowal of his own magical powers.

Despite the mask of exhilaration, the dominant mood in open poetry is one of loss. What the poet utters, he abandons to his evolving form. Open poetry is often a giving up of all things to inhering and surrounding emptiness: "How faint my voice sounds in the lasting sentences. Once it reaches her, my voice is immortal. And I am fallen away into dryness and wetness, into original stuff" (D, 110). Meditating on one of his first major theoretical poems, "An Essay at War," Duncan realizes he was "picturing not a victory but a creative failure ... a giving up to a war of its own things" (BR, viii). "I sensed," he writes, "that I must work not with my abilities but with my inabilities" (BR, ix). Poetry is a medium of minute, particular failures that "puts forward the unsurety it must go by" (C, ii). Each utterance fails its impulse toward achieved and dominant selfhood. The self is audible only in its insistent echoing elsewhere. Like the power Yeats's Leda experiences, what the poet senses in his words is an intrusive force, indifferent, impersonal: "The word moves me. I give ... into it the intent of the poem" (BB, 137). His words yearn but "the delicate trunks of their trees / reach into a cluster of torn flowers" (Y, 8). "The power which comes is only the emanation of the loss of power" (Y, 9). "The idea is elegiac. A poem / of things lost or about to be lost" (D, 23):

> He conceives the poem
> as a shatterd pitcher of rock crystal,
> its more-than-language not in the form
> but in the intrigue of lines, the shattering,
> the inability   •   [D, 23]

Like Williams, Duncan often ends a line with a period removed several spaces. Both use this device partly to signal self-conscious attention, to emphasize that the poem's word-by-word progression is an activity demanding our participation. In Williams, such punctuation revitalizes the poem's language; it stimulates our resources, and we extend the interrupted statement.[50] In Duncan, however, this device is more an economical "measure of the crippled sentence" (*D*, 44). In the passage above, we read "the inability   •" and share the poem's faltering hesitation; we cannot give the words the power to continue. Such fractured speech constitutes "a deconstruction" (*D*, 95); it aborts the self's vocalization and reveals a verbal machinery that operates without our assistance. The wave of the poem proceeds without us, while the wave we ride retreats:

> Troubled surfer seeking the about-to-break line
> of the wave in it to ride
>   toward revelation,
> the tide that would have carried you draws back
>   from the litterd margin,
> and the depth of the sea you would have born forward
> is the depth of an impending failure   [*P*, 11]

Duncan's sense of form is closely linked to such images of failure informed by natural rhythms. Form for him is a beautiful but fateful letting go. Yet images of organic fruitfulness persist in his work despite its sense of dissolution. "The force that words obey in song," he writes, "the rose and artichoke obey / in their unfolding towards their form" (*OF*, 60). Such passages suggest Roethke's early radical vegetalism, and Duncan too is interested in primitive, instinctual components of consciousness: "green shoots of a child inhabit the dark of a man" (*OF*, 21). Yet Duncan's conception of organic growth does not imply the continuous unfolding visible in time-lapse photography of opening flowers. Rather than a fluid unfolding, he wants to convey a fateful coherence of assorted movements, as when he credits butterflies with "tracing out of air unseen roots and branches of sense" despite their erratic flight. They virtually "restore / an imaginary tree of the living . . . by fluttering about" (*RB*, 3). Form thus combines an image of harmoniously unfolding and enfolded space, "robed round in sound, rich as a tree / in full

---

50. For a detailed discussion of this technique, see the chapter on Williams in my *The Incarnate Word: Literature as Verbal Space* (Urbana: University of Illinois Press, 1973).

foliage of metaphor, flower and fruit" (*RB*, 89), with an image of space trembling with diverging excitements, like the "outpouring / spasm of air / that in the sheen of fish-scale's seen" (*RB*, 106).

Duncan deeply wants an image that combines the motifs of cohesion and dissolution. He is not satisfied with poetry that exists along the lines of tension between them. Like the speaker in Roethke's "Meditations of an Old Woman," Duncan would be both pool and river, both the nesting bird and the bird in flight. He has shown that the two properties of form are interrelated dimensions of consciousness. "Reaching out from the brain, the brainstalk flowers at the skin where it meets the world in a concert of vibrations";[51] it is a "radiant alliance": "impulsive skin / covering the soft infolded brain- / meat under the skull" (*RB*, 107). Consciousness is both exploratory and cautious; it has two formal activities, electric branching and sedate convolution, neither static, but each with its residue of design, its formal gestalt.

These two impulses suggest conventional dualities of mind and body, consciousness and matter, categories whose differences Duncan undermines. Each is present in the other; they are each other's most visionary manifestation. The spirit wills its own incarnation; consciousness longs for the peril of embodiment:

> I am not I
> but a spirit of the hour descending into body
>   whose tongue touches
>   myrrh of the morgenrat [*RB*, 8]

The spirit's very mortality enlivens the dross of sheer substance.[52] Poetic language is a descent of spirit and an ascent of body, a materialization of thought and a spiritualization of matter.

Duncan pursues images that bind such opposing terms in a field of force giving the illusion of a dominant source, a constitutive and informing center. "Is there," he asks, " 'a heart-shaped space,' some all but intangible form . . . in the separations and reformations, the

---

51. Duncan, Introd. to *Translations,* p. xii.

52. Cf.: "Soul is the body's dream of its continuity in eternity. . . . Poetry is the very life of the soul: the body's discovery that it can dream. And to perish into its own imagination," Duncan, "Pages from a Notebook," p. 401.

overlappings and differences among the members?"[53] Roethke too
was obsessed with the possibility of describing a paradigm of form,
but Duncan's sense of form includes a more radical element of dissolution.[54] Duncan's "Sonnet 4" expresses his desire for that enduring but erosive center:

> He's given me his *thee* to keep,
> secret, alone, in Love's name,
> for what sake I have only in faith.
>
> Where it is . . . ? How it is near . . . ?
> I would recognize him by the way he walks.
> But it was so long ago and I was never sure   •
>
> except in his regard and then
> sure as the rose scattering its petals to prepare is sure
> for the ripeness near to the perfection of the rose.
>
> I would know the red *thee* of the enclosure
> where thought too curls about, opens
> out from, what's hid,
>
> until it falls away, all the profuse allusion let go,
> the rose-hip persistence of the truth hid therein from me
>
> enduring. [*BB*, 3]

"Sonnet 4" is in the long tradition of love poems that are simultaneously secular and religious. The word "thee' gives the opening
line a studied, self-conscious quality that distances us from its intimacy. "Thee" suggests a formal, sacred rite, but one still radical and
transforming, perhaps the communication of a secret essence. Yet
we cannot be certain whose "thee" is given "to keep." Is it the inner-
most self of the lover or the speaker's own inwardness returned to

---

53. Duncan, "Nights and Days: Chapter One," 132.

54. Unlike Roethke, Duncan also adds a religious and apocalyptic element
to his notion of form. For Duncan, the form of forms is a second coming
when all will be redeemed. Cf.: "The Second Coming is the Form of Forms,
from which all Judgment and redemption of events flows. But here again
I am speaking of the wholeness of a poem in which all its parts are redeemed
as meaning," Duncan, *TL*, 62.

him as otherness worthy of being loved? Then the temporal frame is undermined—"it was so long ago"—and the speaker declares he "was never sure   •" The spaced period emphasizes the uncertainty, "as if there were a stress in silence" (*BB,* ix).

The rest of the poem resolves this confusion by accepting it. "I see now more clearly," Duncan writes elsewhere, "in my loss the continual losing"; there he finds "the deep of home" (*Y,* 30, 32). The unfolding rose, Duncan's recurrent figure for a fertile dying into form, suggests that ecstasy and anxiety are inseparable. The image has the same attraction for Roethke and Kinnell. "The flower of life opens, falls into its seeds," Duncan writes, "over and over again, we ... flower into whatever place and time of being and fall apart into ourselves" (*C,* xlvii f). There is a single formal gesture in an unfolding rose and a sexual embrace:

> Faithless and painful, why does the rose
>   never cease unfolding
>   but grows and unfurls,
>   the swirl, the twist—
>   the hot clasp of bodies, [*FD,* 90]

The curl of petals and the clasp of limbs describe identical arcs in the air. An unfolding rose and enfolding arms celebrate the same form. The center of each cluster of arcs is empty, void, and eternally ripe. They are forms evolved by a calculus of sculptural erosion; they dissolve as they are created.

In "Sonnet 4" the flower is an image of the self fulfilled through its vulnerability. The almost rapturous wish to know "the red *thee* of the enclosure / where thought too curls about, opens / out from, what's hid" combines reverent witness with sexual possession. The form is simultaneously sheltered and exposed. He would penetrate those recesses of thought protected by the first outfoldings of imagination. In that foetal, vaginal enclosure, thought and body undergo a common germination: "the new leaves revolving in their caskets: a dream of origins" (*Y,* 7). All unfolding forms orient themselves about the same source: "a snake-coil of water, / a bird-wheel in the sky ... make their announcement / in the heart of things" (*RB,*

174). At the center, where everything is "let go," these motions cannot be told apart.

Yet form, like sound, flowers "outward without any singleness to define its center" (*W*). This does not mean that the center, like a detached creator, is lodged in a displaced elsewhere. Dispersed in all its parts, the center becomes imminent with every unfolding form. Form is "many-brancht in repeating, / many-rooted in one thing" (*RB*, 90). Yet this center is also an encroaching otherness, a point of absence, a static negative in the midst of everything: "Back of the act, the incarnation, the passions, / the Void He Is" (*RB*, 150). Whether it flees this void or approaches it warily, all variety converges upon it. There we see "space turning upon its brazen hinges / to open wide" (*BB*, 98). The center is stretched open, violated by the poem's progress:

> . . . roses in their
> > first nature burst,
> flare their curling petals wide
> and fall aside from their dark hips, [*RB*, 135]

> How deep the violation goes,
> unfolds, petal by petal, rooted,
> and yet so multiplied,
> inflorescent. [*FD*, 101]

> the slit of an eye opening in
> > time
> vertical to the horizon [*BB*, 14]

The "untrembling center . . . at the heart of the work" (*BB*, 99) is a torn seal that marks every object with the sign of loss. It gives the illusion that time itself has a center, that history has dissipated from a single event to which it continually returns. As poetry weaves its cloth of associations, all speech is seen to be thread spun of that source, but one must "cut the warp / to weave that web" (*BB*, 15). Each increment of design slices and rebinds. Duncan's "let image perish in image" (*BB*, 15), responding perhaps to Yeats's "Images that yet / Fresh images beget," adds the sense of dissolution to the notion of rich, radically transforming verbal association. For Duncan, to enter into any nexus of associations is to encounter endless grieving.

Duncan's most effective poetry either addresses his sense of loss directly or complicates his ecstasy with delicate syntactical and semantic subversions. His more overt subversions rarely work. As in Pound and Olson, the intrusion of unpoetic data sometimes deflates the poetic language. Often, statements flatly antagonistic to the poem's central metaphors work against Duncan's real purpose—to trap us in a net of contradictions. Then we keep our distance and never achieve the imperiled intimacy Duncan seeks. The poetry that succeeds manages both to uplift and to trouble us. It turns its lyricism against itself by careful repetition and variation that seduces and then irritates. These poems have an apparently smooth and fluid surface, one that leads us to read them with only a slight edge of uneasiness to our pleasure. Then, when the text is part of us, its discontinuities are less readily discounted. "I pursue a process of revision and disorganization," Duncan writes, "to keep creation of the poem and consciousness of the poem in interplay" (D, 90).[55] If we are to share in this project, Duncan must make us risk ourselves in the poem's field of multiple occasions; there "the consciousness bent down to a literature lives on its wits in a sulfurous burning."[56]

"Often I Am Permitted to Return to a Meadow" (OF, 7), "My Mother Would Be A Falconress" (BB, 52-54), and "The Torso" (BB, 63-65) exemplify Duncan's sense of form as cohering dissolution. "Often I Am Permitted to Return to a Meadow" is the first poem in The Opening of the Field; the reader thus connects the meadow in the poem with the field in the book's title.[57] Field is a

---

55. Duncan's comments on his use of the term "re-vision" are fairly straightforward: "My revisions are my new works, each poem a revision of what has gone before. In-sight, Re-vision," "Pages from a Notebook," pp. 400-401.

56. Duncan, "Nights and Days: Chapter One," 104.

57. Michael Davidson, "A Book of First Things: The Opening of the Field," in Robert Duncan: Scales of the Marvelous, ed. Robert J. Bertholf and

broad term referring to various landscapes, to the notion of a perceptual gestalt, and to Olson's idea of composition by field. Does the shift to a meadow signal a more specific landscape? A meadow suggests a single harmonious climate, a space protected by its surroundings. "Opening" a field implies a liberating or pioneering gesture, an entrance or exposure. Returning to a meadow implies the recovery of past intimacy, the restoration of secure resources. The poem's title domesticates the revelatory title of the book. The meadow here is a memory to be inhabited; its emotional connotations are private and delicate. Yet we also wonder if this meadow is the field the book would open.

The poem's title is its first line, effecting a beginning *in medias res* that conflicts slightly with the line's strong assertion of composed renewal. The word "permitted" is a gesture of humility, undercutting any connotation of will or urgency. Almost without effort, the speaker finds himself in the presence of this meadow:

> as if it were a scene made-up by the mind,
> that is not mine, but is a made place,
>
> that is mine, it is so near to the heart,
> an eternal pasture folded in all thought
> so that there is a hall therein
>
> that is a made place, created by light
> wherefrom the shadows that are forms fall.

These first three stanzas complete the sentence started in the title. The meadow now seems almost an imaginary *hortus conclusus*, an enclosed garden protected from the outside world. The setting is so "made-up," so constructed, fictional, that its otherness shows little congruence with the imagination that gave it life. Yet intimacy and otherness are inextricably part of the same texture; in the poem they

---

Ian W. Reid, quotes a passage from an unpublished preface to *The Opening of the Field* that makes this connection explicit: "It is the field projected by the poem as its own form (extended here to the field of the book projected by the poem) an effort towards projected verse as initiated by Charles Olson" (Notebook A., p. 102—Bancroft Library, University of California, Berkeley), p. 58.

echo within the same shell of sound. The partial rhyme of "mind"
and "mine" reinforces the meadow's ambiguities. "Made-up" and
"made place," the first implying artifice, the second solid construction, are not mutually exclusive alternatives. Similarly, "that is not
mine" and "that is mine" appear to be opposite, yet visually and
aurally they are mutual reverberations, alternatives reflecting one
another. The very composure and perfection of this made place lend
it a sense of difference, of exclusive containment. But this meadow
is also the place where we always are, the mind's ground and the
setting for its development. It is "so near to the heart," this otherness that constitutes the self.[58]

The word "pasture" broadens the "meadow" of the first line. The
pasture is eternal because it is so thoroughly "made-up" as to last
forever and because it acquires an impersonality and universality
linking it to every other "made place." It is a place, not just a thing,
because its isolation is confirmed by our being there. Enfolding the
pasture in the medium of thought makes it a place with "a hall
therein," with an entrance and a means of passage. The pasture is
the field where the mind feeds on its own substance—the human
body, but the body both specific and general.[59] Like Duncan's image
of the body of primitive man, it is without preconceived outline and
conscious in all of its parts. This makes the mind's energy visible, "as

58. Cf.: "The work of art itself appears as a gift for another but also as a
means for another to be there. Self expression may be an urgency of art, but
the self has no expression except in this other," "The H. D. Book: Part II,
Chapter 2," 29.
59. Cf.: Robert Creeley's comments on Duncan's meadow: "This sense of
a poem—that *place*, that *meadow*—has echoes of so many things that are
intimate to my own sense of the reality experienced in writing," *A Quick
Graph: Collected Notes and Essays* (San Francisco: Four Seasons, 1970), p.
63. Creeley goes on to connect the meadow in "Often I Am Permitted to
Return to a Meadow" with Whitman, with Olson's sense of composition by
field, and then with a passage by Ginsberg:

I always wanted,
to return
to the body
where I was born.

"That body," Creeley concludes, "is the 'field' and is equally the experience of
it" (p. 64).

if it were the mind itself / which descends in the poem / and becomes manifest" (*FD,* 86), while also "encumbering in its concretion and weight the longing for ecstatic flight the soul knows" (*C,* 62).

As we finish the opening stanzas, we sense an uneasiness that also hints of freedom. If forms are mere shadows, they have no special permanence. Yet Duncan will later write of "the ascendancy of the shadow / in the blossoming mass" (*RB,* 169), so even a transient form gives satisfaction in completed structure. Nonetheless, the structure here is also a dissolution:

> Wherefrom fall all architectures I am
> I say are liknesses of the First Beloved
> whose flowers are flames lit to the Lady ·
>
> She it is Queen Under the Hill
> whose hosts are a disturbance of words within words
> that is a field folded.

These next two stanzas present a conventional invocation to the muses, a gesture appropriate to the book's first poem.[60] Again, however, the architectures "fall," and we can read this falling as a loss of variety and innocence, as well as a falling into place, as forms find their necessary order. The tone of these stanzas recalls medieval hymns to the lady and courtly love poems, but that decorous surface

---

60. M. L. Rosenthal, in *The New Poets: American and British Poetry Since World War II* (New York: Oxford, 1967) gives "Often I Am Permitted to Return to a Meadow" special praise:

> None of the other Black Mountain poets, and few other poets of our day, can match the exquisite workmanship and mystical directness of these lines at the beginning and near the end of the poem. The tone is complex—humble, sweet, sad—yet makes for a single curve of feeling. This effect is created partly by a varied incantatory pattern of parallel constructions, so that there is a falling movement at the beginning of lines that shifts, imperceptibly, into a rising movement created by a new turn at the end. Thus the first line (the title) begins with an abstract statement that is a gracious acknowledgment, courtly and bearing a sense of prayer akin somehow to the poetry of the Court of Love tradition, p. 175.

See also Ron Silliman's analysis of the poem in "Opening," *Maps,* No. 6 (1974), pp. 72-80, which includes a list of associations appropriate to Duncan's language: "*meadow:* external to self, physical reality, organic process; *scene made-up:* extended from self, created reality, formal process."

masks a more unsettling communication—that the poem's formal
imperatives, its ordering structures, are really "likenesses" of a much
wider set of verbalizations. This suggests that the poem's progress is
determined by connections inscribed in the words themselves. A "disturbance of words within words," the poem is a ritual performed in
the Lady's honor and in her service—"she," Duncan writes later,
"whose breast is in language," who "sends her own   priestesses of
the Boundless to these councils of our boundaries" (T, 19). A "disturbance" is any reorganization along fresh lines of association. The
"field folded" is an archetype of poetic form: a field of associations
doubling back on themselves to create a formal gestalt. Only within
that limited frame can we glimpse "the Hosts of the Word that
attend   our words" (T, 19).

The result is a fiction, a dream momentarily resisting the larger
pressures of the language:

>It is only a dream of the grass blowing
>east against the source of the sun
>in an hour before the sun's going down
>
>whose secret we see in a children's game
>of ring a round of roses told.

The dream works its changes among the grasses at the surface of the
field of meanings.[61] It troubles the depths briefly, sounding rhythms
that set the poem's pace and establish its configuring image sequences.
Despite its apparent originality, the poem is a variation on a codified
ritual, like a children's game. The secret of this children's game is
the belief (the historical truth of which is irrelevant to Duncan's
purpose) that the rhyme dates back to the bubonic plague, when
flowers were carried to ward off the odor of decay. Elsewhere Duncan describes poetry as an infection of meaning, a disease erupting in

---

61. A passage from Duncan's unpublished preface would have given the
field and the children's game an autobiographical context: "In this book I
take the field as a theme or rather reference point; it is the field which appeared in my earliest remembered childhood dream where children danced
and an omen came of blowing grass where no wind was and a king of the
game was chosen, followed by terror, deluge, by what I do not remember"
(Notebook A., p. 102), quoted by Davidson, "A Book of First Things," p. 57.

the body of language: "The ear / catches rime like pangs of disease from the air," he writes, "For poetry / is a contagion" (*BB, 32*).

With their decorous rhetoric, the last stanzas further the same notions:

> Often I am permitted to return to a meadow
> as if it were a given property of the mind
> that certain bounds hold against chaos,
>
> that is a place of first permission,
> everlasting omen of what is.

The title is repeated and the poem brought round to its origin. But the formal resolution (like the end of the children's game) will also be a falling down. Returning to the beginning suggests that the several stanzas were only the circular unfolding of the first line, a disturbance within its words. The poem is like a first field on which we ventured forth, at once an origin and an initiation. Every return brings unexpected changes: "We must come back and back to the same place and find it subtly altered each time, like a traveler bewitched by lords of the fairy, until he is filled with a presence he would not otherwise have admitted."[62] The poem's field is "where the disturbance is, where the words / awaken" (*RB*, 51) unpredicted changes. It appears to hold a boundary "against chaos," yet "the sound of words waits— / a barbarian host at the borderline of sense" (*FD*, 135). The poem is a "place of first permission" where a universe of words is given one of its voices. Poetic speech has the tension "of the ominous, for a world that would speak is itself a language of omens."[63] So this meadow, giving illusory bounds to infinite speech, becomes an "everlasting omen of what is."

"What is," the governing ground of reality, is for Duncan essentially a reservoir of potential interchanges: "In a field of interacting melodies a single note may belong to both ascending and descending figures, and, yet again, to a sustaining chord or discord."[64] The poem creates its own field within the larger field of words by establishing

---

62. Duncan, "Two Chapters from H. D.," p. 90.
63. Duncan, "The H. D. Book: Part II, Chapter 4," 28.
64. Duncan, Introd. to *Translations*, p. iv.

lines of force between specific harmonies and disharmonies. These "are rimes, Sounding in each other" and "the rimes or reoccurrences are knots in the web or tissue of reality."[65] "That one image may recall another," Duncan writes, "finding depth in the resounding, is the secret of rime and measure. The time of a poem is felt as a recognition of return in vowel tone and in consonant formations, of pattern in the sequence of syllables, in stress and in pitch of a melody, of images and meanings."[66] "Rime" for Duncan covers interactions among both sounds and images, as well as interactions between them.

In "Often I Am Permitted to Return to a Meadow," this net of sound and meaning keeps the meadow image coherent despite the associative digressions. The images of the Queen or Lady and the stanzas about the children's game would disrupt the poem if its verbal ground were not strong enough to support them. The poem's aural design is exactly sufficient, managing simultaneously to sustain and threaten. It includes the antiphonal phrasing of the second line and the first phrase of the third, the assonance of "made place," the consonance of "heart" and "thought" and later of "field folded," the visual rhyme of "near" and "heart," the repetition of "there" with "therein" in the fifth line, the internal rhyme of "all" and "hall" in the second stanza, echoed by "fall" in the third and "fall all" in the fourth. Throughout, there is considerable alliteration. Duncan does not establish a strict sound pattern but employs a variety of devices to make the aural field freely associative and unpredictable. Sound and meaning become mutually supportive, while seeming outside the poet's full control. Sound could, we fear, make the poetry nonsensical. Yet there is considerable attraction in the supreme and empty meaning lodged in the random architecture of sounds:

> rhymes that mimic much of loss,   ghost goings,
>   words lost in passing,   echoed
> where they fall,   againnesses of sound only ·
>
> This failure of sense is melody most. [D, 116]

---

65. Duncan, "Two Chapters from H.D.," pp. 91 and 92.
66. Ibid., p. 82.

"I Compose," Duncan has written, "by the tone-leading of vowels" (*TL*, 67), and he is frequently willing to follow a purely aural lead.[67] In his "Imitations of Gertrude Stein," composed in the early 1950s and most fully collected in *Writing Writing*, *Derivations*, and *Names of People*, Duncan pursues the method at its most fanciful. The results are often frivolous, but occasionally a sound pattern surfaces that encourages our faith in unconscious decision. When syntactical and semantic structures are present, but inextricable from rhythmic playfulness, we experience sudden loss amidst flowering sound.

Duncan's "My Mother Would Be A Falconress" is perhaps his most extreme venture in this direction. The poem is introduced by a prose note that recounts its genesis in an aural compulsion: "I wakend in the night with the lines '*My mother would be a falconress—And I a falcon at her wrist*' being repeated in my mind. Was the word *falconress* or *falconess?*—the troubled insistence of the lines would not let go of me, and I got up and took my notebook ... in the poem there is another curious displacement upward, for the bell which is actually attacht to a falcon's leg by a bewt just above the jess, in the dream becomes a set of bells sewn round the hood, a ringing of sound in the childhood of the poet's head" (*BB*, 51). In effect, Duncan displaces his psychological motivation into a pre-eminently verbal process—the echoing of the poem's first line.[68]

---

67. Cf.: "The materials of the poem—the vowels and consonants—are already structured in their resonance, we have only to listen and to cooperate with the music we hear. The storehouse of human experience in words is resonant too, and we have but to listen to the reverberations of our first thought in the reservoir of communal meanings...." Duncan, "Towards an Open Universe," p. 176.

68. Cf.: Samuel Charters's reading of the poem: "The pulse of the poem is the son's effort to be free of his mother, and Duncan allows only a hint of anything beyond their blind struggle.... The poem's deepest tragedy is in the duality of maturity—that in the man, the child, in pain and torment, is still enclosed," *Some Poems / Poets* (Berkeley: Oyez, 1971), p. 54. This reading is perfectly reasonable, but it is not sufficient to account for the verbal play in the poem, which gives the image of the mother other associations: "Mary, mother of the Logos and of the Living Body of Man in One, may be sound, mother of the word in its letters, and light, mother of the appearance of all bodies" (*SG*); "Mnemosyne, the Mother-Memory of Poetry, is our made-up life, the matrix of fictions," "The H. D. Book: Part I, Chapter 2," p. 28.

The poem begins by challenging the words "falcon" and "falconer." "Falconer" is not mentioned, but we recognize in "falconress" the failure of the established noun to cover both its male and female counterparts. The *OED* lists no feminine form for falconer; Duncan's coined term is an invasion by sound to deprive a word of its authority. The paternal command, signature for father and self, fails or falters. As Duncan writes in a more recent passage:

> And I was immersed into the depths of the Water,
>   let down by that man who stood for my Father
>   into the Element before Intention
>
> (or, in another version, cast into the Flood
> drownd in the rage of the Mother of What Is) [*T*, 20]

In "My Mother Would Be A Falconress" the flood is a confusion of sound: "For she has muffled my dreams in the hood she has made me, / sewn round with bells, jangling when I move." This passage is a narrative version of the poem's verbal situation. The poem's title recurs as the opening line of both the first and second stanzas. Both that line and the second ("And I, her gay falcon treading her wrist") are controlling aural resources, undergoing repetition and variation that builds to an incantatory rhythm.

Against this verbal imperative, the poem's story exerts only limited pressure. The speaker's wish to be a falcon is derivative; he would be falcon to her falconress. He would tread her wrist, then take flight to bring her a bleeding prize. But he must not damage his prey; he must bring it back with its neck broken but otherwise perfect. Then a strain of resentment enters. If she will not honor his instinct, instead limiting his flight and controlling his lust to hunt, he will turn on her and seek her blood. At the end of her will's tether, he spies a land beyond these hills where falcons nest. He would go free, but even when she is dead, he cannot break her hold on him:

> My mother would be a falconress,
> and even now, years after this,
> when the wounds I left her had surely heald,

and the woman is dead,
her fierce eyes closed, and if her heart
were broken, it is stilld

I would be a falcon and go free.
I tread her wrist and wear the hood,
talking to myself, and would draw blood.

These are the last two stanzas. In them, the will to take flight returns to the first line, becoming itself a function of the line's enactment. The narrative developments are variations of the key words and phrases introduced in the opening stanza:

My mother would be a falconress,
And I, her gay falcon treading her wrist,
would fly to bring back
from the blue of the sky to her, bleeding, a prize,
where I dream in my little hood with many bells
jangling when I'd turn my head.

In this first stanza, he treads on her wrist, wanting to bring back a bleeding prize. In the first line of the fourth stanza, the wish is condensed: "I tread my mother's wrist and would draw blood." Wrists themselves can bleed, but the suggestion that he might attack his mother is still constrained by the opening context, in which the only blood is that of his prey. Furthermore, the third stanza details the hunt's violence, thus also helping to block the suggestion that he will turn on the falconress:

She would bring down the little birds.
And I would bring down the little birds.
When will she let me bring down the little birds,
pierced from their flight with their necks broken,
their heads like flowers limp from the stem?

The first three lines are almost identical. The changes read like a litany of prescribed variations, ritually embroidering an unchanging theme. The fifth stanza concludes with a comparable intonation, reasserting the insistence of the pattern: "I would bring down / the

little birds to her / I may not tear into, I must bring back perfectly."
Then, in the first line of the next stanza, the anger reaches for its
voice: "I tear at her wrist with my beak to draw blood." Yet the
fury cannot take flight; it cannot become a separate vehicle of the
falcon-son's will. Every word in the line, as well as the rhythm of the
line as a whole, has prescribed connotations. Each sound echoes what
has gone before. Even the falcon's eventual desire to break loose
from the falconress springs from her own will for flight. It is "as if
her mind / sought in me flight beyond the horizon."

The words for an isolate, individualized self cannot be found.
Each verbal gesture incarnates the total order of the poem, as if
every word branched out from a single trunk. Toward the end of the
poem, Duncan gives explicit evidence that the maternal entanglement is verbal.[69] When the falcon flees, it is as if the falconress's own
remorse at his violence sought relief:

> I flew, as if sight flew from the anguish in her eye beyond her
>   sight,
> sent from my striking loose, from the cruel strike at her wrist,
> striking out from the blood to be free of her.

The changing forms of the verb "to strike" almost encompass and
obliterate the narrative dimensions of the act. If the main drama is
clearly verbal, then the poem is not a parable intended to unveil a
psychological truth. Indeed it is not a parable *about* language. From
Duncan's perspective, the poem has no referential purpose, no alle-
gorical message. It is an instance of the will speech has to break free
of the mothering ground of language, a will itself a function of that
ground.

This is a richly echolalic poem, using perhaps as much repetitive
and self-referential language as a poem can without becoming pure
content-free sound. Yet it exists at the edge of that void. It courts
that Lady of "Often I Am Permitted to Return to a Meadow" whose

---

69. Duncan's own mother died shortly after his birth, and he was later
put up for adoption. There is therefore a specific sense in which his relationship with his biological mother is exclusively verbal. For all of us, however,
the language of family relationships is invested with substantial power.

embrace is emptiness. Each elaboration, each unfolding phrase, renders the center progressively more vacant. The variations are cancellations. The exuberance of the language becomes a decorous melancholy:

> The ever emptying cup,   the vital
>   source that solaces no thirst's throat.
>   Poetry is of this natural vacancy: [D, 116]

Duncan has pursued this formal archetype from his earliest poems. Its sign is evident in every elaborated image of loss. At first, in his more rhetorically verbose poems, we sense this signature of fanciful, foliate emptiness in language whose descriptiveness is exaggerated. Duncan consistently finds himself unable to resist a kind of controlled over-writing. In that respect, his early work resembles W. S. Merwin's; yet Duncan does not develop a spare, concise poetry in response to his initial excesses. Rather, Duncan spreads out his elaborate language, using it more tactfully and adopting the visual appearance of Pound's page. Then the most effusive metaphors have a considerable amount of white space in which to do their work. They seem cleaner, less tightly bound to their surroundings. We can dwell on a passage until we exhaust its resonances. Like Olson, who also followed Pound's lead in using the space of the page, Duncan often deliberately disorders his syntax. He opts for awkward constructions, removes connective language, and violates grammatical rules. Though its results are often precious, the method sometimes forces images into confrontations more sudden and jarring than conventional syntax could achieve. If there are logical, discursive explanations for these conjunctions, the reader must devise them; the poem presents them as rude experience. "In the field of the poem," Duncan writes, "the unexpected / must come" (OF, 35). Indeed the field does not merely guarantee unexpected change and irregular growth; it is their product.

Duncan's stylistic and structural disruptions are designed to orient his poems around their own violated centers. Form is a clustering of dislocations: "The part in its fitting does not lock but unlocks; what was closed is opend" (BB, iv). In his introduction to The

Years as Catches, he announces that "These are poems of an irregu-
larity"; the apparent thrust of a poem, its dominant metaphors, must
contain its own "inner opposition or reproof" (*Y*, i). "I attempt the
discontinuities of poetry," he writes, "to interrupt all sure course of
my inspiration" (*D*, 91). Poetry centers itself only by establishing a
discursive field and then shattering it. There must be, he writes, "no
poem / without such a moment, broken, conquerd," but he continues with "only by what   we did not know / of the design" (*D*,
123). Each betrayal projects a larger, more wounded coherence, a
wider and less secure vision.

   "The Torso" (*BB*, 63-65), number 18 in the "Passages" sequence,
offers a good test of Duncan's aesthetic, for its chief disruption is
one word. The title suggests some of the poem's potential for multiple and ambiguous connotation, since the image of a torso invokes
the realms of both anatomy and sculpture. A torso's formal perfection can imply either its relative independence from the head and
limbs or their actual absence. In either case, a torso invites a studied—potentially ecstatic or skeptical—distance from the human
figure, a distance that is significant in what is essentially a love
poem.[70]

   The poem begins in a rush of natural images: "Most beautiful! the
red-flowering eucalyptus, / the madrone, the yew." The syntax makes
the trees analogues to the torso of the poem's title, but the next line,
surrounded by white space, trails off in ellipses: "Is he . . ." The line
is partly assertive, partly questioning; it makes the opening images
hypothetical—castings of the verbal net for a proper central image.
The speaker's reverie then incorporates a passage from Marlowe's
Edward The Second:

---

70. Cf. this passage from Duncan's early work:

   the torso like the Hapsburg's rock crystal
   pitchers, flawd with its own wonder,
             shatterd visibly
   with immutable perfection. [*D*, 14]

In writing "The Torso" Duncan may also have had in mind Rilke's famous
"Archaic Torso of Apollo," in which the sensuality of the sculpted form, extraordinarily intensified, renders the spectator everywhere visible.

So thou wouldst smile, and take me in thine arms
The sight of London to my exiled eyes
Is as Elysium to a new-come soul

These lines from the play's opening speech are spoken by Edward's young friend Gaveston, who is recalled from banishment when the king ascends to the throne. Since Gaveston is eventually murdered, the quotation adds two connotations to the lover's image—regal and tragic. Those connotations will be foregrounded later in the poem; for the moment, however, the passage serves mainly to elevate and aggrandize the speaker's emotions, effects the next lines extend: "If he be Truth / I would dwell in the illusion of him." The archaic, slightly stilted construction prepares us for the self-conscious avowal of what is very nearly a romantic cliché. Yet the second clause also humanizes and thus comments on the Platonic reference to "Truth." A mixture of resistance and submission suddenly coalesces in the excited wish to be absorbed in the lover's person.

Then a particularly vital image surfaces: "His hands unlocking from chambers of my male body." We can visualize a withdrawal from an embrace, while also reading the line as a spiritual "unlocking," an opening outward of self. The outlines of the image, the meaning of "chambers," is ambiguous, recalling an earlier image of yearning so intense it feels "like the long trunk of another self / turning on his thighs to open life's arms" (*RB*, 90). Like the pronouns in "Sonnet 4," the pronouns in "The Torso" are almost interchangeable; a romantic fusion of self and other is caught in an image of a single pair of unfolding hands. This is the first of seven spaced lines, only one of them punctuated—at once scattered and provisional phrases, a faltering communication, and a verbal field vibrant with transformations. The next lines are ambivalent: "such an idea in man's image / rising tides that sweep me towards him." The tone is reverent, but also slightly compromised by Duncan's tendency to court a deliberately sentimental effusiveness.[71] The mood brings the poem to its major disruption: "...*homosexual?*":

---

71. Duncan's general defense of the sentimental element in his poetry

His hands unlocking from chambers of my male body
             such an idea in man's image
     rising tides that sweep me towards him
             ... *homosexual?*
                           and at the treasure of his mouth
                   pour forth my soul
                             his soul   commingling
     I thought a Being more than vast, His body leading
           into Paradise,   his eyes
                   quickening a fire in me,   a trembling
           hieroglyph:

Duncan is aware that the sexual category can act as a restrictive label that deflates the mythic, transpersonal vision for which the poem is straining.[72] Prefaced by ellipses, it closes the earlier "Is he ..." and cancels the organic allusiveness of the opening listing. Italicized, the word challenges us to question whether his varied emotions and the poem's plural effects can be reduced to this single name. The impulse to include the word is at once political, aggressive, confessional, and purgative. The balance of the poem, he hopes, will demonstrate how inadequate the word homosexual is to describe his full experience. Yet we also need to read "Is he ... *homosexual?*" as a single line, thereby traversing Duncan's romantic, philosophical

---

deserves quotation here:

> had the tone or the tenor of thought not sunk to the level of the "sentimental" or the "philosophizing" (both, vices found frequently in my work by distressed readers since Olson first brought up the matter in *Against Wisdom As Such*), had I not sought to deal with the sentimental as it came, the reader might not have so lost confidence in the matter of the poem. It does not seem to have occurred to Rosenthal that just this tone and tenor of each line as he gets it—the shifts from narrative mode (he calls it the "literal") to pathetic exclamation to projective sentiment—are to be taken not as some affect of the writer's indisposition in need of expression but as content of the poem itself, as poem data, to be read as dream data and feeling-tone are read as factors in the structure of meanings in the dream. It is the constitution of the field of the poem that determines the line. The exclamation *"To be in love!"* does get, very accurately, the tone of the actual dream I am drawing from, but it is not that verisimilitude that determines the line-tone but its belonging to the projective feeling of the poetic structure as I work with it in writing. [*C, i*]

72. See Duncan's "The Homosexual in Society," *Politics*, 1, No. 7 (1944), 209-11, and his preface to the 1972 edition of *Caesar's Gate.* for his comments on the stereotype of the homosexual and its effect on him.

meditation with the single essential question about availability. We must now read "The Torso" both as a fantasy about a stranger—a fantasy constrained by the question of whether a relationship is possible—and as a meditation about an established relationship—one into which language and self-consciousness intrude with their effects of descriptive distancing. For each of these readings the category of homosexuality has the irreducibly double power Michel Foucault has analyzed in *The History of Sexuality*: it is both an exclusionary nomination and one that generates possibilties of action. By saying the name, Duncan wants to deprive it of its nominative power while retaining its subversive force, but it will always serve both as a political challenge and as an element of doubt in the poem. The decision to include it in the text moves beyond an aesthetic of honesty (whatever occurs in the field of the poem must be given its place) to become simultaneously assertive and self-defeating. Duncan breaks the intimate mood of the poem and probably undermines some readers' empathy in doing so. Like so much of the structural deflection essential in American open poetry, Duncan's decision reveals a sense of guilt and its attendant punishment; it establishes "the poet's own duality between doubt and conviction in writing."[73] Moreover, for Duncan, as for Ginsberg, those emotions are given historical impetus by Whitman's comparable sexual anxiety. Personal and historical guilt finally become indistinguishable.

"The Torso" does very nearly surmount these difficulties, but it has been prevented from doing so entirely. The poem continues as if its syntax detours around the intrusive word. The next line, "and at the treasure of his mouth," proceeds from the line before; there he will "pour forth my soul / his soul   commingling." Robert K. Martin uses these lines to argue that the single "occasion of the poem is, of course, an act of fellatio," a reading that is partly accurate but overstated, as any exclusive reading would be.[74] Commingling souls also suggest both breath and a spiritual communion. We cannot choose between an actual physical act, a fantasy, and the ver-

73. Duncan, "From the H. D. Book: Part II, Chapter 5," p. 343.
74. Robert K. Martin, *The Homosexual Tradition in American Poetry* (Austin: University of Texas Press, 1979), p. 174.

bal changes rung on both. Duncan's aesthetic point about referentiality is that poetry demonstrates the world's multiplicity. "I thought a Being more than vast," he writes, and the verb suggests that every lover is partly imaginary insofar as he becomes a kind of supreme being. The interaction of lovers creates in each a representative, universal body "leading / into Paradise." The erotic figure is also religious, the Christian reference reinforced by the figure of the "Orphic Xristos" in "Passages 17," who "lifts me up to him, / lifted me up to him,   embracing   every fear I had" (*BB*, 60). This Being is a communal figure who is also the apotheosis of selfhood. "His eyes," the poem continues, "quickening a fire in me," the body becomes "a trembling / hieroglyph," a signifying field or a sacred text constituted by an alternative, celebratory naming. The body is a joyous cathexis of names:

> At the root of the neck
>
> *the clavicle,* for the neck is the stem of the great artery
>   upward into his head that is beautiful
>
> At the rise of the pectoral muscles
>
> *the nipples,* for the breasts are like sleeping fountains
>   of feeling in man, waiting above the beat of his heart,
>   shielding the rise and fall of his breath, to be
>   awakend
>
> At the axis of his mid hriff
>
> *the navel,* for in the pit of his stomach the chord from
>   which first he was fed has its temple
>
> At the root of the groin
>
> *the pubic hair,* for the torso is the stem in which the man
>   flowers forth and leads to the stamen of flesh in which
>   his seed rises

Although this is a generalized, universal male body, this reading of the body as a text is still one of relatively few successful descriptions of the male body in poetry. There are many unspecific images of bodily life in poetry, images that are essentially nonsexual or pansexual, but very few erotic representations of the male body. The four italicized names, given in descending order as the eye travels down the body, are points of origin or nodes of force in a descriptive field, constituents of the body's textuality. Each name occasions an uplifting of substance, countering the eye's descending glance and paralleling the unfolding description: "the stem of the great artery upward," "the rise of the pectoral muscles," "sleeping fountains...waiting...to be / awakend"; "the stem in which the man / flowers forth"; "his seed rises." The frankness of "nipples" and "pubic hair," the prosaic "navel," will displease some readers. Yet Duncan overcomes the graphic difficulties of the material; he manages to convey the instinctual attractions of his subject and place it in the verbal field of his overall vision. The sequence of vertical motions anticipates the reference to ejaculation in the last section, but the verticality is also overlaid with references to "root" and "stem" that simultaneously reinforce the organicism of the opening lines and recall the etymology of "torso" as the stem of a plant.

But Duncan is compelled again to risk his achievement. The next line almost reduces the vision to infatuation: "a wave of need and desire over   taking me." Yet we are not quite back again to the rhetoric of the earlier line about the "treasure of his mouth," for the space between "over" and "taking" requires us to read this line in two ways as well—as a description of consummated desire and of desire that overpowers. "Cried out my name" risks the same sentiment but survives because of the multiple dimensions of naming established in the poem. We are not only given a lover's cry; we understand naming as instinct vocalized and as a sound bound in a net of words. Naming is fateful, an imposition of verbal destiny. "(This was long ago, It was another life)," he writes, echoing "Sonnet 4," and we sense a wider eros at work—the attractions of a mythic form. A few lines later the mythic references are reinforced: "His look / pierces my side." The look, the sense of being seen, transforms the visionary lover into the wounded Christ; the speaker's

erotic being is crucified. The lovers are caught in a net woven two
millennia before:

What do you want of me?

I do not know, I said.   I have fallen in love.   He
has brought me into heights and depths my heart
would fear   without him.   His look

pierces my side   •   fire eyes   •

I have been waiting for you, he said:
I know what you desire

you do not yet know   but through me   •

And I am with you everywhere.   In your falling

I have fallen from a high place.   I have raised myself

from darkness in your   rising

With delicate echoes of the Gospels, and with clear references to
man's fall and to Christ's incarnation and resurrection, the lovers
undergo a transformation built into the informing power of words
like "falling," "rising," and "gathering."[75] Election as lover, king,
and sacrificial victim traverse one another in these ascending and
descending displacements. "Gathering me, you gather / your Self," he
writes, as the poem gathers its metaphors into an allusive field that
moves outward and inward at the same time. As self and other are
extinguished in an embrace, the lovers also enact a larger story.
Adam, dispersed in all the members of the race, and Osiris, scattered
afield, are gathered together in one figure: "For my Other is not a
woman but a man / *the King upon whose bosom let me lie.*"
   If "The Torso" existed in isolation, we might say that it succeeds

---

75. The archaic quality of Duncan's language helps reinforce the sense
that the interchange between the two figures in the poem echoes Christ's
dialogue with his disciples. Cf. Duncan's "What do you want of me?" "you
do not yet know   but through me" and "I am with you everywhere" with
these passages: "What I do thou knowest not now; but thou shalt know here-
after"; "no man cometh unto the Father, but by me"; "At that day ye shall
know that I am in my Father, and ye in me, and I in you"   (John, 13-14).

in surmounting most of the problems it raises. Its conflation of homosexuality and Christianity—its mixture of anger at conventional American stereotyping with its own romantic effusiveness—its sexual attraction and tension—all these are held together in the poem's verbal net. The formal gestalt Duncan achieves is not one of fully controlled and balanced ambiguity but one of radically fluid though counterpointed allusiveness. Nonetheless, a reader who puts sufficient work into the poem will be rewarded with an experience of a uniquely rich and open kind of textuality. Yet "The Torso" is not simply an isolated poem, and its relationship to the "Passages" sequence radically alters its force, placing it in a network of oppositions that is more disabling than constitutive. Thus the formal dissolution that Duncan courts in "Often I Am Permitted to Return to a Meadow" and "My Mother Would Be A Falconress" is finally achieved when "The Torso" is read in the context of *Bending The Bow* as a whole. The associative field through which the vocabulary of "The Torso" resonates includes demonic echoes that are as strong as those the poem offers. The "rising tides that sweep" the lovers together in "The Torso" recur not only in the conviction that "youth will rise" like "new shoots / of the spring-tide" and in "the blood's natural / uprising   against tyranny" but also in the "sea of toiling men" in the Vietnam poem "Up Rising," men who have "raised this secret entity of America's hatred of Europe, of Africa, of Asia" (*BB*, 94, 114, 81-82). One of the larger contexts of "The Torso," then, is satanic violence, a violence that moves through the poem and takes up its images to use them for darker purposes.

Bending The Bow begins with a prose introduction whose first section is titled "The War" and whose second section, "The Readers," and last section, "Articulations," also invoke the Vietnam war as a designing context the poems cannot escape. Many of the poems deal extensively with Vietnam and other American wars, most notably "Earth's Winter Song," "Moira's Cathedral," and many of the "Passages" sequence, whose titles include "The Fire," "The Multiversity," "Up Rising," and "The Soldiers."[76] Part of Duncan's argument, like Bly's, is that Vietnam repeats an ancient and recurring evil,

---

76. "Passages" numbers 22-27 were first collected as *Of The War* (Berkeley: Oyez, 1966).

though Duncan is more willing than Bly to recognize the tension between historical specificity and eternal recurrence. Yet for Duncan the war also gains a special status from America's destiny as the representative, collective nation that will draw all the world's races into a single community. It is a destiny now fulfilled in conflagration. "We enter again and again the last days of our own history," Duncan writes, "for everywhere living productive forms ... fail, weaken, or grow monstrous, destroying the terms of their existence" (*BB,* i). Duncan's comment reflects the recognition that an historical environment of inexplicable murder and all-too-explicable guilt invades both sexual privacy and poetic creation and makes their isolation impossible. That is a reality to which Levertov and Rich have also testified. Yet Duncan makes a further point when he says that our evolving *forms* of expression "grow monstrous," for then we are faced with a mimicry, satire, and co-optation by history that can alter our faith in both poetry and personal relations. We contract, Duncan writes in "Keeping the War Inside," a disease we cannot cure. Unable to escape its effects, the poet finds himself "drawing into his design the designing invader."[77]

The democratic interconnectedness that Whitman celebrated and that Duncan imagines being verbally fulfilled finds its demonic realization: "with planes roaring out from Guam over Asia, / all America become a sea of toiling men ... in terror and hatred of all communal things, of communion" (*BB,* 81). The "contrapuntal communion of all things," the "Grand Collage" formed by a democratic "increment of associations," is made manifest in this "medley of mistaken themes / grown dreadful and surmounting dread" (*BB,* 78, 99, 11, 13). The "Being more than vast, His body leading / into Paradise" of "The Torso" now confronts us in "Up Rising" as "the swollen head of the nation" and in "The Multiversity" as "the great dragon ... whose scales are men officized—ossified" (*BB,* 83, 70). "The bloody verse America writes over Asia" is not merely an alternative poetry—"(the whole poem becoming a storm   in which faces arise) / Mouths yawn immensely" (*BB,* 113, 128)—but the commanding poem that subsumes all our speech.

77. "Keeping the War Inside," *Journal for the Protection of All Beings,* No. 3 (1969), n. pag.

Earlier in *Bending The Bow* Duncan wrote of "the body of the poem, aroused,   having / what mouths" (BB, 19), an image suggesting the unpredictable plurality of associations at work in radically open forms. Now we see that the image of the poem with many mouths touches both the dream and the nightmare of open poetry. Partly an image of speech as a playful, polymorphous eroticism, its erotic potential is compromised by a latent fear of being consumed. One of those mouths, the poet fears, may belong to "that mothering shark in my childhood sea" (*Y*, 59). Indeed, the poem with many mouths and many voices echoes that very sea of words that overwhelms anyone who dares to converse with it. Nor are we likely to be sung to or caressed by the mouths in the "heads of the Hydra that Pound named *Usura*" (*T*, 21). The hydra has "as many heads as he wants," and once the hydra occupies the poem the "mouth that is the Universe" can only devour us (*BB*, 95, 120). In *The Opening of the Field* Duncan was able to let the poem's mouths converse successfully because the image of the hydra never surfaced. Like Ginsberg's Moloch, the hydra is essentially a social or political monster, though one that retains its connections with a primitive force that is both appealing and threatening; it is ultimately a figure for a "swollen head of the nation" that cannot be controlled or resisted. *The Opening of the Field* kept its inversions and contradictions largely decorous and graceful by limiting its politics, as in Duncan's often anthologized "A Poem Beginning With A Line By Pindar," to a lament for America's failure to achieve Lincoln's and Whitman's vision. The political commentary, in effect, shows the necessity for Duncan's vision of a redemptive poetry of open forms; he does not yet allow political metaphors to invade and compromise his personal vision.

Like Williams, Olson, and Ginsberg, Duncan associates open form with an Adamic, childlike, innocent perceptiveness: "A longing grows to return to the open composition in which the accidents and imperfections of speech might awake intimations of human being";[78] "This is what I wanted for the last poem, / a loosening of conventions and return to open form" (*OF*, 95). To return to open form is also to return to the primal innocence of the nation, or, as

---

78. Duncan, "Pages from a Notebook," p. 401.

Williams and Olson remind us, to recover in imaginative form the
openness that was spoiled in the first physical contact with the continent. With the exception of Ginsberg, who thinks the only barriers
to open form are the society's madness and his own personal fear
and inadequacy, these poets recognize that the writing situation complicates this dream of an America resurrected in verse. For a writer
open to any association, even to interruptions by public discourse,
the very diffusion of influences, let alone the inevitable squalor of
much of public life, will often leave him depressed and unable to
continue. Moreover, the creative will is not so easily separated from
the national will to power.

The wider the poet casts his net, the more open the forms he
employs, the more likely it is that his poem's substance will be e-
quated with the substance of his society. His poem will begin to
have the appearance and texture of the world around him, rather
than the hermetic texture of an alternative world. Its aesthetic, then,
demands external validation. "We can know or imagine," Duncan
has commented, "no more about the good of the poem than we know
or imagine about the good of society."[79] Earlier in the same essay,
Duncan observed that Pound's ideas about distributing material
goods were "an extension of early democratic thought in America—
all men must be citizens, living in the imagination of the common
good, against privilege."[80] The same values are easily transferred to
an idealized image of poetry—no metaphor, no poem, is to assert its
individual privilege over the broad poetic ground. All poets will
participate, forcefully and uniquely, in the common imagination.
Duncan is not speaking here of socialist realism. He does not assume
that a democratic poetry will be socially useful or easily accessible.
He does, however, come to believe that poetry must open itself to
all possible speakers, that it must democratically accept whatever
enters the scene of its activity. Indeed, Duncan writes of the *Cantos*
that "we couldn't have a more extreme example of democratic composition than we had out of that man who kept hoping he'd rescue

79. Duncan, "From the Day Book—excerpts from an Extended Study of
H. D.'s Poetry," p. 41.
80. Ibid., p. 37.

himself by having totalitarian order." Pound, Duncan argues, could
not manage the *Cantos* through authoritarian power: "they didn't
prove to be totalitarian so he was as distressed by them as by the
democracy from which he came."[81] For Duncan the *Cantos* challenge
American poets to accept and extend their troubled commitment to
a democratic form. Duncan thus begins to see his aesthetic as a
displacement of earlier projections of American society:[82]

> The farthest shore is so near
> crows fly up and we know it is America.
> No crow flies. It is not America.
> From what we call Poetry
> a bird I cannot name crows. [*RB*, 121-22]

> I am speaking now of the Dream in which America sleeps, the
>   New World,
> moaning, floundering, in three hundred years of invasions ...
> Tears stream down to feed the Deeps below
> from those eyes in which the spirits of America's yearning
> come and go, broken, reassembling, enduring, defeated ...
>   [*T*, 20]

The first passage above, with its signal melancholy, is written by
a poet for whom only poetry could answer a need to which the
society had hardened. It reflects a basis for poetry in personal need
that animates much of Roethke's and Rich's work, a need that Kinnell too has described: "It is perhaps true that a poem entails a struggle with one's own nature, that it comes partly out of our hunger
to be changed—and so may be an act of longing for what we are
unable to be."[83] Yet what we experience as a personal quest for a
new identity is also a function of the history that shapes us. For all
the social rejection Duncan has endured, the selfhood he wants and

---

81. Duncan, "Robert Duncan's Interview," 82.
82. Cf.: the first section of Duncan's "From the H. D. Book," *Credences,*
1, No. 2 (1975), 50-52, his "Against Nature," *Poetry,* 94, No. 1 (1959),
54-59, and "Changing Perspectives in Reading Whitman."
83. Kinnell, *The Poetics of the Physical World* (Fort Collins, Colorado:
Colorado State University, 1969), p. 18.

the verbally communal poetry he tries to write are still American ideals. Thus in the first passage, poetry and the nation are almost interchangeable. The collective dreams to which both passages allude may be hopelessly mythic, yet they are myths generated anew within the language of poetry. Indeed the last line of the second quotation leads us directly into the aesthetics of open poetry—ambitious, prophetic, collective, pluralistic, open-ended, and often undone, "in which the spirits of America's yearning / come and go, broken, reassembling, enduring, defeated." "There is only the one page," Duncan writes, the continent, like the sea, "moving in rifts, churning, enjambing, / drifting feature from feature" (*RB,* 176). Into that single page, of whose fluid body all poems are members, all of America's past can be projected to be lost again. When Duncan dreams of "that most real where there is no form that is not content, no content that is not form," he does not only dream of a poetry that redeems all its material substance.[84] He also dreams of a poetry that would redeem the nation's past, would uplift even the American land's resistant material bulk into the apotheosis of form.

Bending The Bow brings Duncan closer to that goal than any of his previous collections, but the achievement nearly destroys the book. It is not the first occasion when Duncan recognizes that the play of verbal possibilities reflects the nation's life, that poetry in turn becomes a form of verbal warfare. Duncan indeed has been politicized and has had a politics throughout his career. "An Essay at War" is the fullest exploration of the topic in his early work, but it returns throughout *The First Decade* and *Derivations,* his selected poems from 1940 to 1956. One cannot defeat the poetry of war, Duncan realizes, without becoming oneself warlike—with single-minded plans and stategies. In "An Essay at War" he proposes instead a poetry unplanned and willingly defeated. Yet this will be a poetry so plural that "the language takes fire," becoming thereby "a lantern to read war by" (*D,* 12, 11). Thus for a period of time he devotes himself to working out his Whitmanesque vision of a "medley of voices" (*D,* 22) in a form reactive to history but with a syn-

---

84. Duncan, "Towards An Open Universe," pp. 174-75.

thesis essentially ahistorical. The result is his most lyrical book, *The Opening of the Field*. In *Roots and Branches* he continues to treat some overtly American topics, concluding the book with "The Continent," a poem that partly accepts and partly questions the notion of an American imagination. Then in the mid-1960s Duncan's development undergoes the trial by history visible in the work of so many of his contemporaries; its product is the more fractured achievement of *Bending The Bow*. *Bending The Bow* and *The Opening of the Field* are perhaps the two books where Duncan's vision of a democratically interactive form is most fully realized. In the later book, however, Duncan's incorporation of America's recent history undercuts his vision by showing the field taken up in both antagonistic social interaction and the deadly communality of the battlefield.

Unlike Bly and Levertov, who believe that American openness and American malice can confront one another in poetry, and openness prove victorious, Duncan realizes the two impulses are inseparable. It is not merely, as I suggested in the first chapter, that the satanic figure of the American president is the satiric obverse of the lover in "The Torso."[85] Nor are they simply offered to us as part of a recurrent and partly mythic choice between good and evil, though Duncan may have hoped to structure the opposition in that way. Yet neither is it quite true that the two figures cancel each other. Rather they are linked, opposite but inextricable, acting out a relation between history and poetry in which terror and beauty are joined. Poetry and history in America achieve a special coeval status in

---

85. Charles Altieri, *Enlarging the Temple: New Directions in American Poetry during the 1960's* (Lewisburg: Bucknell University Press, 1979), argues, I think incorrectly, that Duncan "is the only contemporary poet successfully to include the sufferings of the war in Vietnam within his myth.... Combining Heraclitus's view of experience as based on strife, with the erotic urge to incorporate strife into community, Duncan can envision the war as a productive darkness. Underwritten beneath the war and the exiles it has created is the myth of Christmas and natural myths of dying and redeeming gods," p. 168. The first claim seems difficult to sustain in the light of Bly's "The Teeth Mother Naked at Last." The second argument, developed at greater length in James F. Mersmann's *Out of the Vietnam Vortex: A Study*

Duncan's most public work. There the exemplary American poem in which the poet surrenders his "troubled individual isolated experiences to the communal consciousness" comes to an unexpected crisis; we are asked to concede that America's "real art form is an 'empire.' "[86] In Duncan's most public work the spectacle of historical power energizes the poet's will to create.

---

of *Poets and Poetry Against the War* (Lawrence: University Press of Kansas, 1974), ignores the way in which the war takes over the myth instead of being displaced by it.

86. Duncan, "Rites of Participation," p. 62; "Robert Duncan's Interview," 83-84.

CHAPTER FIVE

Meditative Aggressions: Adrienne Rich's Recent Transactions with History

> Trying every key in the bunch to get the door even ajar
> not knowing whether it's locked or simply jammed from long disuse
> trying the keys over and over then throwing the bunch away
> staring around for an axe
> wondering if the world can be changed like this
> if a life can be changed like this [*PSN, 140*] [1]

AS AN IDEOGRAM of Adrienne Rich's aesthetic of willful change, I offer her image, above, of a search for an axe to wield against an unyielding door. The potential violence may seem too harsh and too reductive for the passage to serve, synecdochically, as a figure for her whole enterprise. Yet the affective mix—determination countered by uncertainty—is exactly right. In her best poems the projects consciousness sets for itself are continually complicated both by external events and by consciousness's "bedrock disbelief" (*DW, 6*) in its own clarity and power. At her worst, she offers us the axe and little else. At such times she proposes, singlemindedly, to alter her own perspective and that of her readers, with little evidence of self-doubt. It would be convenient to say that she has gradually outgrown her most flatly didactic poetry and thus that

---

1. The following books by Adrienne Rich are abbreviated and documented internally: *CW—A Change of World* (New Haven: Yale University Press, 1951); *DCL—The Dream of a Common Language: Poems 1974-1977* (New York: Norton, 1978); *DW—Diving into the Wreck: Poems 1971-*

her career shows a clear, linear development. Yet this is not entirely the case. Much more than Roethke himself, Rich has the kind of career Roethke describes in "North American Sequence" as a journey delayed by false starts, reversals, and continual indirection. Her recent work moves back and forth between a moving, complicated aesthetic and varieties of bald, dogmatic address that make for mediocre poetry. Since the common and largely flattering distinction between early and late poetry—imitative or adolescent verse that gradually matures—does not apply here, we have to seek a different explanation for the persistence of her two very different voices.

Rich herself shows no overt preference for either style. For her 1975 *Poems Selected and New* she chose poems that are primarily polemical as well as those that are highly introspective. Her foreword describes the principle of selection: "I think of this book, not as a summing-up or even a retrospective, but as the graph of a process still going on. From the poems of seven volumes and nearly twenty-five years, I have chosen the ones that seem to me to belong, obliquely or not, most truly to that process" (*PSN,* xv). The rhetoric here recalls Robert Duncan's more argumentative loyalty to writing poems intended to be part of a continuum, rather than a series of self-contained achievements. Indeed, since Rich elsewhere uses Duncan's term "re-vision," he may have been an influence on her aesthetic.[2] In any case, they both propose a poetry that is part of a verbal and spiritual activity intrinsically open and unresolved. We can only enter into and appreciate poems as examples of "a process that was tentative and exploratory, both as to form and materials" (*PSN,*

72 (New York: Norton, 1973); L—*Leaflets: Poems 1965-1968* (New York: Norton, 1969); OLS—*On Lies, Secrets, and Silence: Selected Prose 1966-1978* (New York: Norton, 1979); PSN—*Poems Selected and New, 1950-1974* (New York: Norton, 1975); NL—*Necessities of Life: Poems 1962-1965* (New York: Norton, 1966); S—*Snapshots of a Daughter-In-Law: Poems 1954-1962* (New York: Norton, 1967); WTC—*The Will to Change: Poems 1968-1970* (New York: Norton, 1971).
2. In "When We Dead Awaken: Writing as Re-Vision," Rich defines the term in this way: "Re-vision—the act of looking back, of seeing with fresh eyes, of entering an old text from a new critical direction—is for women more than a chapter in cultural history: it is an act of survival" (*OLS,* 35).

xv). The criterion for value becomes the degree to which the poem participates in the developing poetic. A particular poem may be of interest, then, even when it is not very good. Rich, of course, does not actually make the claim in those terms, since her aesthetic requires us to reject evaluative criteria external to a poem and its historical context.

Like Merwin, Rich in the course of her career has become disenchanted with the bravado of sheer technique. Both poets abandoned the traditional craft of their early work, but both continue to be haunted by an element of artificiality: Merwin by the sense that his gnomic lines come too facilely, Rich by poems that opt for exaggerated formalism. As one might expect, it is Rich's most uncompromisingly "committed" poems whose technique seems most obvious and heavy-handed. Since those poems are essential to her awakening feminism, she includes them in her *Poems Selected and New*. There she claims to have "left out poems that felt more like exercises than poems, or that were written out of technique and habit rather than out of strangeness and necessity" (*PSN,* xv). Although she suggests here a uniformly intense but hesitant imperative at the core of all the poetry she favors, the necessities of her two styles are actually very far apart. Those poems armored in moral certitude offer nothing overtly "tentative and exploratory," unless we interpret their polemicism as masking the poet's own inner uncertainty. As a speculation about authorial motivation, however, that possibility is only of interest if the texts themselves can be shown to be more conflicted than their surface conviction suggests.

In retrospect, Rich sees her polemical poems as part of a developing process. We can share her vantage point once she has written poetry that treats the same topics with greater introspection. Her claim that she wrote the poems tentatively is more doubtful, since any sense of distance is complicated by new poems that offer different

---

Duncan used the term in his issue of *The Artist's View* (No. 5, 1953), reprinted as "Pages from a Notebook," pp. 400-407, in Donald Allen's famous anthology *The New American Poetry* (New York: Grove, 1960): "My revisions are my new works, each poem a revision of what has gone before. In-sight. Re-vision" (pp. 400-401).

certainties in equally didactic form. Yet as one kind of militance succeeds another, we can see her attitudes changing. Moreover, each
new posture of conviction lets us see that her most schematic poems
serve a need for sublimation that will not stay satisfied.

Rich's work did not always display such divided and various voices.
Indeed, the changes in her career that led to these diverse styles—
clearly in evidence through the 1960s but culminating in *Leaflets*
(1969), *The Will to Change* (1971), and *Diving into the Wreck*
(1973)—are well known. The reception of those changes, however,
is less than satisfactory, frequently ranging from uncritical enthusiasm for her courage in dealing openly with feminist issues to a
patronizing nostalgia for the more genteel formalism of her first
books.[3] Neither response is fair to what she has achieved so far or
what her career promises.

As others have pointed out, many of the topics that concern Rich
now have always been present in her work.[4] Her rage and despair at
unproductive relationships, for example, is one of her earliest subjects. By 1960, however, and in many of the poems collected in
Snapshots of a Daughter-In-Law and *Necessities of Life,* a new concern enters her work—her place in American history and history's
power over her daily experience. At first this is only new subject
matter. In "Readings of History" (1960) she writes that "history's
queerly strong perfumes" can shape our desires like "seduction fantasies of the public mind" (*S*, 38). The observation does not, however, cause her much difficulty, and it provides no challenge to the
poem's form. Indeed she concludes that stanza with a rather secure
couplet: "Prisoners of what we think occurred, / or dreamers dreaming toward a final word?" The question poses no problem for either
Rich or her readers. Like the gestures toward darkness and emptiness
we will encounter in Merwin's early poetry, Rich's image of historically determined illusion is little more than an excessively ele-

---

3. As an example of nostalgia for Rich's early work see Robert Boyers,
"On Adrienne Rich: Intelligence and Will," *Salmagundi,* Nos. 22/23 (1973),
pp. 132-48.

4. See Helen Vendler, *Part of Nature, Part of Us: Modern American Poets*
(Cambridge: Harvard University Press, 1980), and David Kalstone, *Five
Temperaments* (New York: Oxford, 1977). Vendler's and Kalstone's chap-
ters on Rich are, I think, the two best discussions of her work.

gant conceit. Nor does the next section threaten our security in asking if history can "show us nothing / but pieces of ourselves, detached, / set to a kind of poetry?" If our powers of self-determination are in any way constrained by history, it does not prevent us, with Rich, from exclaiming proudly that "I, too, have lived in history" (S, 39). Fourteen years later, in "From an Old House in America," she will show us how difficult and complex such a statement needs to be—how it testifies to a kind of pride possible when anguish is given both its historical specificity and the terms of its reoccurrence, how any retrospective sympathy gives witness to the impossibility of any final historical knowledge. Here, however, the claim is surprisingly innocent and untroubled.

Necessities of Life, her next book, gives these general statements about history a much more specific American context, and the poems are stronger as a result. We begin to see that the question posed in the preceding book—"Some mote of history has flown into your eye. / Will nothing ever be the same . . . ?" (S, 46)—eventually will be answered, but the answer will give us no comfort: "history is a spider-thread / spun over and over though brushed away" (DCL, 69), and the web remains difficult to see and its terminus impossible to trace. That unresolvability does not yet, however, permeate her rhetoric or her poetic forms. Though poems in *Necessities of Life* like "Face to Face," "Spring Thunder," and "Open-Air Museum" confront us with a heritage of a national consciousness like "a loaded gun," though they show us "underfoot, a land-mass / puffed-up with bad faith and fatigue" that "goes lumbering onward," though they "bring us / face to face with the flag of our true country . . . its heart sucked by slow fire," they also contain those recognitions formally (NL, 49, 44, 20). Powerful though these poems are, they are still confidently *about* the historical nightmare they describe. Unlike "(Newsreel)," which I discussed in my introductory chapter, they do not risk contending with the full destructive effect of the history they name. Nor do they try to change their readers in the way Rich's poetry now would:

> If at the will of the poet the poem
> could turn into a thing

a granite flank laid bare, a lifted head
alight with dew

If it could simply look you in the face
with naked eyeballs, not letting you turn

till you, and I who long to make this thing,
were finally clarified together in its stare [*DCL,* 19]

Her effort to write poetry this demanding, not only of us but also of herself, has succeeded with remarkable frequency. Yet the personal pressure she feels—to "be / more merciless to herself than history" (*S,* 24)—makes it difficult to read much of her poetry except for what it tells us, in retrospect, about her previous work, and what it shows her aching to become. Without at least some sense of achievement in individual poems, that radical version of poetry as a continuing process can also blunt the impact of her work, since we are implicitly urged to delay coming to terms with any given poem. Yet her best poems have found a way to stand successfully on that ruinous ground looking toward both her past and her future. Indeed, they have made her one of the few contemporary American poets with a future that merits the word, i.e., with a future that will not merely repeat previous work. That record of accomplishment grows out of a conjunction of her two main subjects—human emotional and sexual relationships, and the realities of modern history. As she has lived through the history of the 1960s, these two subjects have grown closer in her poetry, and her poetic forms have been nearly dismantled as a result. Yet the cost—of a loss of finished poems and the loss of readers willing to live with her work—is tolerable because of the poems that do succeed. Some of her recent poems, however, are essentially irresolute collages. Others, and these are the most troublesome, are almost one-dimensionally didactic.

A clear example of her didactic style is "Rape" (*DW,* 44-45), in which Rich suggests that a policeman instinctively identifies with a rapist rather than with a victim. "His hand types out the details," she writes, "and he wants them all / but the hysteria in your voice pleases him best." Rich's claim is a useful political challenge, and it may even be valid, but the poem's slick self-assurance is unlikely to convince us. The poem's language undercuts its motivating anger. "In his boots and silver badge," she writes, the cop "and his stallion clop like warlords among the trash." Rich is presumably aiming for tough irony, but the pop machismo is instead mildly comic. "His ideals stand in the air," she continues, "a frozen cloud / from between his unsmiling lips." This strained metaphor develops the comic strip image implicit in the previous line, but its fury chokes on its own resistance to speech. Blocked by an unsuccessful metaphor, the anger returns to its source; the poem is throttled by feeling it cannot articulate successfully.

Strained metaphors and mechanistic form damage many of Rich's argumentative poems. The six stanzas of "Rape," each five lines long, are too regular and secure for an unsettling theme. The poem is also structured by considerable repetition. "You hardly know him," Rich writes of the cop in the first stanza, then repeats the phrase in the second: "You hardly know him but you have to get to know him: / he has access to machinery that could kill you." The familiar play on the verb "to know" is immediately reinforced by the phallic gun, the image of the rider on horseback, and the sexual connotations of the stallion. By the fifth stanza, however, these connections become features of the *poem's* form:

> You hardly know him but now he thinks he knows you:
> he has taken down your worst moment
> on a machine and filed it in a file.
> He knows, or thinks he knows, how much you imagined;
> he knows, or thinks he knows, what you secretly wanted.

The poet also has access to machinery—rhetorical machinery—and she is not willing to abjure its use. The rhythm of recurring phrases here is virtually military. We are intended to sense an inexorable fascist bureaucracy closing in on the woman, but the poem is less the victim of this machinery than its counterpart. This is the final stanza:

> He has access to machinery that could get you put away;
> and if, in the sickening light of the precinct,
> and if, in the sickening light of the precinct,
> your details sound like a portrait of your confessor,

> will you swallow, will you deny them, will you lie your way
> home?

Viewed as a persuasive device, the demagogic metronome in the last line may work, but it may not be working as Rich means it to. This technique is a formal version of a moral authority the poet would ordinarily condemn. It marks the poem's complacency, a complacency at odds with the empathic terror and judgmental anger the poem urges. "Rape" exhibits the casual power it indicts; its knowledge is too easy, its rhetoric lazy. Rich is using her access to print and her established audience to make a political point: "You have to confess / to him, you are guilty of the crime / of having been forced." This argument is not new, nor was it new in 1972 when the poem was written. Rich dates her poetry so that it will serve both to record her interests and ambitions and to document her relation to history. Yet the poem's historical context reduces its force; the poem becomes a rhetorical transcription of existing feminist analyses of police tactics in interviewing rape victims.[5]

Had Rich been able imaginatively to enter the experience of her protagonist, the poem might be more convincing. But there is enough internal evidence to justify doubting that she really wanted to share the consciousness of the woman being interrogated. Far more than the third person, which can often be an effective way of discovering

---

5. Cf. Helen Vendler's analysis in *Part of Nature, Part of Us:*

it is probably just as well to mention its most extreme poem, a poem called "Rape," which begins by announcing that "There is a cop who is both prowler and father," and ends by claiming that as you describe your rape to him, "your details sound like a portrait of your confessor" (who has been carefully described in SS terms, as, with boots on, gun in hand, "he and his stallion clop like warlords"). This cliché (the cop whose eyes "grow narrow and glisten" as "his hand types out all the details") is unworthy of a poet, as is the incrimination of all men in the encapsulation of brothers and fathers in the portrait of this rapist super-cop. Rich would be the first to object to an equally stereotyped description of women—as shrew, as castrating mother, or whatever. The poem, like some others, is a deliberate refusal of the modulations of intelligence in favor of an annulling and untenable propaganda, a grisly indictment, a fictitious and mechanical drama denying the simple fact of possible decency (there are decent cops and decent fathers, and decent brothers, too, but they have no place in the consciousness producing this poem).

It is not hard to imagine someone writing a poem like "Rape," but it is hard to see how such poems pass muster months later when a volume is being gathered for publication. The truth of feeling ("I felt this way, I wrote it down") has never been coterminous with the truth of art [p. 243].

and projecting one's inwardness, the poem's second-person voice is a way of distancing the poet from her subject. This remains true whether we view the "you" of the poem as addressed to another woman or to Rich's uncertainty about what her own reactions might be in similar circumstances. In neither case does the harsh interrogation of the poem's final line read like an extension of the poet's self-doubt. It certifies that Rich is more sophisticated than this woman, that she knows more about social roles. This patronizing sense of class difference may partially explain the language of the third stanza. There Rich tells the victim that she will have to describe her experience while she is still overwhelmed: "you have to turn to him, / the maniac's sperm still greasing your thighs, / your mind whirling like crazy." The last line seems trite, even if Rich is trying to use language a less educated person might use, though the image of the "sickening light of the precinct" is not commonplace. The phrase "your mind whirling like crazy" could also, inappropriately, suggest a passionate swoon. Finally, the overly oratorical line beginning with "the maniac's sperm" exploits a terror that should be unsettling.

None of these difficulties need necessarily ruin a poem, provided that they are handled well. Rich has commented that she wants her "poems to speak for their moment" (*PSN*, xv), which is what "Rape" fails to do. The poem is a function of its moment, but it bears witness to it woodenly, without managing to speak for it. Rich is not willing to risk the poem's politics, yet the lesson is faulted by uncontrolled ambivalences that enter the language anyway. Perhaps, as Duncan often urges, she should have made more conscious use of the full range of feelings present in the writing situation, though such openness about her motives would have its own attendant risks—self-pity and audience indifference, both familiar consequences of confessional poetry. Yet the same political concern that produces inferior poems like "The Ninth Symphony of Beethoven Understood At Last as A Sexual Message" (*DW*, 43) also provides a curative for the problems inherent in the autobiographical impulse. Moreover, the element of personal reflection eliminates the univocal didacticism of her purely political poetry. By playing historical, public themes off against her personal experience, Rich sometimes dramatically possesses the ground of their transactions.

This type of poetry requires considerable self-discipline, for its workable rhetorical range is very narrow. Rich does not have the verbal intuition and quirkiness, like Lowell, to devise metaphors that simultaneously recreate herself and her world. Even in her earliest books, her attempts at crafted and original language have a mannered, self-conscious awkwardness. But the issue is not merely one of skill. In her relationship to her readers, Rich is a much more ethically driven poet; she wants to reach an audience to change it in practical, demonstrable ways. "I wanted," she wrote in 1968, "to choose words that even you / would have to be changed by" (L, 42). Thus we are not in the realm of Rilke's shattering, undecidable "You must change your life" ("Du mußt dein Leben ändern.") but of a demand for specific forms of self-recognition and political awareness. Her poetry therefore cannot turn back on itself hermetically, pursuing its self-enclosure, unless the audience's response is carefully drawn into the enclosing form. The required aesthetic is essentially one of controlled juxtaposition. The public and the private are not so much integrated, as interchanged. The advantage of the method, when it works, is the quality Rosemary Tonks objected to in a review of *Diving into the Wreck*—it is insidious. Tonks is commenting on Rich's use of an objective diction and an accessible, though fragmented, narrative line: "It is the clean diction used by all good reporters . . . and it is insidious because of its invisibility. The subjective factor, with all of its distortions, appears to have been edited out."[6] I would argue that a more exacting evaluation of this technique reveals it not as a weakness but a substantial accomplishment.

Rejection, uneasiness, even anger, are not unreasonable reactions to Adrienne Rich's poetry. In its transactions with the reader, her poetry proceeds by an aesthetic of mutual entrapment. Along the way, we are asked to give up very little. Each individual passage will be grounded in either observable facts or credible responses. That the

6. Rosemary Tonks, "Cutting the Marble," *The New York Review of Books*, 20, No. 15 (October 4, 1975), 8.

responses are insistently analogous with historical circumstances outside our control we accept with the very resistance and annoyance
with which they are catalogued. The effects, of course, are partly
cumulative, and that increases our wariness and our tension. Yet we
go along with the process because the analogies between self and
history stimulate our pleasure in formal repetition. In the end, however, the trap closes. Then we are no longer engaged in making comparisons between inner and outer, between here and there, but in
surviving the obliteration of all such distinctions. In a way, then,
Rosemary Tonks's negative criticism and Richard Howard's exalted
praise are alternate reactions to their similar needs for self-protection.[7]

These extreme positions are essentially defenses against what Rich's
poetry can do to a reader. Her better poems always exact a certain
price from anyone willing to participate in their vision. The kind of
political awareness she advocates may cost a loss of personal freedom.
The voyage into new territory may require us to adopt a generalized,
mythic identity. The reader who accepts her vision uncritically has
probably repressed the real anxieties accompanying self-recognition
and personal change. The enthusiasm for her efforts to create a myth
of androgynous sexuality is a typical case. To applaud the androgynous psyche or to announce this as its historical moment is easier
than actually living out its consequences: "I am here, the mermaid
whose dark hair / streams back, the merman in his armored body
. . . I am she: I am he" (DW, 24). We all have more varied sexual
impulses than we can act on, but will Rich's romanticized androgynous figure, "whose drowned face sleeps with open eyes," help bring
them any closer to realization? While that is not a criterion one
would ordinarily apply to all poetry, it is relevant in Rich's case. Unlike Roethke, she cannot take pleasure in the powerlessness of poetic
solutions to social and historical conflicts. Her poetry continually
testifies to her need to work out possible modes of human existence
verbally, to achieve imaginatively what cannot yet be achieved in
actual relationships. Moreover, she hopes that poetry can transform

---

7. See Richard Howard, *Alone With America: Essays on the Art of Poetry
in the United States Since 1950,* enlarged edition (New York: Atheneum,
1980).

human interaction. Yet perhaps that is not, after all, the point, at
least in poems like "Diving into the Wreck," despite its call for "the
thing itself and not the myth." For what we have here is the myth, as
Rich herself has now implicitly acknowledged: "There are words I
cannot choose again: *humanism androgyny*" (*DCL*, 66). "Such
words," she goes on to say, "have no shame in them." They do not
embody the history of anguish, repression, and self-control that precedes them. "Their glint is too shallow" (*DCL,* 66); they do not
describe either the past or the life of the present. As Rich has recently written of bisexuality, "Such a notion blurs and sentimentalizes
the actualities within which women have experienced sexuality; it is
the old liberal leap across the tasks and struggles of here and now."[8]
Indeed "Diving into the Wreck" demonstrates that one can suppress
difficult feelings by mythologizing them. It may be that both Rich
and her readers are relieved to have their fear and their desire con-
joined in symbols so stylized and abstract.

　　If all of Rich's poems devoted to her sexuality were either didac-

---

　　8. Rich, "Compulsory Heterosexuality and Lesbian Existence," *Signs,* 5,
No. 4 (1980), 637. Cf. Rich's *Of Woman Born: Motherhood as Experience
and Institution* (New York: Norton, 1976): "'Androgyny' has recently become a 'good' word (like 'motherhood' itself!) implying many things to
many people, from bisexuality to a vague freedom from imposed sexual roles.
Rarely has the use of the term been accompanied by any political critique"
(p. 76). Rich extends this analysis in an interview: "It's like the idea of
androgyny which is so seductive somehow as a liberal solution. It's essentially
the notion that the male will somehow incorporate into himself female attributes—tenderness, gentleness, ability to cry, to feel, to express, not to be
rigid. But, what does it mean for women? The 'androgyny' people have not
faced what it would mean in and for society for women to feel themselves
and be seen as full human beings," Elly Bulkin, "An Interview with Adrienne
Rich," *Conditions,* No. 1 (1977), p. 61. In "The Corn-Porn Lyric: Poetry
1972-73," *Contemporary Literature,* 16, No. 1 (1975), Marjorie Perloff
argues that Rich's "assertion of androgyny ... is pure assertion. Whatever experience prompted it remains all too inchoate and elusive" (p. 117). See also
Rich's liberal gesture toward a possible bisexual poetry by men in her "Poetry,
Personality and Wholeness: A Response to Galway Kinnell," *A Field Guide
to Contemporary Poetry and Poetics,* ed. Stuart Friebert and David Young
(New York: Longman, 1980), pp. 224-231, as well as her rejection of the
liberal option in *OLS,* p. 108.

tic or heavily mythologized, I would be inclined to make that judg-ment comprehensive. Yet both the very willful poems and those that seem fully sublimated exist in counterpoint with poems that are much more complicated and meditative. That movement back and forth between poetry as political forum and poetry as personal ex-ploration suggests that Rich's various voices sustain and support one another. It is possible that both her aggressive rhetoric and her most one-dimensional images of androgyny serve a similar function. They may help to bring more private and uncertain experiences to the sur-face, where they can then be verbalized.[9] That is very close to Yeats's notion of how abstract and impersonal images work on human emo-tion, and Rich in her own way is equally persistent in seeking highly generalized masks for the self. On the other hand, the more sche-matic poems may also provide a temporary relief from poems that offer no easy resolutions.

That is not to say, however, that the give-and-take of these two characteristic stances is absolutely regular, or that the kinds of lan-guage identified with each are kept entirely separate. Indeed, in Rich's best poems, her various forms of address compete with one another to form a broader and more open coherence. Rich's pattern seems to be for each new form of address to appear in relatively simplistic poems before being included in her sophisticated work.[10] Thus the generalized sexual masks of *Diving into the Wreck* are only

9. Cf. Rich's comment in an interview published in *Adrienne Rich's Poetry,* ed. Barbara Charlesworth Gelpi and Alpert Gelpi (New York: Nor-ton, 1975): "Some fairly uncomplicated poems hit you at a certain point, when that is exactly what you need. They can make an immense psychic dif-ference—open windows of consciousness—yet lack a certain kind of density. Maybe the poetry that you go on reading over and over all your life, getting more and more out of it, would be a much more complex, dense kind of poetry. But I think there's room for both" (p. 117). In "When We Dead Awaken" Rich says that in her early poetry "formalism was part of the strategy —like asbestos gloves, it allowed me to handle materials I couldn't pick up barehanded" (p. 22).

10. Helen Vendler argues that Rich's career suggests "blunter poems are followed by subtler ones," that she "may need to write explicit *cris du coeur* as sketches, so to speak, for more contained and disciplined later poems," *Part of Nature, Part of Us,* pp. 250, 248.

now undergoing a more complex realization. "Mother-Right" (*DCL*, 59) hints at one direction Rich's depiction of sexual polarization may take—toward a self-regarding irony:

> Woman and child   running
> in a field   A man planted
> on the horizon

There is a trace of humor here, with male rigidity and female responsiveness reduced to such spare images, but Rich is not quite prepared to see her politics so playfully. The rest of the poem succumbs again to her more pretentious mode of presenting the conflict. The woman runs through the grass with her child, the child happily singing as the woman leads them toward open space, while the man compulsively walks the "boundaries / measuring . . . what is his." In "Sibling Mysteries" (1976—*DCL,* 47-52), however, Rich exposes the contrast between male possessiveness and female openness to a more problematic context. There one feels the convergence of many of her concerns of the previous decade. The poem is offered to her sister, and much of it attempts to recover possibilities for communication missed over the years. Yet their particular relationship is also inescapably a collective one, since their lives repeat the experiences of countless other women. "It is strange," she wrote earlier, "to be so many women" (*DW*, 13), and for years she has been working to enter into the texture of women's lives in earlier periods. Now in "Sibling Mysteries" this motif returns in brief, vivid evocations of the separate history women have shared

> in looks exchanged at the feast
> where the fathers sucked the bones
> and struck their bargains [*DCL,* 50]

The image is stark and reductive, but far more complex and widely representative than Rich's comparable efforts have been before; its emotional resonance is remarkably varied, including anger and fear, jealousy, resentment, and contempt, as well as a sisterly fellowship potentially compromised by both its structural resemblance to male camaraderie and its tendency to be limited to shared suffering. She continues with terse, powerful stanzas that reach out to share the anguish of women isolated by the patriarchy at its most terrible,

> in boats of skin on the ice-floe
> —the pregnant set to drift,
> too many mouths for feeding— [DCL,50]

Here the verbal beauty of "boats of skin" draws us into the almost intolerable vulnerability of the full image; the "boats of skin" may be made of animal hide, but the phrase leads us to consider an image of women and their unwanted children banished naked to an ice-floe.

When Rich says to her sister "our lives were driven down the same dark canal," she invokes as well these other women who "were to begin with / brides of the mother." The poem takes the chance of conflating its more limited "sibling mysteries" with the wider history of how "woman's flesh was made taboo" to women. The erotic message in the larger sisterhood addressed with "Let me hold and tell you" how daughters are "brides of each other / under a different law" troubles the poem's autobiographical context. The poem's still very broad analysis of gender thereby acquires an edge of risk and violation that Rich's poems on similar subjects have not had before. Moreover, if the experience of the mother's body is the source of the sexuality Rich urges on women, then she is close to a psychoanalytic model that would include as well the men whose history of war and dominance she rejects. "Sibling Mysteries," then, is a forceful, effective poem, but partly because it takes its notion of female affection and sexuality far enough to be challenged by its own metaphors.

The ideal of a language of female sexuality, linked as it is in Rich's poetry with a disavowal of America's patriarchal history of repression, is inseparable from "the drive / to connect. The dream of a common language" (DCL, 7) that so many American poets since Whitman have shared. Indeed Rich herself draws on Whitman to validate her image of female "community"; it will manifest "what Whitman called 'the hunger for equals'—the desire for a context in which our own strivings will be amplified, quickened, lucidified, through those of our peers" (*OLS,* 214). This new community, Rich repeatedly argues, will be impossible without a language of unique equality and interconnectedness. As we have seen, Kinnell and Duncan, among many poets, have their dreams of a common language as well, dreams that answer to the conflict between the culture's myths of possibility and a constrained sense of historical reality. Another cultural context would present different pressures, but in America a poetry of female interconnectedness is grounded in images of democratic openness. Rich's project is coded within the same field of verbal similarities and differences as Kinnell's and Duncan's; it gets part of its motivation and its appeal from the same culturally produced mix of ambition and regret. Rich's image of sisterhood compensates for the fraternity America has failed to achieve.

As "Sibling Mysteries" and the rest of *The Dream of a Common Language* should make clear, one cannot segregate Rich's concerns and assign them exclusively to those of her poems one likes or dislikes. The topicality of her most well-known poems, particularly those on Vietnam and on issues raised by the feminist movement, extends to her more meditative work. There is no way, then, for her readers to avoid those uncomfortable intrusions of historical circumstances that challenge the self-sufficiency of a poetic vision. History is there, perhaps rather more disturbingly, in the poems that do not settle for either querulous pronouncements or mystified symbols of mermaids.

Although it is not entirely effective, Rich's "Tear Gas" (*PSN,* 139-40), from which the quotation opening this chapter is taken, provides a good example of the relationship between public and private experience in her poetry. The title is not promising, nor is the factual epigraph that follows it: *"October 12, 1969: reports of the tear-gassing of demonstrators protesting the treatment of G. I. prisoners in the stockade at Fort Dix, New Jersey."* The first two lines then set up a challenge the poem accepts: "This is how it feels to do something you are afraid of. / That they are afraid of." The "this" of the first line not only refers to the epigraph; it also attempts to transfer the convergence of public and personal emotion to the poem itself. The poet may be afraid of taking on so unyielding a topic, but "they" are unlikely to be afraid of the poem, so the self-reflexiveness here has to be partly ironic. The poem then moves through a Whitmanesque listing of all the tears shed on such an occasion. Rich also offers a strained and potentially comic analogy to justify the poem's right to address the tears of prisoners and demonstrators:

> beginning to weep as you weep peeling onions, but
> endlessly, for the rest of time, tears of chemistry,
> tears of catalyst, tears of rage, tears for yourself,
> tears for the tortured men in the stockade and for
> their torturers

Whether this was conscious or not, Rich's litany of analogous tears is also a palimpsest of contemporary literary allusions. In the reference to the personal motives that shape public rituals ("at Fort Dix, beginning to feel . . . all you have held back from false pride"), one can detect possible comparisons with Lowell's treatment of similar themes.[11] There are also echoes here of all the lamentations Ginsberg has inscribed in poems he has published during the past twenty years. And in the "relief, that your body was here, you had done it, every last refusal was over" we may hear echoes of Sylvia Plath's rhetoric.

So the poet is here, in the presence of the page, "alone with language" that belongs partly to people who participated in an event she can only empathize with, partly to subsequent newspaper stories, and partly to poets whose work precedes her own. Can her poem master these influences? Rich is aware that it cannot, but she takes these unlikely materials and makes their resistance to verbal transformation the poem's unifying subject. "Tear Gas" is structured by repetition and variation that bind it in a verbal net it cannot escape. This entrapment becomes, curiously, the poem's accomplishment. Rich rejects the need for language that could fully embody the personal and social changes she yearns for, but she wants a language that will at least record her frustration, and that she finds.

---

11. See Thomas Edwards's analysis of several of Lowell's political poems in his *Imagination and Power: A Study of Poetry on Public Themes* (New York: Oxford, 1971), pp. 210-25.

Rich tries literally to compel the poem to represent her needs, to color it with "blood-black, sexual green, reds / veined with contradictions." She casts about for "a word that will shed itself like a tear . . . leaving its stain . . . like sperm or tears." Then she admits, echoing Eliot's Prufrock, perhaps with deliberate self-deflation, that "this is not what I mean / these images are not what I mean." Yet the force of her will does provide for a number of admissions important both for Rich herself and for the wider American political context. Specifically, the most intimate motives in political action are presented as a communal triumph, rather than a trivializing confession:

> The will to change begins in the body not in the mind
> My politics is in my body, accruing and expanding with every
>   act of resistance and each of my failures
> Locked in the closet at 4 years old I beat the wall with my body
> that act is in me still

This sort of observation would ordinarily undermine revolutionary conviction, but here it is unifying and restorative. Thus Rich can also extend the poem's epigraph to account for an incipient sexual change. "These repetitions are beating their way," she writes, "toward a place when we can no longer be together / when my body will no longer demonstrate outside your stockade." Such a passage flickers with multiple contexts. If politics and sexuality display the same organizing structures, the same power relationships, then revolutions in either domain may also re-enact one another. Yet parallelism is not the only mode of repetition invoked here. For the final statement cannot be decisively located within politics or sexuality; it is difference as doubling or duplication, an uncanny division into mirror images that cannot be either entirely separated or combined. The stockade is at once the military prison at Fort Dix and the armored body of a lover committed to an equally historicized politics.

Built into the poem's acceptance of the simultaneous convergence and fragmentation of psychology and politics is a genuinely surprising conclusion—surprising, that is, in view of the historical events the poem cites—that the interaction of public and private life need not be stifling; it can even be liberating. That is, of course, one of America's founding myths, but its less literary precedents are usually unacceptably rhetorical and enthusiastic. Here, however, it is rooted first in failure, then in commonplace experience, and the results are more convincing. The unity of "Tear Gas" is grounded in the mutuality of our discontents. "I am afraid," Rich writes again, and the phrase is now not merely literal but also parenthetical and colloquially amused. Her final line signals a confident pleasure in the poem as inconclusive process, yet its pride is undercut by the poem's circular ironies: "It's not the worst way to live."

The only problem with "Tear Gas" is that neither its personal nor its political revelations are quite vivid enough to sustain the loosely associative form. The poem needs to draw its various elements into a tighter and more dramatic confrontation. The very stark, even schematic and brittle conflicts in Rich's vision cannot be fully served by American poetry's more innocently optimistic versions of a field theory of compostion. Rich's associative fields work best when structured by violent or ecstatic juxtapositions that enable their openness to succeed.[12] The parallels between public and private experience in "Tear Gas" can, however, help us to see how Rich has treated these issues with greater condensation elsewhere, not only in short poems but also in long poems that pursue the linked subversion and restoration of self and other more memorably.

A recent and remarkably poignant poem, "For L. G.: Unseen for Twenty Years" (*PSN*, 232-35), is a good example of these forces working effectively. The poem is an uncertain gesture toward a friend she has lost contact with and a series of difficult moments of self-recognition. While they were traveling together in France twenty years ago, her friend tried, apologetically, to admit his homosexuality and yet give their relationship some physical ground:

---

12. Cf. Rich's observations about Susan Griffin's poetry in Elly Bulkin, "An Interview with Adrienne Rich, Part Two," *Conditions,* No. 2 (1977): "... the poem interrupts itself, where there are two voices against each other in the poem or maybe three or the poet's own voice against her voice, which echoes the kind of splitting and fragmentation women have lived in, the sense of being almost a battleground for different parts of the self" (pp. 55-56).

> *I have to tell you—maybe I'm not a man—*
> *I can't do it with women—but I'd like*
> *to hold you, to know what it's like*
> *to sleep and wake together—*

Her response follows; at the time she may have thought herself to be earnest and perceptive. It is more likely, however, that she was embarrassed, and her quick reaction was to cover for him, unfortunately in a way that was sexually insulting: *"But you're a man, I know it— / The swiftness of your mind is masculine—?"* No doubt she knew that this was more a lawyerly argument and an oblique enticement than the affectionate acceptance he was seeking. Now, however, she sees the conversation politically. It is a function of "the early 'fifties / of invincible ignorance"; she calls her line "some set-piece I'd learned to embroider / in my woman's education." What Rich finds so troubling in this now is not just the personal clumsiness of her response but the sense that her lines were given to her by the times. A moment that had seemed to express her personality is shown to manifest the most commonplace sort of history. That recollection is more convincing than any argument about sexual stereotypes, but it is more difficult to overcome its implications for human action. She is able to recover, with a wider knowledge, her affection for his nervousness: "Your face: taut as a mask of wires, a fencer's mask / half-turned away." And she can admit, as well, that she is still drawn to the superficial fiction she acted out for both of them. Yet she cannot project his image into the present without coming up with other clichés. Maybe, she says, you are now cruising the bars "stalking yourself as I can see you still: / young, tense, amorphous, longing," or perhaps you are married and "live out your double life." When she tries to credit him with a better adaptation her language is wooden and clinical:

> maybe you've found or fought
> through to a kind of faithfulness
> in the strange coexistence
> of two of any gender

In this mixture of curiosity and distance she is closer to her own feelings than in the poems bristling with assurance.[13] Now we can see the somewhat awkward language in the context of Rich's subsequent sexual development. Hesitant self-discovery here is combined with wariness about her audience. Yet her new perspective is no less compromised by its historicity. The fatefulness of action, action dominated by sexual roles she can only identify in retrospect, will counter every self-discovery. At the end, the poem comes full circle and there is nowhere to go:

> and, dear heart, I know, had a lover gestured
> you'd have left me
> for a man, as I left you,
> as we left each other, seeking the love of men.

The ambivalent emotions here very nearly dissolve the poem's conclusion. "Dear heart," recalling the double valence definitively registered in Shakespeare's Sonnet 95, is simultaneously tender and sardonic, and we cannot tell whether the final line points to a gentle acceptance of reality or a kind of ironic resignation. This citation of compromised recognitions is a small victory, but it is all the poem can manage.

That is a characteristically self-reflexive irony for Rich, and it demonstrates how she can master the difficulties of her associative and juxtapositional method. One solution she regularly chooses is to let the verbal echoes that provide a sense of structure also stimulate the most unsettling juxtapositions of individual and public experience. Thus those passages that give us the most confidence in her craft also sometimes reveal the most threatening connections. The devices that order her poems are the very ones that open the field of associations. In "Trying to Talk with a Man" (*DW*, 3-4), the first lines seem flatly factual and public: "Out in this desert we are testing bombs, / that's why we came here." As the poem progresses, the recognition that political and interpersonal violence reflect one another grows. Political violence vents personal frustration that may itself be historically determined. Interpersonal violence is political

---

13. Cf. Rich's discussion of the gradual and somewhat hesitant history of her poetic treatment of her relationship with other women in Bulkin, "An Interview with Adrienne Rich," pp. 64-65.

and theatrical; its destructive, explosive testing mimics public antagonisms. In another poem a woman asks a man what he is feeling and his silent response is at once somatic and political: "Now in the torsion of your body," she realizes, "as you defoliate the fields we lived from / I have your answer" (DW, 30). Here in "Trying to Talk with a Man" the final lines bring these recognitions to a conclusion:

> talking of the danger
> as if it were not ourselves
> as if we were testing anything else.

These lines bring the poem round to its beginning and thereby make it whole. Yet that very unity is a trap for the poem's readers, one from which they cannot easily extricate themselves. Our pleasure in the poem as a verbal construct confronts us with a conflation of self and history that leaves us no apparent margin of freedom. Helen Vendler argues that in this volume the war is "added as a metaphor ... for illustration of the war between the sexes rather than for especially political commentary," but I believe Rich depicts the relationship between politics and personal life as more complexly interdependent.[14] It is not even a case of two separate domains whose traditional metaphors may be used to illuminate each other. In Rich's best poetry politics and personal life act out an unstable mix of mimesis and determinism.[15]

When Rich cannot achieve this kind of verbal and structural dynamic, it often means the poem is not fully realized. "August" (DW, 51), for example, is struggling to become a successful poem, but it does not cohere. The poem begins with a pastoral image reminiscent of James Wright's work: "Two horses in yellow light / eating windfall apples under a tree." Rich wants to rend that calm with a violent recognition. She cannot quite find an image that develops convincingly out of the initial vista, so she resorts, as she did in "Dialogue"

---

14. Vendler, *Part of Nature, Part of Us,* p. 259.

15. Cf.: "The power politics of the relations between the sexes, long unexplored, is still a charged issue. To raise it is to cut to the core of power relations throughout society, to break down irreparably the screens of mystification between 'private life' and 'public affairs' " (OLS, 196).

(*DW*, 21), to a use of italics to signify cold hysteria. Her night-mares, she concludes, are beginning to "open / into prehistory"; it "looks like a village lit with blood / where all the fathers are crying: *My son is mine!*" These powerful last lines evoke a complex of essential male anxieties at threatened paternity—a need for authority over the male heir, a denial of Oedipal impulses, fear of castration, and a desire to claim sole responsibility for procreation—but the lines also break away from a poem that has lost its center. They divest themselves of the rest of the poem to create a forceful image that is entirely self-sufficient.

This is not to say that Rich's less tightly knit poems always fail. "Shooting Script," a two-part sequence totalling fourteen poems, uses a simple structure quite effectively: a series of separate lines linked frequently by repeated phrases and syntactical forms. Throughout, the language is direct and spare. Recurrent concerns (like the Vietnam war) tie the sequence together thematically. Yet the sequence as a whole also testifies to the way history attacks the poem from the center, fracturing its stanzas into individual fragments: "read there," Rich tells us in the last poem, "the map of the future, the roads radiating from the / initial split, the filaments thrown out from that impasse" (*WTC*, 67). To apply one of the words Rich uses, the poem is defoliated, its leaves falling from its trunk.

"Shooting Script" begins with a poem, recalling the method of Duncan's "Often I Am Permitted to Return to a Meadow," that works variations on its first two lines: "We were bound on the wheel of an endless conversation. / Inside this shell, a tide waiting for someone to enter" (*WTC*, 53). Immediately, a cluster of possible readings is suggested. The first line, which is the poem's only complete sentence, may bring to mind a recurrent scene in Rich's poetry: a relationship between two people, closed to outside influence and largely fixed in a pattern of repeated interchanges. This is, of course, an impersonal template for a relationship. Moreover, if we hear an echo of one of the more famous lines in *King Lear,* "I am bound / Upon a wheel of fire," along with the images of the wheel of fire in medieval legends and the Apocrypha, we will read the line with a typically modernist sense of belatedness and deflation. Thus the line has enough general connotation for us to hear in it reverberations of all contemporary conversation; it is an image of the way we are situated in language, another of Rich's regular concerns. This is the endless conversation which the poem must repeat, even as the poem tries to differentiate itself from it. The "we" of the first line therefore includes the poem's readers as well, and the shell in the second line figures in an infinite number of sites, from the closed circularity of particular interactions to the encapsulation of a period of history in its own verbal repetitions.

The rest of the poem is a sequence of appositives, each echoing the vocabulary of the first two lines and offering a definition of the poem as a text to be experienced: "A cycle whose rhythm begins to change the meanings of words" (*WTC*, 53) is one of the subsequent lines; "A monologue waiting for you to interrupt it" is another. In a miniature version of a technique comparable to Kinnell's in *The Book of Nightmares*, clusters of related words—conversation, monologue, dialogue; tide, waves, ebb and flow; melting, pulsing—are interchanged, interrelated, and finally bound into a net that holds together their differences and similarities. The possibility of change within language is held out to us, but the poem's erosive intermingling of human interaction and natural process tends to take it away. That this aesthetic of opposition becomes echolalia (human speech echoing nature's dialogue of substances) is not entirely negative. The will to change is enacted even as it is undone. And the "meaning that searches for its word like a hermit crab," therein to dwell in isolation, will eventually outgrow its shelter.

The poem extends to us an ambivalent offer to enter this text and its cycle of changes. The imagery of natural rhythms is enticing; even the roughly mock-heroic rhythm of the opening line is appealing. Indeed the whole poem coheres as an appreciative phenomenology of the connotative web woven by its key words. Yet the hermeticism of this phenomenology is also stifling. This "conversation of sounds melting constantly into rhythms," linked to the "dialogue of the rock with the breaker," is also the claustrophobic "turning of an endless conversation," or the apocalyptic stasis of "an ear filled with one sound only." However beautiful we find the poem's rhythmically overlapping meanings, we will also find its entrapment sterile; this "tide that ebbs and flows against a deserted continent" can be picturesque while suggesting, in human terms, repeated contacts that fail to evoke a response. Rich's mixed feelings about the verbal tapestry she weaves amplify the doubts we began to see in Duncan's and Kinnell's comparable efforts.

These affective uncertainties contribute an element of instability to the poem's overall form and to any judgment we might try to make about its originality. The verbal connections worked here seem both to exist before the poem begins, as part of the texture of our language, and to exist only because of the poem's creative energy. As a verbal act, the poem is unresolvably unstable; it must seem at once involuntary and willed. Its field of relationships is neither altogether given nor altogether artificial. We cannot account for this unresolvability by faulting Rich for being indecisive; nor can we recuperate it, in conventional New Critical fashion, by characterizing it as a set of tightly controlled ambiguities.

The whole tone of formal control here is toward increasing our uncertainty, not toward containing it. She begins the sixth poem in "Shooting Script" by writing "You are beside me like a wall; I touch you with my fingers and keep moving through the bad light." The last line repeats this opening, except now she writes of merely "trying to move through the bad light." As she puts it in the middle section, "This light eats away at the clarities I had fixed on." The light is the poem's light as well, a strained light that brings with it "the smell of a smell of burning."

More than anything else, it is the issue of history's presence in the poem that accounts for this twice removed, altogether supplementary, but ineradicable scent. History operates as the continual counterpoint to the will to change, to a conviction that individual freedom is decisive in any way. The fourth poem in the sequence begins "In my imagination I was the pivot of a fresh beginning," an assertion that the following lines essentially undo. They juxtapose a series of archeological sites that no longer communicate with a sequence of contemporary acts that are either misguided or unthinking. The result is an image of the present burdened by a totemic silence that makes a fresh beginning impossible. Elsewhere in the sequence history operates to shape individual character into a few unvarying roles. "They come to you," she writes to a young woman, "with their descriptions of your soul." A few lines later, sounding for a moment like Merwin, she adds, "They believe your future has a history and that it is themselves." Here, however, at least a measure of rejection is possible. They may have "old bracelets and rings they want to fasten onto you," but you remain beyond their comprehension. "You are a letter written, folded, burnt to ash, and mailed in an envelope to another continent." She is thinking here both of a woman's indifference to male history and of the process of composition. Yet these options offer only escape or opposition—through either an intense but private consciousness or a ritual gesture of disavowal.

In the last poem, however, she moves beyond these alternatives, as she did in "(Newsreel)," by turning history's devastation into a mode of deliberate composition. History has taken its definitive toll on every option but one—the verbal miming of and implicit mastery of history's own effects. She will "give up the temptations of the projector"; no longer will she replay the images of a past that was never hers in any event. Now she will possess instead the shattered blank ground on which the images were projected, the idealized American field now uniformly splintered, "the web of cracks filtering across the plaster." She presents us with a sequence of aesthetic injunctions—addressed simultaneously to the ruins of our history and to the ruins of the poem's form: "To reread the instructions on your palm; to find there how the /lifeline, broken, keeps its direction"; "to know in every distortion of the light what fracture is." We are given a phenomenology of willed rupture. Its final images are colloquial and playful but nonetheless sobering in their forceful usurpation of both her personal history and Williams's, Olson's and Roethke's notion of the primacy of place in American poetry: "To pull yourself up by your own roots; to eat the last meal in / your old neighborhood." "Shooting Script" succeeds because its disciplined language turns a nearly dismantled form into a vehicle for historical awareness. In the end aesthetics and history converge to become prophecy, as a deconstructed verbal matrix shows us American space in its final form.

In Rich's best poems the claims she has made for her own aesthetic are central and demonstrable. "The poem itself," she has written, "engenders new sensations, new awareness in me as it progresses." In "Tear Gas" and "For L. G.: Unseen for Twenty Years," or in her long poem "From an Old House in America" (*PSN*, 235-45), connections occur and risks are taken that Rich herself did not seem to plan and that we cannot anticipate. Each of these changes requires a further tentative complication of poetic form. Like "Shooting Script" her best poems skirt the edge of disaster. The poems that open themselves to subversion by past history and by current politics take the chance of being disordered or trivialized. Rich has found ways of structuring the relationships she discovers, yet she cannot expect to resolve "the irreducible, incomplete connection / between the dead and living" (*PSN*, 237). What unifies her most important work is the willingness to record the continual loss of security without the loss of a certain very American innocent expectation. "I was looking," she writes in "Shooting Script," "for a way out of a lifetime's consolations." Yet a few years later she can still say that "a dream of tenderness wrestles with all I know of history" (*PSN*, 241-42). When the tenderness persists, her readers may be willing to admit that their own experience has also been shaped, whether brutally or comically, by history's undecidable presence.

The act of setting an historical incident against a moment of personal experience has virtually become Rich's poetic signature since *The Will to Change*. Yet it is not a method that lends itself successfully to casual composition or predictable results. Any individual poem will seem incomplete, the problems it raises beyond solution. Moreover, there will always be new material not yet subjected to the ruthless confrontations that take place in the process of composition. There is a feeling of reluctance, and a genuine poignancy, each time another area of experience is exposed to this political testing. The mixture of will and vulnerability in Rich's own reactions is perhaps nowhere more visible than in "Twenty-one Love Poems," first published separately and then included in *The Dream of a Common Language.*

The sequence begins with what sounds like a typical speaking voice in the presence of an American city's decay. "Whenever in this city," she writes, "sirens flicker / with pornography... we also have to walk" (*DCL,* 25). The passage may appear to be a complaint, but "have to" actually serves as ethical insistence: "We need to grasp our lives inseparable / from those rancid dreams." The mode, as with so much of contemporary American poetry, is an ironic continuation of the Whitmanesque embrace in a landscape that has degenerated into tenements and "rainsoaked garbage." She does not, however, want the irony to blunt the discomfort of the contradictory impulses, and the last lines state her willed hopefulness dramatically:

No one has imagined us. We want to live like trees,
sycamores blazing through the sulfuric air,
dappled with scars, still exhuberantly budding,
our animal passion rooted in the city. [*DCL,* 25]

This tension between desire and actuality persists in Rich's poetry no matter how thoroughly her emotional aspirations are countered by American history. From the negative poems about America in *Necessities of Life* through the more decisively compromised poems in *The Will to Change,* her despair and anger at American culture coexists with her wish for a renewed vision of American communality. It is not until Merwin that we find an unremittingly bleak inversion of the Whitmanesque aesthetic. Yet even Rich's feminist version of Whitman's democratic interconnectedness is convincing only when it is completely interwoven with historical impossibility. Rich works steadily at this effort to depict female power amidst "the earth deposits of our history" (*DCL,* 13) through the recent poems in *Poems Selected and New* and *The Dream of a Common Language.* One failed version of the effort is "Not Somewhere Else, But Here" (*DCL,* 39-40), which is almost a feminist recapitulation of the technique of "Shooting Script," but with its associations transcribed too loosely:

Death of the city   Her face
   sleeping   Her quick stride   Her

running   Search for a private space   The city
caving from within   The lessons badly
learned   Or not at all   The unbuilt world
This one love flowing   Touching other
lives   Spilt love   The least wall caving

In "Twenty-one Love Poems" we can see where this work must lead. Through most of the sequence, she succeeds in interweaving the ordinary, unspectacular environment, the special social pressures always at the edge of her awareness, the historical forces ranged against two female lovers, and their shared intimacies.[16] The relationship is always "a flute / plucked and fingered by women outside the law." Yet she reserves a privileged site—sexual intimacy—for a poem that voices the desire to break free of public history, their individual past, and the politics of the relationship. Between the fourteenth and fifteenth poems she places "(The Floating Poem, Unnumbered)." Enclosed, as its title is in parentheses, it is surrounded by and grounded in the twenty-one numbered poems. It is at once protected and threatened by them, and its opening and closing lines provide a passage to and from the concerns of the rest of the sequence: "Whatever happens with us," she writes at first, "Your body / will haunt mine," and closes with "whatever happens, this is" (DCL, 32). The sequence as a whole testifies widely to the paradoxical stresses in "whatever happens," but this single poem, like Duncan's "Sonnet 4," reaches for a temporality all its own. The sequence's structure

---

16. See Rich's discussion of her poem sequence: "One thing I was trying to do in *Twenty-One Love Poems* was constantly to relate the lovers to a larger world. You're never just in bed together in a private space; you can't be, there is a hostile and envious world out there, acutely threatened by women's love for each other.... So many of these things enter in when two women are together: joy like none other, vulnerability like none other, the breaking of the core prohibition at the heart of patriarchy," Bulkin, "An Interview with Adrienne Rich, Part Two," p. 57. *Twenty-One Love Poems* was first published in a limited edition by Effie's Press in California. In an interview with Blanche M. Boyd in *Christopher Street*, 1, No. 7 (1977), Rich recounts her decision to publish the sequence this way: "I wanted these poems to come out from Effie's Press because I have a special kind of love for them, and wanted them to be...how shall I say?...touched by women's hands through the whole process" (p. 15).

simultaneously gives and denies this poem that inviolability. This is Rich's most overtly erotic poem to date, and she may have simply been unable to politicize its intimacies:

> Whatever happens with us, your body
> will haunt mine—tender, delicate
> your lovemaking, like the half-curled frond
> of the fiddlehead fern in forests
> just washed by sun. Your traveled, generous thighs
> between which my whole face has come and come—
> the innocence and wisdom of the place my tongue has found
>   there—
> the live, insatiate dance of your nipples in my mouth—
> your touch on me, firm, protective, searching
> me out, your strong tongue and slender fingers
> reaching where I had been waiting years for you
> in my rose-wet cave—whatever happens, this is. [*DCL*, 32]

Except possibly for one excessively sentimental phrase—"the innocence and wisdom of," a phrase whose conventionality suggests how difficult Rich found the poem to write—"(The Floating Poem, Unnumbered)" succeeds in being both tender and sensual. The comic playfulness of the alliteration in "half-curled frond / of the fiddlehead fern" and the edge of comic self-regard in "insatiate dance" give the poem's rapture a tonal complication from which it benefits. We may even hear in these lines a wry echo of the pervasive garden imagery of her earliest work, but in this poem at least we are not altogether removed from those "paths fern-fringed and delicate" of *A Change of World* where "innocent sensuality abides" (*CW*, 73-74).

One reads the first part of the sequence wondering if any of the poems will risk more frank physical description. Given that sense of hesitant anticipation, it is emotionally appropriate that this pivotal poem be unnumbered and symbolically free of all historical entanglement. Yet one can also say that Rich has left the sequence with a project unfinished and perhaps still to come, one that would be even more challenging to her audience—a historicizing of erotic pleasure. As Foucault has argued, the privileging of sexuality as a special site for authentic self-expression is itself historically determined. Foucault's challenge to our confidence in the ahistorical character of sexuality is implicit in much that Rich has previously written about relations between the sexes. Indeed her recognition here that lesbian sexuality is "outside the law" is historicized exactly as Foucault argues: it is both a prohibition and an inducement to a form of sexuality conceived in opposition to the dominant culture. As Rich herself has written, lesbianism is a conflux "of the self-chosen woman, the forbidden 'primary intensity' between women, and also the woman who refuses to obey, who has said 'no' to the fathers" (*OLS*, 202); the impulse toward "the breaking of a taboo" cannot be separated from that "electric and empowering charge between women"—"an engulfed continent which rises fragmentedly to view from time to time only to become submerged again."[17] If Rich follows this project through to completion, it may lead her to write poems about female sexuality that have the deconstructive force of poems about American history like "(Newsreel)."

Yet Rich will have to acknowledge the cost of these insights—both to herself and to her audience. For where history and politics are concerned, knowledge does not necessarily produce freedom. And history touches even our simplest pleasures. *"The moment when a feeling enters the body,"* she writes, "is political. This touch is political" (*WTC*, 24). By focusing on what the poem itself can actually do (or fail to do) in the presence of that unacceptable, undeniable reality, Rich also creates a compelling record of our other human options. They are fewer and they are more problematic than her exhortatory poetry would lead us to believe. Yet we are also more driven to choose that small ground on which some witness can be given, for we are ourselves already being chosen by "the cruelty of our times and customs" (*PSN*, 234).

---

17. Rich, "Compulsory Heterosexuality and Lesbian Existence," 649, 658, and 647.

CHAPTER SIX

The Resources of Failure: W. S. Merwin's Deconstructive Career

> Certain words now in our knowledge we will not use again, and
> we will never forget them. We need them. Like the back of
> the picture. Like our marrow, and the color in our veins.
> We shine the lantern of our sleep on them, to make sure, and
> there they are, trembling already for the day of witness.
> They will be buried with us, and rise with the rest. [*HT,* 58][1]

PERHAPS, AS MERWIN SUGGESTS in this little hieratic meditation, the very words most central to our selfhood must remain
unspoken. Yet any reader of Merwin's recent poetry—with its insistent, recurring vocabulary—will suspect that this poet thinks he
knows what those words are. At the least, Merwin clearly feels that
certain words and images give witness to what cannot be said. These
words have gradually become the core of his poetic language; there,
they infiltrate the rest of the language, reducing the whole of dis-

---

1. The following books by W. S. Merwin are abbreviated and documented
internally: *CF—The Compass Flower* (New York: Atheneum, 1977); *CL—
The Carrier of Ladders* (New York: Atheneum, 1970); *DB—The Dancing
Bears* (New Haven: Yale University Press, 1954); *DF—The Drunk in the
Furnace* (New York: Macmillan, 1960); *HT—Houses and Travellers* (New
York: Atheneum, 1977); *GB—Green with Beasts* (New York: Alfred A.
Knopf, 1956); *L—The Lice* (New York: Atheneum, 1967); *MJ—A Mask
for Janus* (New Haven: Yale University Press, 1952); *MT—The Moving
Target* (New York: Atheneum, 1963); *WA—Writings to an Unfinished
Accompaniment* (New York: Atheneum, 1973).

course to a single ineffable and refracted meaning. Not so long ago—
no longer in any case than 1939 and *Finnegans Wake*—a work demonstrating the interconnectedness of language could be a source of
continuing pleasure. In American poetry, as we have seen, this verbal
interconnectedness imitates a democratic ideal. That cultural pressure
keeps the aesthetic alive somewhat longer in America, but through
the 1960s it becomes increasingly ironic and impossible. With
Roethke, the project is uncertain and unstable, though still possible
as a verbal gesture that is politically gratuitous but emotionally
gratifying. For this generation, Duncan may be among the last un-
qualified believers in this central part of Whitman's poetic, but the
historical events of the 1960s undermine even Duncan's faith in
verbal community. With Kinnell, the aesthetic of verbal connections
becomes frenetic and compulsive; Roethke's graceful rehearsals of
verbal ecstasy now require elaborate connections whose powers of
democratic transformation are fatally damaged by American history.
This development culminates in Rich and Merwin, in whose poetry
history finally triumphs. Yet both Rich and Merwin regularly opt for
radically deconstructed forms that manage to capture history's powers
of dissolution. Rich, however, reserves one possibility for a restorative
verbal democracy—a female interconnectedness that can at least
counterpoint America's less successful history. But with Merwin's
poetry that joy in tracing the endless relationships among words
seems irrecoverable. One feature of Merwin's aesthetic is that our
delight in watching words echo one another is relentlessly undercut.

The use of such words, then, involves specific risks that are apparent the first time they are spoken. The selfhood they reveal is intimate but impersonal. The knowledge they bring is therefore deflating,
an evacuation without much attendant drama. To speak these words
is to experience an uneasiness that cannot be resolved; yet the poet
who speaks them may appear, paradoxically, as Jacques Derrida has
come to be viewed in contemporary criticism, the master of irresolu-
tion. The challenge Merwin sets himself in his best work is to occupy
exactly that position—to become the anonymous American figure
who announces the harmonizing dissolution of the language. Merwin
thus offers us one final, dark incarnation of a poetic of democratic

openness. In doing so, of course, he has claimed that signal voice as his own. The contradiction provides him with a sardonic version of Whitman's prophetic stance, and it gives his poetry its own grim humor. To be successful, both the inverted prophecy and the humor must remain muted, for they tend toward the sententious. At the same time, they must be compromised at every opportunity.

As anyone even casually familiar with his career knows, Merwin has not always written poetry that radically undermines each assertion. In effect, his recent work offers us what remained after he rigorously pruned the excesses of his first poems and then turned what was left back on itself. The result has been a poetry of extraordinary force, a poetry that inherits the despair of the century but gives it a prophetic new form, a form that ruthlessly deconstructs its own accomplishments. There would have been, to be sure, no way of predicting this intense condensation, but the foundation for Merwin's development is present in his language from the beginning. "Silence," "emptiness," "distance," "darkness"—there are others, but this diction that Merwin shares with Kinnell includes some of his most recurrent words. At first they serve to lend mystery to Merwin's initial romanticism, a romanticism in which Keats's melancholy is mediated through Yeats's antimonies.[2] To read his first four books in the light of what he has published since 1960 is to discover these key terms, potent and isolated in the later poems, present with all their thematic resonance surprisingly spelled out.[3] These early poems almost provide a

---

2. Harvey Gross, "The Writing on the Void: The Poetry of W. S. Merwin," *Iowa Review*, 1, No. 3 (Summer 1970), 92-106, compares Merwin's stylistic elegance to that of Keats. There are numerous parallels with Yeats: "as though a man could make / A mirror out of his own divinity, / Wherein he might believe himself, and be" (*DB*, 72);

> What is a man
> That a man may recognize, unless the inhuman
> Sun and moon wearing the masks of a man,
> Weave before him such a tale as he
>   —Finding his own face in the strange story—
> Mistakes by metaphor and calls his own
> Smiling, as on a familiar mystery? [*DB*, 41]

3. Jarold Ramsey, "The Continuities of W. S. Merwin: 'What Has Escaped Us We Bring With Us,'" *Massachusetts Review*, 14, No. 3 (Summer 1973), 569-90, argues that "in every one of Merwin's books there is his peculiar

semantic glossary to the imagery of the later work. In a way, this development duplicates two early modernist concerns: the reaction to Romanticism and the interest in formal condensation. Merwin, however, has now moved toward a typically contemporary irony about the possibility of any kind of formal perfection.

Merwin's first two books offer pleasant and engaging reading. His metrical skills, as Auden notes in his introduction to *A Mask for Janus* (1952), are considerable; his mastery of a wide variety of traditional forms is impressive. Yet the poetry is so ornately complacent that a line like "We survived the selves that we remembered" (*MJ,* 5) is almost cause for self-congratulation; in the later poetry it would be more claustrophobic than ironic, free from choice or potential for change and free as well from much conviction about either survival or memory. Yet the line does anticipate his recent work; it is among those passages in his first books that read almost like recipes for his later poetic: "We turned from silence and fearfully made / Our small language in the place of the night" (*MJ,* 8). In isolation, the content of these lines suggests the precarious quality of Merwin's recent language, and it also reflects a verbal helplessness before history that is present, in less definitive form, in all of the contemporary poets I have discussed. But a few lines later Merwin indulges in a dream of "the last oceans where the drowned pursue / The daze and fall of fabulous voyages," and "the place of night" becomes a Romantic conceit. We can permit ourselves to contemplate "drownings / In mirrors," and to "dream of distances," because these transformations occur in a secure rhetorical territory.

Merwin's longest poem, "East of the Sun and West of the Moon" (1954), retells the Norwegian folktale known by the same title; the plot structure is similar to Apuleius's *Cupid and Psyche.* Unlike the more tightly organized poems in these books, this poem is not managed with Merwin's formal grace. The lack of control, however, allows

---

grammar of emblems, the signatures of his imagination: The bells, mirrors, gloves, stones, doorways; the birds, the whales; and behind them all, inexhaustible in its numinousness, the sea" (p. 569). I agree that this vocabulary runs through all of Merwin's books, but I also feel that it functions quite differently at each stage of his career.

more of his main concerns to surface. His key terms occur more frequently, but they are almost inundated by elegant description. "I sing," he writes, "to drown the silence of far flowers"; "white-tongued flowers shout / Impossible silence on the impossible air" (DB, 57, 46). Any threat in such images of silence, or in the several descriptions of the empty distance over which the girl must pursue her lover, is deflected by the elaborate language. Poetic tradition and Merwin's own effusive rhetoric combine to protect her journey "beyond the hueless sighing of drowned days / Into the dark where no shades sigh" (DB, 53).

With Merwin's third and fourth books, however, a note of desperation enters the invocation of his key terms. This sense of desperation marks a second stage in his work. Many of the poems in *Green With Beasts* (1956) and *The Drunk in the Furnace* (1960) are over-written, repetitive, almost garrulous. But they are not clumsily written, nor do they lack craft. Poems like "Leviathan" (GB, 11-12) seem designed instead to exhaust their subject matter through continual variation and reiteration of the same terms and images. Where silence earlier involved a kind of rhetorical swooning, it now acquires obsessive resonance. The subject matter is generally more explicit; he stops calling so many poems "Song," "Carol," or "Fable," and gives them precise titles. He seems to be confronting brute reality more directly. Yet the apparent attempt to exhaust the subject really signals the poet's need to exhaust his own perceptions, a motive that may also be present in Kinnell's "The Avenue Bearing the Initial of Christ into the New World." Merwin wants to render the mechanism of his verbal apprehension finally knowable and given; if he cannot do that, he will be satisfied to extinguish it.

The poetry presses toward a silence achieved through self-depletion. Thus the descriptive lines piled on one another, as well as the recurring topic of the sea, tend in their massiveness to suggest their obverse —emptiness and evacuation. This traditional connection between everything and nothing, between whales or oceans and nothingness, later develops into the intimate loneliness of Merwin's vast landscapes—landscapes whose empty American immensity suggests the loss of historical possibility—landscapes where distance penetrates everything in sight. Formally, these poems seem wholly unlike the

thin, spare poems for which he has become famous. The relationship
between the two groups of poems is one of radical difference, and the
change in his career with *The Moving Target* (1963) is one of re-
versal and rejection. At their core, therefore, they have an essential
resemblance—the verbose poems so full of themselves and the meticulously honed poems retaining only the last vestige of speech—each
is supremely "a vessel at anchor in its own reflection" (*DF*, 4). Internally, the language in each type of poem is highly consistent. As
artifacts, however, the early poems are overblown, whereas the recent
poems are contemporary objects that almost eliminate themselves.
There is one other crucial comparison: within each group the poems
resemble one another to an extraordinary degree. Yet "there must
be," Merwin writes toward the end of his second book, "in a kingdom
of mirrors a king among / Mirrors" (*DB*, 77); within the two sets
of poems, each individual poem would be that king. The earlier
poems compete for that honor, but the later poems try to win by
losing most thoroughly. For to be a king among mirrors is to pro-
claim a sovereignty of absolution, to be the perfect image of all
otherness. Seen in the light of what he has done since 1960, the excesses of Merwin's overwrought poems reveal a need to create poetry
so empty it could contain the world. That covert desire is eventually
fulfilled by a poetry that becomes empty in the very act of opening
itself to the world. As with the other poets I have discussed, not
until the 1960s does a substantial postwar world exist even as a background in Merwin's poetry. Once it does, Merwin's tone undergoes its
definitive change.

Judged according to its influence on Merwin's subsequent development, *Green With Beasts* (1956) is the most important of the first
four volumes. In this book his prolix descriptiveness is most closely
tied to the thematic investigation of a self-reflexive emptiness. The
book begins with a sequence of five animal poems. We anticipate
a bestiary of creatures uniquely individuated through poetry, but the
continual reiteration of the same themes and images soon eliminates
that expectation. Nor is he quite attempting to pinpoint the otherness
common to all animal life. He uses animals to control the redeeming
otherness inhering in the whole external world. "When I speak," he

wrote earlier, "it is the world / That I must mention" (*DB*, 61), but the world, it seems, has no need to speak of us. Despite his continuing interest in animal poems, then, they do not constitute a separate strain in his poetry. These animal poems actually represent the first fruition of his insight into our dependence on physical objects in general. One of his main purposes is to undermine our security by disclosing the way objects dominate the entire spatio-temporal environment.

A rooster, in this sequence of poems, has a cry that "frames all the silence" (*GB*, 13); he hovers motionless, "his wings as though beating the air of elsewhere," though everything, as Merwin tells us, becomes elsewhere in that moment. His one eye glares "like the sun's self (for there is no other)," and the center of our self is suddenly displaced. Similarly, a dog summons in his unfixed gaze the "shimmering vista of emptiness," the whole summer afternoon around him, "the shining distance that weighs and waves / Like water" (*GB*, 17). He guards "the empty / Distance, the insufferable light losing itself / In its own glare." The dog is used to focus the world's indifferent gaze on us, to render us seen in the blind eye of sheer material substance. Perhaps the dog is simply unaware of our presence. No,

> Look again: it is through you
> That he looks, and the danger of his eyes
> Is that in them you are not there. [*GB*, 18]

The terms of the paradox are clear, but Merwin is forced to restate them again and again: "behind his eyes / You will be seen not to be there, in the glaring / Uncharactered reaches of oblivion." Pray, he tells us, that we "be delivered / From the vain distance he is the power of," but the real imperative is apparent in the confident irony of his diction: he casually sketches everything we depend on as "the dust you stand in / And your other darlings." Throughout his career, Merwin suggests that naming makes us a possession of the thing named. The real wish is to be consumed.

In the next poem, "White Goat, White Ram," the self-reflective quality in description becomes too conscious. We are not interested in the animals themselves, he writes, but in "conjuring by their

shapes / The shape of our desire, which without them would remain / Without a form and nameless" (*GB*, 20). The whiteness of
the goat and ram is a symbol, "as we should say those are white who
remember nothing"; their whiteness is a mechanism for transforming "the dying riot of random generation," our own "mad menag-
erie, / The body behind bone" (*DB*, 70, 34) into "a circle of silence,
a drying vista of ruin" (*MJ*, 45). But the impulse is too obvious to
communicate with any sense of necessity. The poetry becomes slack.
He tries unsuccessfully to draw an organizing symbolism from Christ's
story by adapting it ironically to fit our situation, "so that our grace-
lessness may have the back of a goat / To ride away upon." Kinnell
makes similar efforts to secularize religious imagery with equally uneasy results. Only Duncan succeeds at this for a time, because of his
belief in mythic universality, though the dark history of the 1960s
troubles Duncan's religious imagery as well. Merwin is not temper-
mentally suited to un-ironic religious imagery except as a way to invoke inexplicable ritual violence. However romantic Merwin once
may have been, he was not as well (unless much earlier) an unquali-
fied believer. It rings false when he says we would "give speech to
the mute tongues / Of angels."[4] If the goats "browse beyond words,"
then they only recede further beyond this poem.

   In the second section of the book, Merwin attempts to derive some
structural benefit from his compulsion for repetition. Particularly in
"The Prodigal Son" and "The Annunciation," he aims for a musical
sense of thematic variation and recurrence. Yet he repeats his key
words more overtly than before, without the camouflage of different
adjectives. In "The Prodigal Son" (*GB*, 28-32) the echoes are so
numerous that the whole poem would have to be quoted to account
for all of them. "Distance" occurs sixteen times in the poem's five
pages, "emptiness" seventeen times, and there are continual references to silence, vacancy, nothingness, hollowness, illusions, and mi-
rages. The poem, like the familiar hot afternoon in which it takes
place, should presumably begin to shimmer in our mind's eye "as in

---

   4. At times Merwin's attitude toward religion is almost sardonic, as when
he describes a rocky landscape: "nowhere else / Pillows like these stones for
dreaming of angels" (*DF*, 23). Or, with more bitterness: "Unable to endure
my world and calling the failure God, I will / destroy yours" (*MT*, 13). Yet
he is also both attracted to and irritated by religious mystery.

its own / Mirage." The metaphysics of this enterprise probably has its roots in Wallace Stevens, but Merwin has rejected Stevens's verbal intricacy for a heavy metronome that approaches self-mimicry.

The poem's story serves primarily to delay and, less successfully, to occasion the resolution we expect from the outset. The images of dissolving forms will collapse into a single harmonious field—the prodigal son will return home. In a setting of motionless summer heat, the father of the absent son sits brooding on empty distance with vacant eyes. His house itself is "an image merely / By which he may know the face of emptiness"; like the poem, it is "a name with which to say emptiness." He is obsessed with his son's absence, though the departure only brought about the inevitable, for "emptiness had lodged with him before." Meanwhile the son, too, contemplates emptiness, having left home in search of "something / Vague because distant," something

> Which, unknowing, he was leaving behind, yet
> Which he had to leave to be able to find. And wasted
> His substance in wild experiment and found
> Emptiness only, found nothing in distance,
> Sits finally in a sty and broods
> Upon emptiness, upon distance.

Abundance and desolation are now more openly connected by the tedium associated with sexual abandon. "My sex," Merwin later writes, "grew into the only tree, a joyless evergreen" (*MT*, 2). The son indulges in women and silks, only to find "his mind turns among / Those vacancies as a mirror hung by a string / In a ruin." Seemingly separated by space and extended in time, the son's gloom and the father's gloom are actually copresent to one another. Out of the same field of mirrored heat and shadow, out of the same silence in which "distance is dead," the son and the father move together. The story comes full circle; in the ghost-like substance of the poem ("unto this / Has been likened the kingdom of heaven") the trinity is restored. Past and future are indeed folded together in the present of this poem, but the reader is left the bemused spectator of a bucolic round.

If Merwin were to issue a selection of poems, this text should surely be included, not because it is a good poem—it isn't—but because it is dissatisfied with its own inadequacy. The poem's restlessness prepares us for the great shift in his technique. As the epigraph for *The Dancing Bears,* Merwin chose Flaubert's observation (here in Richard Howard's translation) that "human speech is like a cracked kettle on which we pound out tunes fit to make bears dance, when what we want is to win over the stars." As Howard points out, this is "the ironical sign . . . under which Merwin inscribes his elegance and his eloquence."[5] As an epigraph for this book, the quotation is mostly a gratuitous afterthought, the kind of precious disavowal that both distances and protects; he is not yet troubled by the self-conscious element in verbal artifice. The epigraph is really a bridge to the next two collections and their genuine anguish at the limitations of his language. "The stars," he will write, "that came with us this far have gone back" (*MT,* 32). And more poignantly, "the stars do not believe in each other" (*CL,* 136); when their light reaches us, they are already dead.

There is a lesson here for those reviewers who are unhappy that Merwin's most recent poems reflect some self-imitation. Stylistic consistency often edges toward self-imitation—a fact that many contemporary authors have consciously exploited. Yet Merwin has managed to use this sometimes fruitless reflexiveness to force substantial changes in his style. Each of his stylistic metamorphoses has followed from a self-conscious craft that turned into self-parody and even revulsion, a process perhaps more complex, though no more anguished, than Rich's deliberate rejection of formal perfection in the 1960s. I would sing, he wrote in one of the elaborate love poems at the end of *The Dancing Bears,* "till you have become / The poem in whose arbor we may kiss," but the air of impossibility has already invaded the quest: "in the fraying / Edges of patience the teased harpies / Hone the incredible silence against their tongues" (*DB,* 82, 83). Not so surprisingly, we open the next volume to the unpretentious futility of the dedicatory poem: "In this world how little can

5. *Alone With America: Essays on the Art of Poetry in the United States Since 1950* (New York: Atheneum, 1969), p. 361.

be communicated" (*GB,* 5). He proceeds, in the next poem, "past bone-wreck of vessels, / Tide-ruin, wash of lost bodies bobbing" (*GB,* 11), and the resources of the sea bring the book full circle and carry him into the opening poems of *The Drunk in the Furnace.* But there the florid rhetoric, with its echoes of Dylan Thomas, is at war with its empty subject: "Virtues / That had borne us thus far turned on us, peopling / The lashed plains of our minds with hollow voices" (*DF,* 6).

The most significant features of *The Drunk in the Furnace* are its melancholy, more discursive and less at ease with itself than in his first book, and its self-deprecatory and liberating comedy. The melancholy lacks the force it will have when it find its true, eroded form. We learn of the fated circularity of Odysseus's journey, of the foghorn that calls "to something men had forgotten, / That stirs under fog" (*DF,* 3), and of a ship that had passed by the poem's speaker only a few hours before going down in a storm (the old notion of being brushed unknowingly by disaster). The poems are competent, but too self-consciously thoughtful. The wildly ironic poems in the book are closer to the roots of the change at work in Merwin's career. In "Fable" a man clinging to the top branch of a tree accepts the advice of a passerby who says he must save himself by jumping, because the tree is falling. He is killed in the fall, and the passerby kindly remarks to the corpse that he really let himself drop because he wanted to die. The macabre is also evident in the story of the one-eyed man, king in the country of the blind, who so tires of describing the visible world to his subjects that at the end he does not even mention "the black thumb as big as a valley" descending on them out of the sky (*DF,* 35).

Two poems are especially relevant to Merwin's next book. In "Sailor Ashore" a drunk's vision reveals ironically "what unsteady ways the solid earth has / After all" (*DF,* 7). There follows, masked with buffoonery, the kind of unnerving perception so frequent in Merwin's work since *The Moving Target:* "the sea is everywhere. / But worst here where it is secret and pretends / To keep its mountains in one place." The drunk's classic perception of the animacy of inanimate objects and forces anticipates what will become one of

Merwin's characteristic syntactic and semantic devices.

The final poem in the book, which is also the title poem, is an irrevocable perspective on his work to that point. An empty iron furnace rusts in a trash-ridden gully by a poisonous creek, until a derelict decides to make it his "bad castle." He brings his bottle, bolts the door behind him, and carouses in drunken solitude until he passes out. Written in careful septets, the poem's formal concern for a frivolous occasion mocks all the sonorities of Merwin's previous books. The poem ends with a description of the local adults listening to warnings from their preacher, while their children crowd to the irresistible furnace:

> Their witless offspring flock like piped rats to its siren
> Crescendo, and agape on the crumbling ridge
> Stand in a row and learn. [DF, 54]

With this burlesque of all his own overwrought rhetoric, Merwin can never return to his earlier style. It is a deliberate aggression.

This rebirth out of willful failure is a singularly American trait. It is common to many of our foremost poets, and crucial to many ruined or limited careers whose poetry nevertheless holds us. Of the several hundred poems Merwin has published since 1960, many do not succeed; some, like the run-on Beckettian sentence of "Fear" (CL, 83-86), are simply not appropriate to his new form. A few, like "Line" (CF, 26), which describes the ritual interactions in a supermarket line, deal with prosaic topics that resist Merwin's powers of transformation and thus become comic. Many, like most of his short prose pieces, seem glibly designed to indulge a lazy audience's pleasure in effortless and unspecific mystery. Others demand too much of themselves and of their readers, as when Merwin—like Rich in "Not Somewhere Else, But Here" in *The Dream of a Common Language* and Duncan in "The Fire" in *Bending The Bow*—tries to render a series of unconnected images into a condition of heightened apprehension: "an end a wise man fire / other stars the left hand" (WA, 101). Many, such as the haiku-like fragments in "Signs" (CL, 116-

18), pale before the overwhelming power of his best work. Yet the production, like Whitman's work, is a single enterprise; the volumes beginning with *The Moving Target* are all one book. The poems reflect one another endlessly, repeat the same messages tirelessly, clarify one another and simultaneously complicate one another until no image can ever be resolved.

It is not merely that we must judge the body of poems entire. It is rather, as with Rich, that the finest poems are always in dialogue with the worst. Though new subjects are frequently introduced, many of the major poems use a vocabulary (silence, emptiness, distance, darkness, whiteness, death) and create images with words (gloves, hands, eyes, feet, shoes, water, birds, mirrors, sky, trees, nests, wings) whose familiarity surpasses a verbal signature and becomes almost a form of self-betrayal. What we experience in the best poems is a cohesion *despite* this omnipresent diction. These poems wrest themselves from their rhetorical ground and make themselves simultaneously unique and typical. Merwin exploits the most impossible fact of language—that words and images are riddled with received meaning and historical context. Like Kenneth Burke, Merwin believes that language is not merely a web of connotations but also a structured source of motivation. Unlike Burke and Duncan, however, Merwin does not feel that play amidst these verbal connections will be liberating. Language is already a democratic resource, but it is suffocating. Our words speak through us to override any fresh use we may have for them. "On the way to them," he writes, "the words / Die" (*L,* 7); they are used, given, and they will not live for us. "I can put my words into the mouths / of spirits," he tells us, "but they will not say them" (*CL,* 17).

Merwin is not the first to have wrestled in this way with poetic tradition; indeed, his first books are damaged by influences never made truly his own. Merwin is, however, unique in so daringly disclosing the echolalic qualities of his own language. Beckett and Burroughs, along with many younger novelists, have taken that risk in prose, but our preconceptions about the formal integrity of poems make the choice more difficult there. Because of those expectations, the ironic formal repetition and verbal self-subversion so common in experi-

mental fiction have yet to be attempted with much success in contemporary poetry.[6] Moreover, most open-form contemporary American poetry retains some Whitmanesque hope of projecting an ideally
open and democratic society. Merwin's open forms, however, have
succeeded in mirroring the loss of any real historical possibility. Unlike those poems of the 1960s that are grounded in a reaction against
historical actuality, or even those poems that seem to be victimized
by history, Merwin's poems manage to give our history its most
frightening voice. The revolution in Merwin's style must, then, be
understood as an exacting and necessary discipline, one which is
highly responsive to the general political environment. (A specific
example is his decision, two-thirds of the way through *The Moving
Target* and again early in *The Lice,* to abandon all punctuation.[7])
This discipline is undertaken, somewhat like Beckett's decision to
write in French, in the face of considerable self-doubt and a sensitivity
to the supremely self-conscious state of language in this historical
moment. He recognizes that poetry exhibits some of the most terrible
and most transcendent dreams identified with American culture. "Is it
with speech," he asks, that "you combed out your voice till the ends
bled" (*L*, 39). "In / our language deaths are to be heard / at any
moment through the talk" (*CL*, 56). To give voice to those deaths,
as Eliot did in *The Waste Land* and as Merwin has succeeded in doing, is to become for a moment the single voice of an age.

Merwin's failures are parings essential to the carving of that central voice. A device which works in one volume (such as the twice-

6. For an analysis of the relationship between Merwin's poetry and contemporary fiction, see Evan Watkins, "W. S. Merwin: A Critical Accompaniment," *Boundary 2, 4,* No. 1 (Fall 1975), 187-99.
7. Eliminating punctuation allows for some special effects that might be
more self-conscious in a conventionally punctuated poem. Occasionally he will
let the last line of a stanza bleed off into empty space: "but when she opened
it" (*CL*, 126). Alternatively, he can limit that uncertainty with the following
line, in this case the first line of the next stanza: "Someone has just / but no
sound reaches the gate" (*CL*, 36). He will frequently embed a quotation
within a line, without distinguishing punctuation, so that what would ordinarily be isolated seems instead to emerge inexorably from the preceding
words: "I hear the cry go up for him Caesar Caesar" (*L*, 19); "I have
prayed O wounds come back from death / and be healed" (*CL*, 96).

repeated words which come to fruition as a technique in *The Lice*) is
exorcised by repeated use in the next. Obviously latent possibilities,
which we expect to find but which we know will not convince us,
appear in the poetry, as if they must ritually be undone:

> there is no memory
> except the smoke writing *wait*
> *wai*
> *w* [CL, 101]

We can excuse this as an amusing visual game, but it will nonetheless
persist in our memories as a reduction of Merwin's whole enterprise,
a reduction which is therefore implicit throughout his work. Even
that value judgment, however, cannot be maintained complacently,
for in the same poem he revises an older image and raises it to a new
level of discovery:

> the white
> invisible stars they also
> writing
>
> and unable to read

Merwin often generates one splendid line in an otherwise ordinary
poem that leaves us indifferent to the quality of the rest. And some
poems introduce images weakly, only to have them fulfilled some
pages later. Such conflicting levels of quality within a single poem are
not in themselves problematic or unusual. But neither individual lines
nor individual poems are very easy to isolate from the surrounding
intertext of Merwin's output. His best poems are still those that cohere, though they achieve their formal integrity by dominating a
score of comparable metaphors which work from other poems to
undo the internal relations. That achievement, perhaps we should say
counter-achievement, reverses what we ordinarily expect to experience
through poetic form. It has the effect of an aggression against the
core assumptions of New Criticism. It also serves as an attempt to
displace the modernist revolution and relocate it in the present moment. The disruptions and discontinuities of *The Waste Land* reap-

pear in Merwin's poetry without recourse to any mythic synthesis and with little implied priority for the poetic text itself.[8]

These accomplishments might seem of small consequence, if they were not so closely tied to a sense of a surrounding culture. With each of Merwin's formal self-subversions, we sense our mutual destiny at work in his poetry. If the hesitance, the repetitiveness, and the runic suggestiveness of his poetry border on preciosity, the fault seems to be ours as well as his. We cannot, in effect, fault him with inadequacies he seems to have drawn out of the language we share. Thus his failed poems are important precisely because they

> Appear
> not as what they are
> but as what prevents them   [*CL*, 118]

"It has taken me this long," he writes, "to know what I cannot say" (*CL*, 28); this is a universal silence—visionary, figural, and full of its own throttled speech. Only Merwin could dare to give us "and when" as an entire last stanza (*WA*, 109); it is intolerable, of course, but we knew such a provisional gesture was imminent in our language, so we are relieved to have it taken from us, to see it written. "My words," he writes, "are the garment of what I shall never be / Like the tucked sleeve of a one-armed boy" (*L*, 62). This takes to its conclusion an impulse present in each of the four preceding poets— to achieve in poetry a vision of selfhood not yet possible in actual life. Merwin, however, gives the goal its true historical futility, for

---

8. Eliot's influence on Merwin could be the subject of a separate essay, but I should at least note that the relationship goes beyond the ambience of *The Waste Land*. It extends to similarities in diction and rhythm, to the point where Merwin seems to have deconstructed the early Eliot. Thus Eliot's "the bone's prayer to Death its God" seems almost to belong more properly to Merwin, whereas Merwin's "in this country of stone and dark dew" seems as though it should be returned to Eliot. On the other hand, Eliot's "rats' feet over broken glass" and Merwin's "Large brotherhood of broken stones" could be inserted into poems by either of them. Consider this sequence of lines: "I can hear the blood crawling over the plains" (Merwin); "Over endless plains, stumbling in cracked earth" (Eliot); "its horizon beyond which nothing is known" (Merwin); "Ringed by the flat horizon only" (Eliot); "the horizon I was making for runs through my eyes" (Merwin).

the vision now "shall never be." The words of this vision, never consummated in speech, remain at the edge of each unsatisfied utterance.
They are not merely his words, he insists; they are not centered in
some unique selfhood verbally achieved. They are our words, and he
is merely their agent. This role is common to the prophetic impulse in
American poetry since Whitman, but it finds in Merwin its most
anonymous and universal incarnation.[9] "It would be enough," Merwin says, "for me to know / who is writing this" (*CL*, 35). In most
other poets this Borgesian comment would simply be mystical. We
only tolerate Yeats's claim and its attendant system because of the
poetry it produced. Yet Merwin's poetry is so close to the destiny of
the language he uses—to the pressure the words themselves exercise
toward their day of witness—that we must entertain the notion of a

---

9. Merwin generally eliminates personal references from his poetry even
when he knows a poem to have part of its impetus in a particular event in his
life. At a reading (University of Illinois, February 4, 1974) Merwin commented that "My Friends" (*MT*, 80-81) was based on a demonstration at
the San Francisco Post Office in support of the people who had sailed into a
nuclear test site. "My friends without shields walk on the target" becomes a
quite specific reference in that context, gaining a particular poignancy and
some political force but losing some of its broad power to threaten us with a
universal image of a meticulously targeted vulnerability. Similarly, at a more
recent reading (Beloit College, April 3, 1981) Merwin introduced "Before
That" (*MT*, 69-70) by talking about the kind of urban renewal that wan-
tonly destroys our architectural heritage. He glossed the "City unhealthy pale
with pictures of/cemeteries sifting on its windows" by telling the audience
that white crosses are painted on buildings about to be demolished. For an
audience familiar with Merwin's poetry the effect of restoring this kind of
referentiality is partly deflationary and reductive. Moreover, the suggestion
that his poetry is grounded in a narrow kind of referentiality is misleading
to the extent that it directs our attention away from the poetry as a writing
practice. Yet the poetry itself resists a reductive reading, in effect asserting
its own plural, aggressive, ironic relation to referentiality. Merwin's impulse in
introducing his poetry in this way is therefore likely to be equally ambivalent.
The impulse is partly a friendly effort to make the poems accessible and to
provide relief from a reading's intensity. Yet the poem itself will then force
an open, apocalyptic reading of its referent. Thus the introductory comment
at once betrays the poem and proves that it cannot be betrayed. This double
quality can be most easily demonstrated by citing Merwin's rather different
introduction of "The Last One" (*L*, 10-12) : "I wish it would become so un-
topical that no one would understand it at all."

collective will: "Again this procession of the speechless / Bringing me their words" (*MT*, 97).

"Looking for Mushrooms at Sunrise" (*L*, 80) offers a fine image of poetry as a response to necessities inhering in language itself. As in many of the most effective poems in *The Lice,* he retains the sense of a specific topic, while simultaneously making the poem reflect the mood and vocabulary of the rest of his work. Before dawn, he walks "on centuries of dead chestnut leaves": the surface of the earth is a matrix of every depleted past. It is "a place without grief," seemingly with no human consciousness present to it:

> In the dark while the rain fell
> The gold chanterelles pushed through a sleep that was not mine
> Waking me
> So that I came up the mountain to find them

No sleep, he suggests, is entirely our own; we dream collectively. Our speech then flows from the reservoir of things said. The soft, almost shapeless thrust of new mushrooms rising through darkness is a perfect image of the half-awakened consciousness. But the stanza goes further, hinting that our sleep is not exclusively human, that our sleep is the earth's sleep. So the search for mushrooms is also part of a waning hope that mute, essential substances will continue speaking to us in the light. The day seems familiar, as though the landscape were a tapestry woven of past anticipations: "I recognize their haunts as though remembering / Another life." The poem ends in a spirit of unsettled possibility. It resonates in the mind until we choose to break with it. The conclusion is full of pathos controlled both by verbal economy and by hope indistinguishable from anxiety. "Where else am I walking even now," he writes—and the metrical pause before the next line seems endless—"Looking for me."

These poems have a tone of quiet prophecy, as though the final whimper Eliot foretold continues to dwindle forever. In "The Room" (*L,* 48), he writes of a frail survivor whose apparently approaching death is really the imprint of inexhaustible renewal. Of course one version of poetic renewal is reading. Thus "The Room" is also about our reading the poem. "I," therefore, is not only a poet speaking; the

pronoun belongs equally to the reader, and "all this" is the text he contemplates:

> I think all this is somewhere in myself
> The cold room unlit before dawn
> Containing a stillness such as attends death
> And from a corner the sounds of a small bird trying
> From time to time to fly a few beats in the dark
> You would say it was dying it is immortal

Finality, for Merwin, is endlessly repeatable. If we are, as Olson writes, the "last 'first' people," we may continue in that role forever. That conviction begins in Merwin's earlier work with his narratives pursuing silence and emptiness, then matures in his later work to where it no longer needs narrative support. Distance and vacuity are eventually inescapable conditions of all presence: "The horizon I was making for runs through my eyes. / It has woven its simple nest among my bones" (*MT*, 10). This is an image of consciousness alienated from its own substance. We have "been made," Merwin writes in lines that echo with increased fatalism Olson's sense of the constitutive role of space in American culture, "Of distances that would not again be ours" (*L*, 74). Eventually, this image of selfhood as embodying communal absence brings him to attempt poems of considerable presence which have no apparent subject at all. In *The Moving Target* and *The Lice*, however, he first explores the tonality of the void, at the same time linking it to a sense of history as an untraceable but pervasive disease.

"December Among the Vanished" (*L*, 45) is one of the major poems addressed to the texture of absence:

> The old snow gets up and moves taking its
> Birds with it
>
> The beasts hide in the knitted walls
> From the winter that lipless man
> Hinges echo but nothing opens
>
> A silence before this one
> Has left its broken huts facing the pastures

> Through their stone roofs the snow
> And the darkness walk down
>
> In one of them I sit with a dead shepherd
> And watch his lambs

The atmosphere of this poem offers snow, but no reviving moisture. Change is only loss; the snow "gets up"—it drifts or evaporates with the insistence of inanimate force, the winter birds (or their tracks) following its course. The beasts hiding in knitted walls anticipate the unprotected sheep of the last stanza, since we may take "knitted walls" as an image of sheep's coats, but the phrase also suggests predators in a forest, or even an animal furtiveness inhering in all matter, as when he wrote of "the night green with beasts as April with grass" (*GB*, 15). In any case, the sense of threat and tension is clear. The winter is a "lipless man," sere and skeletal. The next line, "Hinges echo but nothing opens," is intended to be a complete sentence; the rattling door frames, or even the hinge of potential seasonal change, are the empty vestiges of possibilities now extinct. Yet Merwin's unpunctuated poems often create syntactical ambiguities, so we may also read that "lipless man Hinges" echo the winter. But this human presence, perhaps the hinged jaws of a skull, can neither speak nor alter the landscape. The second stanza begins with an image of broken huts, belonging by virtue of their common origin to a silence receding into the past. We cannot remember if this silence once followed Armageddon; we suspect that it has a historical cause, but we can no longer isolate one. The lines also imply, more metaphorically, that even silence is now unhoused, even nothingness is exposed and unprotected. The pastures are no vista of openness but an encroaching distance. There are no barriers against fortune; with insensible willfulness, the snow and darkness "walk" down through shattered roofs. Everything is penetrated by loss.

The poem to this point is directed toward the last lines, where the tension becomes intolerable. They are among the most anguished lines in contemporary poetry, and their pain has no outlet. In one of those vacant huts, he writes, "I sit with a dead shepherd / And watch his lambs." The ceremony of shepherding is gone out of the world,

whether that of gods or of men; the lambs are born too late to understand their danger. The poem's tone makes the speaker seem a powerless witness, brought forward to watch in paralysis. Yet the resonances of the final verb are very complicated. "Watch" suggests not only mere observation but also protective vigilance, as in "watch over." We are not, however, convinced that the speaker could intervene if the lambs were threatened. The verb also implies the watch kept over the dead, an association which makes the lambs appear even more helpless. What is definitely missing here, what will never return, is the particular, secure relationship between the shepherd and his flock, a relationship ordinarily renewed each December. The act of writing the poem is perhaps an act of witness, though the poet cannot quite become the new shepherd. Inevitably, too, our own loyalties are torn. We yearn to reach out and care for the lambs, but we are also part of that flock whose shepherd is dead.

In a larger sense, the poem itself is very nearly paralyzed. As the poem proceeds, its imagery is filled out, its emotional resonance intensified and newly dramatized, but the poem is also nothing more than another fragment of the world *The Lice* has evoked for forty pages. From that perspective, its broad tonal consistency suggests stasis rather than creative variation. Like so many of Merwin's recent poems, or like Rich's "Shooting Script," it is a sequence of equivalences impinging on one another; if there is a definitive key to their similarities, the poem both desires and evades it. Even the title, "December Among the Vanished," straddles redundancy and contradiction—suggesting at once a double extinction and the inconceivable winter of those no longer present.

Many of Merwin's poems do not develop through logical or syntactical progression. They proceed by accretion. Syntax sometimes connects lines and occasionally stanzas, but even syntactical progression is often deliberately subverted by line breaks at awkward points within clauses. The impulse to speak is always threatened by closure; the poem at any moment may abort itself into silence. Indeed, many of Merwin's poems seem to end more than once. Often, when the poem reaches the bottom of a page, the internal evidence combines with the physical layout to suggest the poem has concluded. Yet we can only be certain after turning the page. New Criticism has trained us to take the published text as final. Yet with this poet we must admit that even his more tightly organized poems could easily be expanded with lines or stanzas from other poems. Similarly, many poems could be cut or rearranged without necessarily altering their effect. This verbal equalization, the ultimate opening and democratization of form, is entirely appropriate to Merwin's vision. All the poems since *The Moving Target* may be read as though they were written simultaneously—in the winter of an eternal present.

All seasons, for Merwin, have winter at their core. There is no longer any cruelest month: "April April / Sinks through the sand of names" (*L*, 29). Seasonal change and historical occurrence extend desolation to each new moment. Of spring he writes: "The dead bowmen buried these many years / Are setting out again" (*MT*, 96); they are in motion, but we cannot assume they are alive. When the walnuts fall to the road and split open in the autumn, he observes: "Here is the small brain of our extinct summer. / Already it remembers nothing" (*MT*, 32). "Extinction," he writes, is "my ancestor" (*MT*, 74); with each arrival, "once more I remember that the beginning / Is broken" (*L*, 24). Time in Merwin has been entirely spatialized. We have finally been given that spatial absolution that haunts so much of American literature since the nineteenth century; our history has been given over to a geography of omnipresent distance. "Seeing how it goes," he writes, "I see how it will be" (*MT*, 49); "the past" is "like a day / that would burn unmoved forever" (*WA*, 20). The present is neither a point of departure nor even an origin true to itself; it is merely that eventfulness in which both past and future recur. "We are the echo of the future" (*L*, 33). "The present" is "a wax bell in a wax belfry" (*MT*, 81); in it, "the future woke me with its silence" (*MT*, 97). When he says, "I am the son of the future but my own father" (*CL*, 92), he points to no romantic rebellion against a paternally-imposed destiny, but rather to the self-conscious irony with which he recreates the inevitable. "I am the son of ruins already among us" (*CL*, 96).

Appropriately, then, Merwin's poetry is always called post-

apocalyptic. The term is frequently applied to contemporary literature, but it requires some elaboration before it will exactly fit Merwin's vision. Like the silence in "December Among the Vanished,"
the holocaust that leveled our sense of possibility cannot be named
or dated. Moreover, even the most tangible of present events lose
their outlines rapidly. Those few of Merwin's poems that retain specific historical references, such as "The Asians Dying," which I discuss
in the first chapter, demonstrate how history disappears by infiltrating
everything. Not only, however, do such poems individually recount
the loss of historical awareness; each is surrounded by poems virtually
identical in tone and import that have no traceable historical refer-
ents. Thus the quality of particular historical events is dissipated and
generalized as soon as we read any quantity of Merwin's poetry.
Finally, though Merwin's desolate landscapes are unquestionably post-
apocalyptic, they are also pervaded with a sense of uneasy expectation.
The apocalypse in our past survives only as a kind of vague dread, as
if it were only about to occur. If "it is / the broken windows that
look to the future" (CL, 87), then the air of impending doom is
undercut when we realize the windows are already broken. "It had
been many years," he writes, "since the final prophet had felt the hand
of the future how it had no weight" (L, 13). Both our dreams of
transcendence and our dreams of disaster are false sympathies, maudlin and self-serving dramas. "I am sure now," he writes in "Glimpse
of the Ice" (L, 46), death is "a light under the skin coming nearer."
Yet the death will never occur; even if it has already happened we
are unable to move beyond it. Post-apocalyptic, surely, but obsessed
with "The End / That great god . . . Leaving behind it the future /
Dead" (L, 68). Moreover, the sense of a faded apocalypse in Merwin
is distinctly American. It transcends the conventional references to
the Nazi holocaust and to nuclear war to refer more broadly to a sense
in America that our origin and continuing presence as a people is
apocalyptic. We live in the midst of a resolution we cannot possess,
we "sit in the dark praying as one silence / for the resurrection" (CL,
37). Again and again, we rush forward to come into the emptiness of
ourselves; we reach out to embrace our special destination. "We run /

down onto the wharf named / for us" but "the harbor is empty"
(*WA,* 38) :

> . . . our gravestones are blowing
> like clouds backward
> through time to find us
> they sail over us through us
> back to lives that waited
> for us
>
> and we never knew [*WA,* 38]

This is the end of a poem, and its rhythm is part of the poem's communication. The onrushing tempo builds, hesitates, and then expends
itself in indecision. Many of Merwin's last lines are like that, intentionally undercutting the mounting energy, delivered almost flatly.
In other cases, the final touch is heavier, and the content tends to be
anticipatory, creating a new beginning rather than a conclusion. Such
incomplete beginnings leave us hanging with nowhere to go, for the
poem is at an end. The two characteristic methods move us from different directions toward the same stasis. Occasionally, he manages
both effects at once. "Come back" (*L,* 76) ends with a line without
period or question mark: "Is it the same way there"—a line that is
thus both query and statement. Our absolution is everywhere around
us, but it is like water which "flows through its / Own fingers without
end" (*L,* 43). So Merwin can dedicate a poem to "The Anniversary
of My Death," an uncertain day he can celebrate every morning. That
day will arrive like the constant beam of a star already extinguished.
Another poem of dedication is titled "For the Grave of Posterity"
(*MT,* 71). The poem celebrates a "stone that is / not here and bears
no writing"; the stone "commemorates / the emptiness at the end
of / history." The conclusion, properly without final punctuation, is
one of vague erasure in the guise of finality: "Whatever it could
have said of you is already forgotten."

Each of the dead, Merwin writes, offers us his message: "*I know
nothing / learn of me*" (*CL,* 51). It is also the message of each of
his poems. In a little prose statement titled "On Open Form," Merwin
speculates rather paradoxically about a poetry whose forms are each

uniquely anonymous; each form is to have "an unduplicatable resonance, something that would be like an echo except that it is repeating
no sound."[10] In "To Where We Are" (*MT*, 61), he concludes with
a description of "our neighbors" that is also an invocation to his
readers:

> Natives of now, creatures of
> One song,
> Their first, their last,
>
> Listen.

The poetry he has written, since that moment of self-reflexive laughter
in *The Drunk in the Furnace*, has been poetry of this univocal, de-
moniacally democratic song. Its forms are wholly unhinged; they are
a species of "Nothing / On which doors were opening" (*L*, 20).

One of the foremost of these poems is "Beginning" (*CL*, 123):

> Long before spring
> king of the black cranes
> rises one day
> from the black
> needle's eye
> on the white plain
> under the white sky
>
> the crown turns
> and the eye
> drilled clear through his head
> turns
> it is north everywhere
> come out he says
>
> come out then
> the light is not yet
> divided

---

10. *Naked Poetry*, ed. Stephen Berg and Robert Mezey (Indianapolis and
New York: Bobbs-Merrill Co., 1969), pp. 270-72.

it is a long way
to the first
anything
come even so
we will start
bring your nights with you

One early source for this poem is Merwin's "The Frozen Sea" (*DF*, 6), a poem about antarctic exploration and about the human experience of that landscape. The ice and snow are "the very flesh / No different only colder, as was / The sea itself"; they reflect a "whiteness that we could not bear. It / Turned bloody in our carnal eyes." The wind there shrieks of a violent purification; it would "freeze out / The mortal flaw in us." Its "screaming silence" fills the explorers' minds with hollow animal voices that boast "their / Guts would feed on God." The absolute whiteness and sheer antagonism of the setting invoke comparable human extremes—transcendence and violence. The men are at the center of a vortex; they are so small, these figures "around whom the howling / World turned." Only "a soulless needle" can tell them where they are, though even the magnetic compass is useless near the poles, where the dipping needle stands vertical. They have come to a point of origin that inversely suggests closure. Merwin describes this journey to whiteness in lines he will later directly echo in "Beginning": we have come, he writes, "to the pure south, and whichever way we turned / Was north, the sides of the north, everywhere." The choices of direction are infinite, but they are all the same. With the sides of the north surrounding them, they are not liberated but confined. Time seems to have stopped; it awaits only the imprint of the law. In a poem called "The Present" (*MT,* 51), he writes: "The walls join hands and / It is tomorrow."

"Beginning" realizes the figural potential of the earlier poem. The ambiguous title, without the restricting definite article, is at once noun, verb, and adjective; it makes this creation-poem co-extensive with all time. It is an eschatology of origins; it binds the course of history to a single core of emptiness. The landscape is again pure whiteness—a white plain under a white sky, possibly separated by the thin seam of the horizon, but perhaps not distinguishable at all. Yet this whiteness is not of substance but of essence; like the sun, it

"hangs / in a cage of light" (*CL*, 96). The poem begins "long before spring," which sets it not only before the first spring or the first
birth, but also as a seed or source within every renewal. The poem's
distance is one of inaccessible proximity; within us and outside time,
its beginning is a true origin—an end.

Within these hemispheres of light is, like the germ of the poem's
movement, a black needle's eye. The image of the needle's eye combines a sense of the compass, its needle now ascending directly out of
its center, with an allusion to Christ's words, "It is easier for a camel
to go through the eye of a needle, than for a rich man to enter the
kingdom of God." The biblical reference occurs in three earlier poems
about Merwin's grandparents (*DF*, 41-44), as in his grandmother's
belief that you could get "through . . . the needle's eye if / You made
up your mind straight and narrow." The needle's eye is a nexus for
these past connections and also an image of vision as a rite of passage.
As he writes later in "The Way Ahead" (*WA*, 63):

> An eye is to come
>   to what was never seen
>   the beginning opening
>   and beholding the end
>   falling into it

Out of this eye, whose pupil is a doorway into the nothingness of
all things, out of this eye which is his nest, rises the king of the
black cranes. Metaphorically, kingship here suggests that he is the
foremost of his kind, selected to bear a destiny of dark flight. Merwin
may be aware of the legend alluded to in Christian art that there is
indeed a king of the cranes whom the other cranes, each standing on
one foot to stay awake, encircle and guard as he sleeps at night. If the
legend is relevant here, it can add another dimension to the nest
image: the king of the cranes rises out of pre-existent watchfulness.
In both Western and Eastern art the crane is frequently a positive
symbol of justice, vigilance, loyalty, and good works. In Egyptian
iconography the crane is associated with the ibis-headed god Thoth,
spokesman and arbiter for the gods, patron of wisdom and the arts,

and inventor of writing.[11] Yet the crane is also known in a wide range of myths as a sly and wily bird, whose enticements to humans are offered in duplicity. So the crane, dark lord over the bleached plain at the beginning and the end of time, here, at least, is an ambivalent figure.

His crown turns, and his indifferent gaze falls on us. His gaze is empty; it is only a hollow cylinder through which the white landscape is focused. The eye is "drilled clear through his head"; it is an image familiar to us from modern sculpture, a more ruthless version also of the drilled eyes in ancient Greek sculpture. The image is startlingly mechanical, like a periscope or a gun turret. As the eye turns, it progressively renders the crane's whole head empty. The image of the crane's eye is a verbal successor to the black needle's eye in the first stanza. This vacant stare, the eye through which white light fills his black head, makes the opposite colors equivalent. It heralds the collapse of all alternatives, although it is proffered to us as a first moment when distinction is only a perceiving eye moving through uniform white light. "Come out," the crane encourages, "it is north everywhere." In Merwin's work, such enticements are double-edged. "Well they'd made up their minds to be everywhere because why not," he writes in "The Last One" (L, 10); the line presages an empty possessiveness that will cover the earth. Come out, he reasons, and we are tempted, as with his power of flight, by an image of the end disguised as a new beginning. If the light is not yet divided, then we need not fear our own darkness; it will be transparent. If it is north everywhere, then every failure will be an ascent, every cruelty a transfiguration. Come out, the crane demands, we shall now make everything in our image; we no longer need know ourselves at all. Dream, the crane suggests, that no things are yet to

---

11. Carol Kyle, "A Riddle for the New Year: Affirmation in W. S. Merwin," *Modern Poetry Studies,* 4, No. 3 (Winter 1973), 288-303, mentions the possible reference to Thoth. Her reading of "Beginning" argues that the poem is essentially affirmative. Kyle also finds Merwin's series of cultural avatars — figures like Columbus or John Wesley Powell — to be entirely affirmative. Since Merwin uses these men as figures for American initiatives that have failed or turned demonic, I find her reading inexplicable.

be seen; thus everything can be undone. "Everything that does not
need you," Merwin wrote earlier, "is real" (*L,* 35). But these things
can be undone. It is a long way before anything will happen, and the
crane's offhand "come even so" is the sardonic justification for the
death we would want anyway. When "the first / anything" appears
it will occur under the sign of everything. "Bring your nights with
you," he commands, as though we had any intention of doing otherwise, as though we had any choice. These "nights" are composed of
the darkness we have inside us even in the brightest light. From the
black needle's eye, our shadow rises to fall over the earth. "Beginning" extends the American myth of a second chance to a dream of
a decisive chance—an opportunity to eliminate all uncertainty. Moreover, we may feel uneasily that we have already made the choice, for
the crane's invitation, past the mid-point of "Beginning," also reads
like a belated invitation to encounter the poem, one we accepted in
venturing forth to read.

The poem seems inexorable, yet its form is almost dismantled. Its
achievement is to pursue its own deconstruction with sufficient discipline to triumph over it. Full of long pauses, particularly in the last
stanza, it has been pushed to the point of faltering. Although a narrative line is maintained throughout, it is reduced virtually to a series
of isolated images. Whiteness, blackness, emptiness—the poem pivots
about a hollow center which is nonetheless human. It comes almost
as close as a poem can to containing nothing; yet it is broadly prophetic, cohering through a coldly democratic generosity that summons all subjects. It attempts to be, and largely succeeds as, an
allegory of all situations.

Into its resolving emptiness "Beginning" draws all the political and
social poems from *The Moving Target* to *The Carrier of Ladders.*
There are no overt references to American history here, but the anguished mixture of loss and hope at the core of poems like "The Trail
Into Kansas," "Western Country," "Other Travelers to the River,"
and "The Gardens of Zuñi," the last two addressed respectively to
William Bartram and John Wesley Powell, culminates in this poem
of ultimate beginnings and endings. In effect, "the black heart of

Andrew Jackson" (CL, 50) is traced here to its abstract origin outside any ordinary sequence of events. But the poem is also radically
anticipatory, bringing America's first and last dreams together. Thus
"Beginning" also generalizes Merwin's merciless vision of American
history as the representative eschatology of our times. Through the
tunnel of the crane's eye pass our celebrations, our songs, our pronouncements of victory and glory, and our incessant violence. A few
years earlier, Merwin had written two bitterly sardonic lines indict-
ing and connecting everything that is best and worst in us: "The
beating on the bars of the cages / Is caught and parcelled out to the
bells" (MT, 87). By the time we get to "Beginning," however, the
reciprocal halves of this social contract have coalesced into a single
wave of sound. Our complicity with our leaders, or our enthusiasm
for them (and there are no other choices), is a convulsive "applause
like the heels of the hanged" (CL, 57). In a poem like "Beginning"
the cultural accusation is implicit in the metaphors of sight and light
and darkness, worked into that vocabulary in such a way that it cannot be extricated. Thus we hear echoes of his earlier political judgments ("You born with the faces of presidents on your eyelids," he
wrote, "and your lies elected"—MT, 93, 94) even in this language,
which is reduced to its bare essentials.

This harsh analysis of all of us began, in Merwin's early poetry,
with a heavy irony directed toward his own verbal excesses. It has left
him, even now, with a sense of guilt about formal accomplishment.
He is one of the very few good poets to consider aesthetic satisfaction
not the highest of all emotions, but almost a herd instinct born of
fear. There is, of course, no scarcity of poets who reject the notion
that the individual poem has to prove itself. The result is most often
poetry of little verbal interest; even those more talented poets who
take that position, like Duncan and Rich, regularly produce weak
poetry as a result. Merwin, however, has realized the necessity of
taking meticulous care in deconstructing his poems. Moreover, he
has understood the place of a fascination with failed visions in
America's controlling myths. So in all his poems we hear the collective movement of our culture's language toward its ends. "How
many things," he muses, "come to one name / hoping to be fed"

(*CL*, 131); his poetry continually names, but the relief we feel in naming and being named is either pathetic or despicable. "By the time you read this," he writes, and he is willfully playing with his reader, "it is dark on the next page" (*CL*, 131). He has a tendency to give us less and less in his poetry, to demand ever more of us as readers. There is no poet of comparable talent whose work is so exhausting to read; each thing given becomes meaningful only when taken away.

Merwin's poems become a mirror for all of us, one we thought we wanted, but the glass gives no comfort; in it we see the "cold lakes / from which our eyes were made" (*WA*, 42). Yet even that relief, for the vision of our own evil is tantalizing in its finality, is denied us. In his recent work the mirror invites hysteria. In "Glass" (*WA*, 107), a mirror opens and "where the eyes were" is a gray road with a little figure running away. It is Alice's story with a shrill edge to it, for there is no secure return. The figures suddenly multiply, as though the anonymous men who hang like suspended rain in Magritte's famous painting "Golconde" (1953)[12] began to flail in uncontrolled descent: "with their backs to you and their arms in the air / and no shadows." All the visible world flees with them, the stones, the birds, the dust—symbols also in Merwin's art—and it seems "all your terrors" are "running away from you." But it is, he writes almost amusedly, "too late." So "you fall on your knees and try to call to them / far in the empty face."

In poems like this, in *Writings to an Unfinished Accompaniment* and *The Compass Flower*, at times a loss of control threatens. Some

---

12. The comparison with Magritte can be extended. When Merwin's surrealism is most visual, in lines like "the glass knights lie by their gloves of blood" (*L*, 8), or "you can see / Eyes lined up to ripen on all the sills" (*MT*, 26), or "at the windows in the knives / You are watching" (*L*, 4), I am reminded of those of Magritte's paintings whose surrealism depends on the improbable juxtaposition or displacement of distinctly bounded objects. One of Merwin's recurring images, that of the human hand, is frequently cast in this mode: "I have seen streets where the hands of the beggars / Are left out at night like shoes in a hotel corridor" (*MT*, 27); "flocks of single hands are all flying / southward" (*WA*, 18). "Dead Hand," a two-line poem, reads: "Temptations still nest in it like basilisks. / Hang it up till the rings fall" (*MT*, 14).

of the images seem uncommunicatively runic, and the irony is almost manic. In some of the poems in *The Compass Flower,* Merwin's favorite nouns are used so casually that they are almost trivialized. Unlike Kinnell, whose vocabulary for emptiness and revelation often fails in short poems, Merwin's repeated vocabulary does not require long and elaborate contextualization. Merwin's vocabulary rather needs concise but continually new and unexpected realization. Only then can he use a familiar vocabulary "to make language itself almost something you cannot catch hold of."[13] Nonetheless, Merwin's weaker poems are necessary to his career. For the poems that do cohere, the weaker poems provide a background of unhinged emotion in which suffering loses its hold on prophecy. In the midst of poems whose echoing of past work suffocates, in the midst of fragmentary poems exhibiting the imprint of a form that now has an insistent life of its own, we discover poems of remarkable strength. In only three lines, "The Old Boast" (*WA,* 13) demonstrates Merwin's new power:

> Listen natives of a dry place
> from the harpist's fingers
> rain

An impossible disjunction exists here between the title and the text. The title is voiced with a deliberately antagonistic irony. It pushes the poem toward alluding to the false sustenance in aesthetic pleasure. But the text is inescapably felicitous. It displays a visionary synesthesia in which sound is water and the harpist's moving fingers appear as falling rain. The harp traditionally implies an unresolved tension between transcendence and sensuality. The poem maintains those forces in ambivalent poise.

Another almost ineffably vatic poem is "Folk Art" (*WA,* 67). The title signifies, with flat irony, Merwin's fondness for inadvertent revelation:

> Sunday the fighting-cock
> loses an eye

---

13. Merwin, "An Interview With W. S. Merwin," *Road Apple Review,* 1, No. 2, 36.

a red hand-print is plastered to its face
with a hole in it
and it sees what the palms see from the cross
one palm

In the same volume, Merwin writes that "we were severed / from the animals / with a wound that never heals"(p. 22). In this poem, the wound is not healed, but it does speak. The imagery is reminiscent, not necessarily intentionally, of Lawrence's "The Man Who Died," and it is also relevant to Lawrence's fascination with primitive, violent ritual in Mexico.[14] With a gesture almost too swift for sight, the fighting-cock's eye is pecked out. The image is hardly pleasant. But the shape of the wound suggests a mock benediction, the laying on of bloody hands. It is our own violence, visible, rude, and tangible across a mysterious biological distance. We flinch and are given the second sight we secretly wanted, made possible as it always is by a rite of blood. There is a hole in this red hand, and it is permitted to see what we cannot. We fear, Merwin wrote earlier, that our lives do not go all the way, so we will send this messenger there. We gather again to "call crucify / crucify him" (CL, 87). This is no ordinary vision, for the eye is blind. Its sight is a form of mutilated touch: It reaches out to envision a mortality for all substance. It "sees what the palms see from the cross," death, for a moment both fleshly and eternal. That single palm is bared in every open hand.

These two poems include characteristics shared by the most successful poems in *The Compass Flower*. There Merwin attempts to write positively about love and nature, but regularly fails. Straightforward affirmation is a mode Merwin may never be able to recover, a mode as well that public life may have made difficult for other American poets. Merwin needs to write about nature in such a way as to raise essential doubts about our epistemology. His best nature poems display a shocked wonder at the consubstantiality of natural things, displayed, almost inaccessibly, in language. Thus Merwin can write that the sun mysteriously shows "all the colors of

14. The imagery also resembles the description of the "Blue Cockerel": "the spread red hand / Of his comb thrown back and the one eye / Glaring like the sun's self" (GB, 13).

autumn without the leaves," but he cannot convincingly say that "marjoram joy of the mountain flowers again" without making that personification more troubling (*CF*, 49, 48). "The Horse" (*CF*, 14), however, shows that Merwin can achieve a radical beauty that seems to obliterate the necessity for human witness:

> In a dead tree
> there is the ghost of a horse
> no horse
> was ever seen near the tree
> but the tree was born
> of a mare
> it rolled with long legs
> in rustling meadows
> it pricked its ears
> it reared and tossed its head
> and suddenly stood still
> beginning to remember
> as its leaves fell

Because there is a dark ecstasy in "The Old Boast," "Folk Art," and "The Horse," readers will mitigate their nervousness by convincing themselves that their energy is optimistic. It would be more accurate to say that these three poems present images of epistemological transformation radically indifferent to our need for affirmation. In most of Merwin's work, however, his vision is more coldly antagonistic. There is an ordinary human reluctance to face a vision so uncompromisingly negative. Merwin himself faces it in the moment of writing, but it would be foolish to expect him to underline his honesty in some less ambiguous confession. Of course this vision does not prevent him from writing; it is not a nihilism that blocks discourse. Indeed his vision is a form of verbal productivity—a highly successful one, judging from the number of poems he has published since 1960. Yet the fact of continuing production is not in itself a form of affirmation. Nor does it seem accurate to say that Merwin provides us with a phenomenology of inhabited absence. If he did, we could argue that, like all phenomenologies, even negative ones, it shows an affectionate, affirmative empathy for its subject matter. Yet the obsessive, almost mechanistic repetition of Merwin's central vocabulary runs counter to the responsiveness we expect from a phenomenological method.

Criticism often capitulates, in its final pages, by finding affirmation in the most bleak of modern works; it is part of the impulse to socialize the experience of reading literature. In criticism of American literature these affirmative conclusions also show that the critic wishes to push the culture's myths toward a positive fulfillment. Yet the easy optimism of American poems in open forms is essentially dead. A criticism that glibly seeks visions of democratic communality in poems devoted to moments of self-extinction or visions of collective dread is a criticism perhaps unwilling to cope with its own relation to history. In Merwin's case the impulse toward affirmation should be resisted. "This way the dust, that way the dust," he writes, sounding for a moment like Roethke, "I listen to both sides" (*MT*, 50), but Roethke's nervous playfulness in Merwin becomes a weighing of dark alternatives. On balance there is little comfort in this stasis. He ends that poem with lines that will be quoted many times as evidence that his vision is finally positive:

> This must be what I wanted to be doing,
> Walking at night between the two deserts,
> Singing. [*MT*, 50]

Merwin himself has commented that "absolute despair has no art," but a poetry which reveals "the existence of hope" need not be hopeful.[15] There is a trace of pride in the passage above, a pride in speech giving witness to pain. Yet the desert does not bloom. The pain cannot be mastered or transformed. And the first line implies that he has no real choice. Even in his earlier work he knew his poetic terrain to be

> No landscape but a demeanor of distance
> Where interchangeably the poles are death
> And death, as in an opposition of mirrors
> Where no beginning is, no end .... [*DB*, 77]

---

15. "Notes for a Preface," *The Distinctive Voice*, ed. William J. Martz (Glenview: Scott, Foresman, 1966) pp. 269-72.

He concludes *Writings to an Unfinished Accompaniment* with a poem, "Gift," that will also be enthusiastically misunderstood. The title applies not only to poetic inspiration, to the words he is given to utter, but also to the gift we receive in reading. He has to trust this gift, or he can trust nothing. He will be led by it, as streams are, as are the "braiding flights of birds / the gropings of veins." The first image is unashamedly beautiful. He often gives us, as in the final poem of *The Carrier of Ladders,* a poem whose language seems superficially beautiful without complication. Yet in that earlier poem his final plea, "Sing to me," is addressed to the music of a tree that will not bloom in the time of blossoms. Here, too, the final tone is insidious through its compromised rapture. The braiding flight of birds, for all its pleasure, is a rope endlessly woven and unwoven. It tantalizes, like the uncomprehending "gropings of veins," with a vision of unity always imminent and never forthcoming. The next lines, despite their dry economy, are more openly sardonic. He is led by this gift as are "the thankful days / breath by breath." From this inexorable movement of a destiny indifferent to human difference, the last stanza, a passage of extraordinary force, separates itself. No more decisive plea exists anywhere in Merwin's poetry: I shall be named by this gift, I shall choose willfully to be emptied and undone in this irreversible giving. It is a call, voiced for all of us, not simply to be freed, but to be possessed:

> I call to it Nameless One O Invisible
> Untouchable Free
> I am nameless I am divided
> I am invisible I am untouchable
> and empty
> nomad live with me
> be my eyes
> my tongue and my hands
> my sleep and my rising
> out of chaos
> come and be given

This plea to be taken over by a destiny finally free of uncertain hopefulness seems universal. Yet we diminish its singular appeal and terror if we deny the passage its historical ground. We have to understand "Gift" as a last, dark invocation of Whitman's solitary role as the representative American speaker. In it we should hear an answer, an alternative conclusion, to Merwin's earlier depiction of America's unresolvable communal yearnings:

> Each no doubt knows a western country
> half discovered
> which he thinks is there because
> he thinks he left it
> and its names are still written in the sun
> in his age and he knows them
> but he will never tread their ground [CL, 48]

This passage is from "Western Country," one of the series of poems in *The Carrier of Ladders* that use figures from American history as avatars of our national psyche. The poem that follows it, "The Gardens of Zuñi," is about John Wesley Powell (1832-1902), an American geologist and ethnologist who lost his right arm at the battle of Shiloh. Powell later led a number of expeditions into the American West, worked on a scheme to classify Indian languages, and argued for careful agriculture in the dry high plains and irrigation programs in arid portions of the West. At the core of Powell's mixture of pessimism and ambition Merwin sees an exemplary American fatefulness:

> The one-armed explorer
> Could touch only half of the country
> In the virgin half
> the house fires give no more heat
> than the stars
> it has been so these many years
> and there is no bleeding
>
> He is long dead with his five fingers

and the sum of their touching
and the memory
of the other hand
his scout

that sent back no message
from where it had reached
with no lines in its palm
while he balanced
balanced
and groped on
for the virgin land

and found where it had been

Acting for all of us, Powell pursues a vision that compels us despite its temporal and spatial distance. Only his right hand, severed in the nation's fratricidal war, can still reach for the invisible virgin land we cannot forget. Our own body, lost to us and insensible, touches in an irretrievable past the virgin country that cannot be possessed.[16] Only fifty years ago, Williams could still imagine that a sacrificial marriage between the explorer and the virgin land might provide us with a model of a restorative American identity. In one of the chapters of *In The American Grain,* De Soto dies and his body is literally consumed by the continent. Yet a few chapters later a new kind of American is born, symbolically, of this grisly union. Even if the continent is no longer virginal, poets can, Williams would believe, continue to explore its image in us. In the first poem of "North American Sequence," just before the 1960s, Roethke can declare himself, unlike Eliot, still willing to see the poet as an explorer in American landscapes:

Old men should be explorers?
I'll be an Indian
Ogalala?
Iroquois.[17]

16. Cf. these lines quoted earlier: "my words are the garment of what I shall never be / Like the tucked sleeve of a one-armed boy" (*L,* 62).

17. Roethke, *Collected Poems* (New York: Doubleday, 1966), p. 189.

Now, with Merwin, we are no longer free to decide whether to choose an American identity. That "blindness a hollow a cold source" is guaranteed for each of us, citizens whose forefathers moved out "over the prairie" (*CL,* 47). A poetry of open forms imitating a democratic geography is no longer difficult to achieve. Yet the current harvest of Olson's and Williams's composition by field is not always appealing. Seeking America in verse, the poets of the 1960s "found where it had been" and what it had become.

Index

A Note on the Author

CARY NELSON teaches modern literature and critical theory and directs the Unit for Criticism and Interpretive Theory at the University of Illinois. Professor Nelson received his B.A. from Antioch College and his Ph.D. from the University of Rochester, where he was an NDEA fellow. He has also been an Associate Fellow of the University of Illinois Center for Advanced Study. He is the author of *The Incarnate Word: Literature as Verbal Space* (University of Illinois Press, 1973) and is presently completing *Reading Criticism: The Literary Status of Critical Discourse*, chapters from which have been published in *MLN, PMLA, The Denver Quarterly, Critical Inquiry*, and in the collections *Psychoanalysis and the Question of the Text* and *What Is Criticism?*